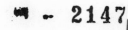 

INDIAN RELIGIONS AND PHILOSOPHIES

CONSCIOUSNESS AND REALITY

An Indian Approach to Metaphysics

JOHN B CHETHIMATTAM

ORBIS BOOKS
MARYKNOLL, NEW YORK

First published by Geoffrey Chapman, London, 1971

This edition, first published 1971
© 1971, John B Chethimattam

LCC 73-164417

This book is set in 10 on 12pt Baskerville
Made and printed in Great Britain

CONTENTS

Abbreviations used in the footnotes

Upanishads:—

Ait Up	Aitareya Upanishad
Brih Up	Bṛhadâranyaka Upanishad
Chând Up	Chândogya Upanishad
Isa Up	Isavasya (Isa) Upanishad
Kath Up	Katha Upanishad
Kau Up	Kauṣitaki Upanishad
Ken Up	Kena Upanishad
Mait Up	Maitrâyaṇi (Maitri) Upanishad
Mândy Up	Mândûkya Upanishad
Mûnd Up	Mûndaka Upanishad
Pras Up	Praśna Upanishad
Svet Up	Svetasvatara Upanishad
Tait Up	Taittîriya Upanishad

Sûtras:—

Bad S	Badarâyama Sûtras
Br S	Brahma Sûtras
Ny S	Nyâya Sûtras
Vai S	Vaiśeṣika Sûtras
Ved S	Vedânta Sûtras
Yog S	Yoga Sûtras

Bhâṣyas:—

G Bh	*Śankara's* Gîta Bhâṣya
Sank Bh	Śankara's Bhâṣya
	(e.g. Ved S Sank Bh = Śankara's Bhâṣya on the Vedânta Sûtras; Tait Up Sank Bh = Śankara's Bhâṣya on the Taittîriyopanishad; etc.)
Sri Bh	Râmânuja's Śrî Bhâṣya

Miscellaneous:—

AV	Atharva Veda
BG	Bhagavad Gîta
Mândy K	Mândûkya Kârikâ
RV	Ṛg Veda
Sâm K	Sâmkhya Kârikâ
Vedârth	Vedârtha Samgraha
VP	Vishṇu Púrâṇa

PREFACE

'Christians, Jews, Buddhists, Hindus, Muslims and others are all faced today (for the first time) by a joint challenge : to collaborate in building a common world,' said Dr. Wilfred Cantwell Smith in his inaugural Convocation Address as Director of the Centre for the Study of World Religions of the Harvard University. This modern challenge is something which India faced all through her millennia-old history. India is a world in miniature. In her long history, all the major world cultures, philosophies and religions met together, interacted and converged to form a single tradition.

Hence, the story of this long dialogue in Indian tradition has a message for the contemporary world : only in an intimate inter-action or transaction can a real dialogue take place. Information gathered by scientific study may create an academic interest in other traditions. Only an interpretation as if from within the tradi-tions, by a sort of empathy through contact with persons belonging to the respective traditions, will provide an insight into the inner dynamism of the faith behind the traditions. Only when the con-vergence of these various approaches to man and his life's problems is taken into account will a true dialogue emerge. To keep up the dialogue, the identity and uniqueness of each tradition also have to be kept intact. With regard to India, this authentic dialogue among the various cultural traditions, philosophical thought-patterns and world religions is a historical fact.

The scope of this short study is to provide a sort of introduction to the millennia-long dialogue in the Indian sub-continent. This limited scope restricts the study to generalities, leaving further details to more specific works.

My intention here is to show that no single tradition can claim a monopoly of truth, and none can pretend to be a perennial philo-sophy all by itself. Each tradition has its own particular mode of approach, its own specific problems to handle and peculiar solutions

PREFACE

In recent times, East-West religious dialogue has gained momentum. The world looks too small to be split up into opposing religious camps. But, what often stands in the way of a mutual appreciation of religious positions is the radical difference in philosophical thought-patterns between East and West. Hence, a clear understanding of the Indian philosophical approach is essential for evaluating the religious contribution of India. The scope of this book is to explain briefly the physiognomy of Indian thought in contrast to the Western mode of thought.

India is the homeland of the major Eastern religions and her traditional philosophy was greatly instrumental in formulating their religious ideas. What is often only a particular way of looking at things and expressing one's ideas is taken by people of other traditions as some exotic religious concept. For this reason a great part of Western criticism of Hinduism and Buddhism has missed the mark. The confusion has been increased by Indian scholars educated in the West who appeal to Kant, Hegel, Berkeley and Bradley to interpret Indian philosophical ideas. They bring in all kinds of superficial parallels with Linguistic Analysis, Logical Positivism, Phenomenology and Existentialism to explain the ancient Indian tradition!

For any fruitful dialogue, each one has to be conscious of his own identity as well as of the individuality of his partner. Hence, a right understanding of the metaphysical genius of India is indispensable for an East-West religious dialogue. I have attempted here to rethink the principal questions discussed in Western metaphysics from the Indian angle of vision. I have not dealt with all the different schools of Western thought, nor mentioned the shades and differences of opinion in Western contemporary philosophy. This is a book on the Indian tradition. The West is considered only as a point of reference, and in this I have restricted myself to the

ix

main stream running down from Plato and Aristotle through Augustine and Aquinas.

I owe a great debt of gratitude to Rev. Dr. Norris W. Clarke, s.j., of the Fordham University, New York, who by his criticism of the book from the Western point of outlook helped me to clarify several questions. I was also greatly assisted in the writing of this book by the discussions in the Seminars on Comparative Religion directed by Dr. Wilfred Cantwell Smith at the Harvard University, as well as by the Sanskrit course on Ramanuja's Philosophy given at the same University by Dr. Daniel H. H. Ingalls. A remark made by Dr. Ingalls while discussing a Sanskrit term can serve as a useful caution to those who approach the Indian thought from a Western background : A wrong translation of Sanskrit terms can make Indian Philosophy look very similar to Western Philosophy!

BANGALORE   JOHN B. CHETHIMATTAM, C.M.I.
NEW YORK   *Dharmaram College*
1 May 1970   *Fordham University*

PART I

HISTORICAL BACKGROUND

CHAPTER I
INTRODUCTION

RELEVANCE OF THE INDIAN APPROACH TO REALITY

The Approach to Reality is different in different philosophical traditions. Greek Philosophy took an objective and ontological view of reality and emphasized the interrelation and hierarchical order of beings. Hebrew tradition gave a strong action-connotation to the verb 'haya' = is, and emphasized the personal side of reality. Indian philosophical tradition placed the accent on the interioristic and self-centred unity of reality in consciousness. Perhaps this diversity in approach to the basic problem of Philosophy—the question of Reality—may be the basic reason for the existence of different schools of Philosophy.

I shall not discuss here the Hebrew approach, which is unique in its own way. However, it is necessary to indicate briefly the general trend of Western thought to understand by contrast the physiognomy of the Indian tradition.

WESTERN VIEW OF REALITY

In the history of Greek thought, Parmenides is considered the father of Metaphysics since he seems to be the first to deal with the world of experience under the transcendental aspect of being. The goddess told him : 'That which may be spoken of and thought of is what is : for it is possible for it to be; but it is impossible for nothing to be.'[1] For Parmenides, being is unique and necessary : 'What is, is without beginning, indestructible, entire, single, unshakable, endless; neither *has* it been nor *shall* it be, since it *is*; all alike, single, solid.'[2] But Parmenides is concerned with truth as such, and not about an existent absolute reality. Being is, for him, the object of speech and thought. Hence, for him 'things, though

---

[1] Parmenides, Frag. 6; Hilton C. Nahm, *Selections from Early Greek Philosophy* (New York : Appleton-Century-Crofts, 1964), p. 93.
[2] *Ibid.*, Frag. 8.

3

far off, are firmly present to the mind'.³ 'What can be thought is the thought that it is.'⁴

Plato made use of the Parmenidian terminology, but gave a different meaning to it. For him, reality is 'being that veritably is', and non-being is becoming.⁵ It is still a unity gathered together by reasoning from a plurality of perceptions.⁶ Reality is conceived as the ideal of thought removed from the change of experience, 'subsisting of itself and by itself in an eternal oneness, while every lovely thing partakes of it'.⁷

Aristotle, on the other hand, deals with reality from the aspect of being, nature, namely, *that which is* : leaving aside the accidental sense in which something is said to be, he thinks that 'the kinds of essential being are precisely those that are indicated by the figures of predication', namely the predicaments.⁸ But primarily it stands for the substance,⁹ especially for the form which makes the substance what it is. Here the emphasis is on essence, though in a text there seems to be a reference to actual existence in inquiring the first cause of existent things.¹⁰

Plotinus makes a judicious synthesis between Plato and Aristotle : making use of the hylemorphic terminology of Aristotle, he follows the Platonic method of transcendence and rises from the reflected and participated beauty of the external world, through the beauty of the soul to the ultimate One, which is beyond being and thought.¹¹ St Augustine follows Plotinus in the use of the Platonic method. But he is more interested in the human facts of freedom and sin, and hence rises from existence, life and knowledge to pure

---

³ *Ibid.*, Frag. 4, p. 92.
⁴ *Ibid.*, Frag. 3.
⁵ Plato, *Phaedrus*, 247c. Cf. *Theaetetus*, 152d.
⁶ *Phaedrus*, 249c.
⁷ *Symposium*, 211b.
⁸ Aristotle, *Metaphysics*, V, 7, 1017a, 23–30.
⁹ *Ibid.*, VII, 1, 1028a.
¹⁰ *Ibid.*, IV, 1, 1003a, 27–33.
¹¹ Plotinus, *Enneades*, V, ix, 2; IV, viii, 1; V, v, 9 : 'And this has nothing else to be in; so It is in nothing at all, and therefore in this sense nowhere. Where then are other things? In It. It is therefore not far from the other, nor in them, and there is nothing which contains It, but It contains all things. It is in this way the Good of all things, because It exists and all things depend upon It.' The One is beyond all multiplicity, and hence beyond all being. (Cf. *Ibid.*, VI, ix, 1; VI, ix, 3 : 'After one has pronounced the word "Good", one should ascribe nothing further to it because any additions of whatever sort will make it less than it really is.')

and infinite wisdom as the Supreme Reality, which alone can give intelligibility to evil and be the object of human choice.[12]

St Thomas brought the evolution of metaphysical thought in the Western tradition to a certain fulfilment by pinpointing the act of existence as the core of reality : 'Now being is predicated absolutely and primarily of substances; it is predicated secondarily and in a qualified sense of accidents. . . . But in simple substances it is present more truly and excellently, in as much as they also have the act of existing (esse) in a more excellent way.'[13] This 'being' of St Thomas is not the Aristotelian one, the form, but that which gives actuality to the form : 'Being is the actuality of every form or nature; for goodness and humanity are spoken of as actual, only because they are spoken of as being. Therefore, being must be compared to essence, if the latter is distinct from it, as actuality to potentiality.'[14] The act of being in this sense 'is the perfection of all perfections' and 'nothing can be added to the act of being that is extraneous to it, since nothing is extraneous to it except non-being'.[15] This act of existing points to 'the First Being which is simply the act of existing'.[16]

Thus we start thinking about a reality struck by what is presented to our thought and speech (Parmenides), and recognize that it is in itself and by itself (Plato); we understand its nature and form as coming in our predications (Aristotle); but, at the same time, recognize its objective reality beyond all form (Plotinus). In relation with our human existence bound in life, understanding and freedom, Supreme Wisdom has to be recognized as the culmination of all reality (Augustine). But, what is most basic in the objective reality, whether finite or infinite, is the act of existence, and God is subsistent existence (Aquinas).

The great contribution of Western Philosophy starting from the sixteenth century to contemporary times is the increasing emphasis placed on consciousness and personality as the central objects of philosophical inquiry. Descartes with his 'Cogito' showed that the subject of thought is the focal point of the objective world. Kant with his autonomous Reason indicated that knowledge of reality is

---

[12] St Augustine, *De Libero Arbitrio,* II.
[13] St Thomas Aquinas, *De Ente et Essentia, c.*1.
[14] *Summa Theologica* I, q.3, a4c.
[15] *De Potentia,* III, a2, ad9.
[16] *De Ente et Essentia, c.*4.

not a passive reception, but an active construction. Fichte and Schelling showed the complementarity of consciousness and reality. Even Empiricists and Logical Positivists, who deny all metaphysics, place thought as a process in the foreground.

But these developments have not affected the consistency of Western thought as a rational objective approach to reality. Descartes' 'Cogito' has only presented the Logos of Heraclitus in a new light, and Kant's *a priori* forms and categories of Reason are on objective system as idealistic as that of Plato.

Of all modern thinkers, the philosophers known loosely as Existentialists have concentrated attention on the conscious human being as the centre of all reality. He is the *Dasein* that stands in the midst of beings and understands their Being;[17] he is the pure 'For-Himself' in opposition to the things, the comprehensive knower who embraces subject and object at a single point. Still, even with the Existentialists the integrity of the rational approach is preserved. The basic approach of Existentialism is phenomenological : examine the *Dasein* as it is in itself.

The Hindu Thought-Pattern

The Hindu tradition approaches reality from a different angle. It does not attempt to analyze an object or find a system or framework to give order and meaning to the external world. It is primarily concerned with a personal problem, the problem of one's own suffering, experience of pain and pleasure, and bondage to material conditions. It seeks *môksha* or release from change, stability of existence. In this quest it has fixed its attention on conscious experience, the 'I-hood'; for, in all the changing vicissitudes of life's experience, only the sense of 'I' remains unchanged.

Looking into my own self, examining my sense of 'I', I cannot discover a beginning or an end or any limitation to it. I cannot imagine a time when I was not, nor picture to myself a condition when I will not be. Only looking outward to my objective experience am I confronted with this state of instability, flux and limitation. Hence, in the quest for an ideal reality to fix thought upon—the model of permanence and stability—Indian tradition has chosen the conscious Ego rather than the objective world.

[17] Martin Heidegger, *Introduction to Metaphysics,* trs. Ralph Manheim (New York : Doubleday, 1961), pp. 45–115.

Our scope

I intend to examine how, from this particular angle of vision, the most basic metaphysical problems can be discussed. I have taken the Metaphysics of Ramanuja as a point of departure for this discussion, because he is generally acknowledged as the most representative philosopher of the Hindu tradition. Almost a contemporary of St Thomas Aquinas, coming a few years ahead of him in history, his work was also one of synthesis, combining and reconciling the various divergent schools of Hindu thought into a synthetic whole.

In the next chapter I shall briefly examine the historical currents of thought which formed the background of Ramanuja, and his own synthesis of them. This will enable us to understand the basic metaphysical principles which emerge from an analysis of reality from this particular angle.

CHAPTER II

CONCEPT OF REALITY
IN THE UPANISHADS

Even in the mythological period, when philosophical thinking had very little evolved, India fixed on life and vital evolution as the model of its world conception. The cosmological myths for the most part conceive the origin of the world as something like a biological generation : the universe is said to have evolved from the primeval golden seed, the *Hiranyagarbha*. The origin is at times traced to the cosmic egg, which split into two, forming heaven and earth.[1]

In the famous *Purushasûkta* of the *Rig Veda,* the evolution of things is ascribed to the *Purusha,* the Supreme Person :

> A thousand heads hath Purusha, a thousand eyes, a thousand feet. On every side pervading earth he fills a space ten fingers wide. This Purusha is all that yet hath been and all that is to be. . . . All creatures are one-fourth of him, three-fourths eternal life in heaven.[2]

With the evolution of thought, the notion of Being, *sat* (participle of the verb *asti,* 'to be'), is introduced. But *asti* in Sanskrit is no mere copula, as the *esti* of Greek. Hence, *sat* has a strong existential meaning. In the light of the evolution and emergence of *sat,* the state before it is characterized as *asat* or non-being : *sat* is said to

---

[1] *Chând Up,* III, xix, 1. The chronology or relative antiquity of the Upanishads is of secondary importance for us in this discussion. Since they are productions of different schools, they bear the stamp of the respective school, and show us the different currents of thought. For a summary of the discussions on the chronology of the Upanishads, cf. Joseph Nadin Rawson, *The Katha Upanishad* (London: Oxford University Press, 1934), pp. 8–12; Dr. S. Radhakrishnan, *The Principal Upanishads* (New York: Harper & Bros., 1953), p. 22: 'Modern criticism is generally agreed that the ancient prose Upanishads, *Aitareya, Kaushitaki, Chândogya, Kena, Taittîriya,* and *Brihadâranyaka,* together with *Isa* and *Katha,* belong to the eighth and seventh centuries B.C. They are all pre-Buddhistic.'

[2] *RV,* X, 90.

8

emerge from the womb of *asat,* in which was the embryonic water, as yet 'unaccented', i.e., without the aid of any other principle, but solely by the orgasmic heat of procreative impulse or *kâma* : 'Thereafter arose desire in the beginning : desire, the primal seed and germ of spirit.'[3]

Several Upanishads repeat this Vedic doctrine of the origin of being from non-being :

> In the beginning this was non-existent. From it was born what exists. That made itself its Self, therefore it is called the self-made.[4]
> In the beginning there was nothing here whatsover. By Death indeed all this was concealed—by hunger, for death is hunger. Death thought, 'Let me have a body'.[5]

THE PRIMACY OF BEING OVER NON-BEING

But soon the primacy of being is realized and affirmed clearly. Being is the beginning and origin of all things. Thus in the *Chândogya Upanishad,* Uddalaka instructing his son about the nature of reality, says :

> My boy, just as through a clod of clay, all that is made of clay would become known; all products being due to words, a mere name; the clay alone is real.
> My boy, just as through a single ingot of gold, all that is made of gold would become known. . . .
> Just as through a single nail clipper, all that is made of iron would become known. . . .
> In the beginning, my dear, this was Being only—one, without a second.—Some say that, in the beginning, this was non-being, only one, without a second. From that non-being sprang Being. But how could it be so, my dear?—said he; How could Being be born from non-being? In fact, this was Being only, in the beginning, one, without a second.[6]
> All these creatures, my dear, have their root in Being, reside in Being and rest in Being. . . . Now that which is this subtle reality,

---

[3] *RV,* X, 129. J. A. B. Van Buitnen points out that we need not look for any mystical or abstract metaphysical thought here, but only a spontaneous projection of the biological processes in one's own immediate experience to the cosmic order. Cf. *Râmânuja's Vedârtha Samgraha* (Poona : Deccan College, 1956), p. 6, note 11. Yet, one has to admit that even this biological symbolism implies a true metaphysics.

[4] *Tait Up,* II, vii, 1.
[5] *Brih Up.* I, ii, 1.
[6] *Chând Up,* VI, i, 4–6; VI, ii, 1–2.

in that has all this its Self; that is the Truth; that thou art, O Svetaketu.[7]

This clear affirmation of the primacy of Being over non-being became the key statement in the Indian philosophical tradition, so much so that every metaphysician who came later felt constrained to give a commentary on the text, even though each one put on it a meaning according to his own special shade of opinion.

The similarity of the text with the words of Parmenides on Being is striking. But the difference of outlook is evident from the context : Parmenides is seeking what is the real object of thought and speech. Uddalaka, on the other hand, starts inquiring into 'that by which the unrevealed is revealed, the non-understood understood, and the unknown known',[8] namely the ultimate basis of all reality that remains hidden from ordinary experience. This *'sat'* is said to be unique, the source and origin of all things.

Similarly, in the *Brihadâranyaka Upanishad,* Maitreyi, who cares for no worldly goods but immortality alone, is told by Yâjnavalkya, her ascetic husband, that only the knowledge of *Atman,* the Self, can lead to immortality : 'The Self is to be seen, to be heard, to be perceived, to be marked, and everything else only for the sake of the Self.'[9]

The *Atman* is in everything as sound in individual notes of music, as salt in water. According to a special line of thought proposed by the *Brihadâranyaka Upanishad,* being and non-being, material and immaterial, mortal and immortal, solid and fluid,

---

[7] *Chând Up,* VI, viii, 6–7. Emile Senart warns us against giving a strict meaning to the technical terms of the Upanishads, for the Upanishads come before the scholastic period of Indian thought when terms got fixed in their technical meaning. The Ancients easily passed from the concrete to the abstract and back again. The liturgical use of the Upanishads places their statements in a symbolic, ritualistic and mystical context, where a single statement, and even individual words and syllables, could bear a variety of meanings which could be understood only by oral tradition.

The ritualistic emphasis of the Upanishads may be shown by the predominant role 'Agni', or fire, plays in the discussions. On the one hand, fire is the instrument of sacrifice, and on the other, it symbolizes the principle of change or transformation which is the cosmic energy at work behind the whole world of manifestation. Cf. Emile Senart, *Chândogya Upanishad* (Paris : Societe d'Edition 'Les Belles Lettres', 1930), pp. 78–9; Govindagopal Mukhopadhyâya, *Studies in the Upanishads* (Calcutta : Sanskrit College, 1960), p.9.

[8] *Chând Up,* VI, i, 3.

[9] *Brih Up,* II, iv, 1–8.

are two forms of Brahman, the Supreme Reality. The two together make the world of our experience : *Sat* (= being) + *tyat* (= indefinite) = *satyam* (= true). Brahman, who is beyond both these opposites, can be only indicated by 'not this', 'not this' being a designation in terms of our experience; for He is *satyasya satyam,* the truth of the true.[10]

In the *Kathopanishad,* the pious Brahmin boy Naciketas, who chides his father for the latter's lack of generosity and upright intention, is sent by the angry father to the god of Death. There at the palace of the god in the latter's absence, Naciketas receives a bad welcome. Death, on his return, comes to know about the dishonour done to a Brahmin in his home and grants Naciketas permission to ask for any boon he wishes. Naciketas asks for knowledge about the nature of Ultimate Reality. After testing the constancy and sincerity of Naciketas, Death explains that the Real symbolized by the mystic word 'Om' is Brahman, who is :

> The Self, smaller than small, greater than the great,
> Is the Atman that is set in the heart of a creature here. . . .
>   Sitting, he proceeds afar;
> Lying, he goes everywhere. . . .
> Him who is the bodiless among bodies,
> Stable among the unstable,
> The great, all-pervading Atman,
> On recognizing Him, the wise man sorrows not.[11]

It is significant that the doctrine about the Ultimate Reality is placed in the mouth of Death. Death is the teacher of Reality. Naciketas, immediately after receiving the doctrine from the mouth of Death, becomes freed from all worldly attachment and attains Brahman.[12]

---

[10] *Brih Up,* II, iii, 1 and 6.

[11] *Kath Up,* I, ii, 16–22. J. N. Rawson says that, in spite of the impression got from Sankara and Deussen, the standpoint of the *Kath Up* is 'definitely theistic, sometimes emphasizing the unity of all in a way that approaches positive or realistic pantheism, but never recognizing the doctrine of illusion, and therefore never teaching the negative idealistic pantheism or acosmism of Sankara'. (*The Katha Upanishad,* p. ix). Perhaps the ascription of 'idealistic pantheism' and 'acosmism' to Sankara is at the basis of his whole misunderstanding.

[12] *Kath Up,* II, vi, 18.

THE METAPHYSICAL METHOD

Some think that this realization of Ultimate Reality other than by sense experience and reasoning is a form of mystic experience.[13] But this is not correct. Reality belongs to a level which cannot be attained by sense experience and by generalizations from sense perception. But the procedure by which the Upanishads rise to Reality is very much similar to the Platonic method, though it is in an interioristic direction.

Thus, in the *Brihadâranyaka Upanishad,* Yâjnavalkya in his discussion with the priests shows how one has to proceed from the crude material earth, through the elements of water, air and fire in the increasing order of subtlety to the general notion of being : 'He who dwells in all beings, and within all beings, whom all beings do not know, whose body all beings are, and who rules all beings from within, he is the Self, the ruler within, the immortal.'[14]

But beyond this general aspect of material being (*adhibhûta*) are the levels of consciousness : one has to go up the ladder of life, speech, the senses of hearing, sight and others, the internal sense of mind, and knowledge, to the inmost core of our conscious self which is the pure aspect of witness. Hence, ultimate reality has to be conceived as pure witness : 'He is thy Self, the ruler within, the immortal; unseen, but seeing; unheard, but hearing; unperceived, but perceiving; unknown, but knowing. There is no other seer but he, . . . there is no other knower but he. This is thy Self, the ruler within, the immortal.'[15] Thus the search for reality ends in the pure conscious Self, which is the purest and subtlest core of all things.

The same method of procedure appears in other Upanishads also. *Kena Upanishad* begins with the word *kena,* 'by whom' : 'Impelled by whom, at whose will does the mind move, do the vital airs act, by whose movement does the speech speak, the eye

---

[13] Cf. S. N. Dasgupta, *Indian Idealism* (Cambridge University Press, 1933), pp. 30–1. Walter Ruben, in *Die Philosophen der Upanishaden* (Bern : A. Francke Ag. Verlag, 1947), proposes a theory of historical development in the Upanishads clearly distinguished into five periods : B.C. 700–670— period of the absolutization of elements of nature; 670–640—cosmic vision; 640–610—generations of Idealism and Realism; 610–580—Mysticism; 580–550—Moralism and Anti-Moralism culminating in the birth of the scientific attitude. To say the least, the theory seems artificial.

[14] *Brih Up,* III, vii, 15; III, viii, 7, 13–23.

[15] *Brih Up,* III, vii, 23.

and the ear and their presiding deities attain their objects?' The answer is that the ear of the ear, the mind of the mind, the speech of speech and the eye of the eye is the Real beyond, who is indicated by the key-word of the Upanishad, *Tadvanam*, namely the goal and object of all aspirations. He is so subtle that none of the human faculties can grasp him.

A parable makes the matter clear : Once, the gods were standing together and bragging about their feats in a victory they gained against the demons. Suddenly an unknown deity appears in the vicinity. God *Agni*, fire, is deputed to find out his identity. As a condition for answering his question, the stranger challenges Agni to prove his power by burning a straw he puts forth; Agni fails and is turned back. Then the god of air, *Vayu*, approaches and is turned back, since he fails to blow the straw away. Finally, *Indra*, the god of the sky, approaches the stranger. Then, suddenly, the Deity vanishes. *Umâ*, the goddess of divine wisdom, appearing in mid-air, tells them that it was Brahman, the Supreme, who appeared to them, and that only through Him had they achieved the victory. The lesson of the parable is that action, represented by fire, and sense experience symbolized by the god of air, cannot in any way attain Ultimate Reality. Even the intellect, symbolized by the god of the sky, Indra, cannot directly attain Reality, unless it is manifested by divine wisdom in mid-air, i.e., in the cave of the heart, by a sort of intuition.[16]

The Real is so subtle and so beyond all sense and imagination that those who think they know it, do not know it, while those who think they do not know it may very well have attained a real knowledge of it.[17] But the mode of procedure is clear : go beyond the senses to ultimate and immutable reality, that is, the basis of all intelligibility and consciousness.

DIFFERENT SCHOOLS OF METAPHYSICS

Though there is a common method of approach to Reality in the Upanishads, all do not have the same view of reality itself. Three distinct trends can be distinguished in particular according to their conception of the coexistence of the Supreme Being and finite beings : Non-Dualism, Dualism and Qualified Non-Dualism.

[16] *Ken Up*, II and III.
[17] *Ken Up*, II, 3.

Non-dualist trend of thought

The simplest form of procedure from experience to the Real is shown by the Non-Dualist school. *Mûndaka Upanishad* launches the inquiry into Brahman asking, 'What is that through which, if it is known, everything else becomes known?'[18] The answer is simple : it is Brahman, subsistent and infinite consciousness, the self of all things. Everything beside Brahman is only a reflexion and a shadow. The world of finite beings, including 'the seven faculties, the seven lights (acts of perception) and the seven kinds of fuel (the objects)', is only a bow for us to shoot the arrow of concentration on Brahman[19] : 'The Sun does not shine there, nor the Moon and the stars, nor these lightnings, and much less this fire. When He shines, everything shines after Him; by His light all this is lighted.'[20] Brahman is Truth and the world is 'un-true'. This true self of all things is not known by perception or Scripture or reasoning. 'He whom the Atman chooses, by him the Atman can be attained.'[21] One who knows Brahman loses himself in the Brahman as the rivers lose themselves in the sea.[22] The key-word of this Upanishad is *Jnânamayam tapah,* the asceticism of knowledge; it is through intensification of consciousness that the Real is realized.

Mândûkya Upanishad, which belongs to the same trend of thought, proceeds through the states of consciousness—namely waking state, dream, and dreamless sleep—to the fourth state of Brahman realization. In the waking state we are in contact with the gross aspect of the world. In dream we go beyond this gross aspect to the purely mental forms of things, which are lightsome. But in the condition of dreamless sleep, one is blissfully at home in one's own self and the self is unaffected by any external object. According to this Upanishad, the final and ideal state of consciousness should comprise the reality of all the three and go beyond them in the pure selfhood of Brahman shining by itself. Hence it is symbolized by the mystic word OM (A + U + M), 'A' standing for external experience, 'U' for internal experience, and 'M' for involution in oneself. What the Upanishad states is that the Ulti-

[18] *Mûnd Up,* I, i, 3.
[19] *Mûnd Up,* II, ii, 3–4.
[20] *Mûnd Up,* II, ii, 10.
[21] *Mûnd Up,* III, ii, 3.
[22] *Mûnd Up,* III, ii, 8.

mate Reality is beyond all our finite conditions of experience : it is the condition of pure selfhood, unseen, unchangeable, indescribable, incomprehensible, undefinable, unthinkable, and unindicatable.[23]

Taittirîya Upanishad reaches the same non-dualistic conclusion, but taking the levels of human interest and activity for the stages of inward abstraction : one who is interested in worldly pursuits and wealth has his consciousness concentrated on the outermost level, the self of food. Inner to this self of food is that of vital breath, the level of animal life, and beyond it is the self of mind or sense experience. But different from it and farther beyond is the level of knowledge, which is conceived to form the *vijnânamayât-man*, or self of knowledge. Higher still is the level of pure bliss or happiness, which constitutes the self of bliss.[24] Interior to all these sheaths of selfhood is the one Ultimate Reality which is defined as *satyam-jnânam-anantam*, infinite and immutable consciousness.[25]

This Non-Dualistic trend of the Upanishads found its chief defender in a later period in Sri Sankara, who made Advaita or Non-Dualism the chief metaphysical school in India. According to him, the world of our experience has only a relative value, namely that of a stepping-stone towards the realization of the Real. This Real is immutable existence, pure consciousness and pure bliss : *saccidânanda*. Infinite existence is immutable, since it cannot acquire or lose anything; it is pure consciousness, since it cannot lack anything. Once this Brahman is realized as the one Reality, the world and individuality of finite beings have no more meaning. The opposition between the Real and Unreal is found in our conscious experience itself : the areas of the I and the Thou, the subject and the object, split up everything into irreconcilable camps opposed to each other as light and darkness. Hence, of these we have to choose one as real and reject the other as unreal. Real is evidently that which remains unchanged in all states of consciousness, the common factor in all experience. This is pure I-hood or Self. Hence Brahman, the Ultimate Reality, can be defined only as pure and infinite truth and consciousness. By the side of that absolute selfhood, the individuality of finite beings can be characterized only as un-real (*an-rita*), non-knowledge (*avidyâ*) and illusion (*mâyâ*). But the world is not nothing; it does exist. But it

[23] *Mândy Up*, no. 7
[24] *Tait Up*, II, ii, 8.
[25] *Tait Up*, II, i, 1.

is not real. It has only a practical and temporary meaning and has to cease when finally Brahman is realized as the ultimate self of all.[26] We shall discuss the position of Sankara in detail in another chapter.

Dualistic trend

From the same basis of consciousness there developed in the Upanishadic period a dualistic trend of thought about reality. The *Prasna Upanishad* starts with the assertion that Prajâpati, the Creator, produced in the beginning the basic pairs of all things, spirit and matter, Sun and Moon, day and night and the like.[27] The spirit is he 'who sees, hears, smells, tastes, perceives, conceives, acts, he whose essence is knowledge, the person, and he dwells in the highest, indestructible self'.[28] On the side of matter appear the various factors of the changing world, the gross and subtle elements, the faculties of action and sensation, the mind, intellect (*buddhi*), and individuality itself.[29]

The same idea is developed in the *Maitrâyani Upanishad* where a certain identity between the individual spirit in man and the Supreme Person is affirmed.[30]

This trend of thought appears especially in the philosophical system of the *Sâmkhya* and *Yoga* schools.[31] The metaphysical abstraction implied in this dualistic procedure is clear enough : it is an analysis of our conscious experience reducing it to ultimate factors; in our experience we find certain factors which are of the pure spirit, unaffected by the conditions of space and time, such as pure I-hood which unites all our acts of experience. These factors have to be traced to a spiritual principle transcending space and time, called *Purusha*.

The activities dependent on time-space conditions are easily

---

[26] *Ved S Sank Bh,* Introduction.
[27] *Pras Up,* I, 13.
[28] *Pras Up,* IV, 9.
[29] *Pras Up,* IV, 8.
[30] *Mait Up,* II, 5.
[31] The origin of the Sâmkhya-Yoga school is shrouded in obscurity. Scholars generally agree with A. B. Keith that it is impossible to find any real basis for its doctrines in the Upanishads. (Cf. A. B. Keith, *Sâmkhya System,* p. 7.) At best, it is a system built on to the Upanishads, rather than coming out of them. In all probability, it has to be traced to the non-Vedic sources of Indian thought.

reduced to three irreducible functions of a principle of evolution : there is a function of reflexion manifested in thought, which is reduced to *sattva,* a function of dynamism and creativity termed *rajas,* and a function of limitation and individuality called *tamas.* These are not three principles, but three irreducible functions of a single principle of evolution.

The *Purusha* is pure consciousness, and hence a mere witness unaffected by the evolutions of matter, though its pure light can be obscured and hidden by the evolutes of matter which surround it. The ideal condition is when the spirit remains all by itself in isolation, and the matter in itself in a perfect balance of its three functions.

Unity in multiplicity or *qualified non-dualism*

If the first group looks at Reality from the side of the Absolute and fails to give a proper account of the multiplicity of beings, the second group looks at it from the side of multiplicity and fails to account for unity. A third group takes its stand, as it were, in the middle, and tries to reconcile the absolute unity with the conditioned multiplicity.

The *Isa Upanishad* comes first in this line. As a handbook of the Vâjasaneya school its opening prayer itself is indicative of this intention : 'that is Fulness, this is fulness; fulness is derived from the Fulness. Even after the fulness is drawn from the Fulness, Fulness remains as such.' The first verse of the Upanishad is a statement of the presence of the supreme in all things : 'Everything that moves on the earth is enveloped by the Lord. . . .'

On the one hand, those who deny the Atman, the inmost Real, enter the densest darkness. Those who see the Atman in all things and all things in the Atman go beyond all suffering and desire. Though motionless, the Atman is swifter than thought, and nobody can overtake him; though standing still, he overtakes even the fastest runners. He envelops all, is bright, incorporeal, scatheless,, pure, untouched by evil, omnipresent, self-existent, witness and disposer of all things.[32] Hence, those who embrace the world of becoming and ignorance in preference to the Atman enter the densest darkness.[33]

[32] *Isa Up,* no. 8.
[33] *Isa Up,* nos. 9–14.

On the other hand, those who embrace exclusively the knowledge of the Absolute and the world of the immutable, neglecting the world of change and relative knowledge, enter into greater darkness. One should rather cross over death with the help of non-knowledge and the world of becoming, namely the paths of action and moral life, and attain immortality through the knowledge of the true Reality.[34]

This third trend of thought found in the Upanishads formed the Vedic background for the Metaphysics of Ramanuja. He strove to save the value of the relative and finite world, human personality, and the usefulness of religion and personal devotion to the Supreme Lord, the personal God. In his choice of this Upanishadic trend, he was guided by the Dravidian tradition of which, too, he was the representative.

[34] *Ibid.*

CHAPTER III

RAMANUJA AND HIS
IMMEDIATE BACKGROUND

The importance of Ramanuja in studying the Indian approach to reality is that, according to scholars, he is more in agreement with the whole of Indian philosophical tradition than any other important philosopher, especially than Sankara, who is held in esteem by all for his outstanding original contribution to Metaphysics. Coming more than three centuries after the great Advaitic thinker, Ramanuja[1] built up his system in reaction to the growing influence of Sankara's *Advaita* or 'Non-Dualism'. Educated first in the Advaitic tradition, he soon fell out with his teacher Yadavaprakasa, a militant *Advaitin,* because he found that the *Advaita* philosophy was doing great damage to the religious spirit of the people through its abstract concept of the Absolute and purely theoretical approach to the problems of religious philosophy. Hence, in deep meditation in a Vishnu temple he tried to formulate his own system.

In this reaction against *Advaita,* he drew inspiration from the *Bhakti,* or devotional movement of the Alvars of Tamilnad in South

[1] Ramanuja was born in 1017 A.D., son of Kesava Jâjnika at Sriperumbudur, a village some thirty miles south of Madras. After his marriage at the age of sixteen and the premature death of his father, he moved to the famous temple city of Kanchi (or Canjeepuram) a few miles away, where he devoted his time to the study of religious Scriptures, and made pilgrimages to various holy places like Benares. After the death of Sri Yamunacharya he became the leader of the Vaisnavait religious group and head of the *mutt* at Srirangam, at which post he remained till his death, except for a period of twelve years (1096–1118) when, owing to the displeasure of the Chola king Krimikantha (1070–1118), he had to leave Srirangam and live in the state of Mysore. He wrote his treatises for the instruction of his religious subjects. For the composition of his works he is said to have travelled as far north as Kashmir to consult the writings of the ancient Masters. He is said to have died at the advanced age of a hundred and twenty. Cf. Krishna Datta Bharadwaj, *The Philosophy of Ramanuja* (New Delhi, 1958), pp. 2–8; Alkondaville Govindacharya, *The Life of Ramanujacharya* (Madras, 1906).

19

India, and ended up as the official head of the movement and its greatest metaphysician. He achieved a synthesis of the tradition with *Vedânta* and provided a solid rational basis for Hindu devotionalism.

THE AGAMIC 'BHAKTI' MOVEMENT

Alongside the Upanishadic tradition of thought there evolved another approach to reality, especially in South India, drawing its inspiration from the religious tradition of the *Dâsyus,* the original settlers of India, whom the Aryans expelled from the Indo-Gangetic plain. The *Agamas,* books dealing with the worship of *Siva, Vishnu* and *Sakti,* seem to draw their spirit from this original philosophical tradition of India. In opposition to the Veda,[2] which is *apaurusheya* or impersonal, *Agamas* are personal—they are supposed to be revealed by the personal deities *Siva, Vishnu* and *Sakti.*

This emphasis on personality is the dominant note of this tradition. While the Vedic literature is intimately connected with sacrifices and rites, and tries to interpret the world of experience with ritual symbolism, the *Agamas* are doctrinal treatises with four distinct sections, *carya, kriya, yoga* and *jnâna*—worship, ritual, self-discipline and doctrine. The last portion, which is philosophy proper, discusses not the unitary aspect of reality as do the Upanishads, but the world of concrete being in its three modes : God, individual souls and matter.

The Vedic cult consists of fire rites, in which offerings are consumed by fire. The Agamic cult is fireless; offerings are merely presented to the Lord, who is supposed to extract and accept from them only the subtle portions along with the spirit of the offerer, the material parts being given back to be consumed by the offerer and his friends. The Agamic worship is centred on a single personal God, who would not allow any other god to be worshipped along with him, while the Vedic cult accommodates a multitude of gods. In the Vedic cult, the *mantras* or prayers and the rites are very important as being automatically productive of results, while the *Agamas* place the emphasis on pleasing the Deity, who is supposed to live in the midst of the people like a king in the temple consecrated to him, sharing in their daily lives, partaking of the food

---

[2] P. T. Srinivas Iyengar, *History of the Tamils from the Earliest Times to 600 A.D.* (Madras: C. Coomaraswamy Naidu & Sons, 1929), pp. 103–6.

regularly offered to him, and accepting the devotion of the people. The Vedic cult did not admit any visible form of the deities; all gods were represented by fire. For the Agamic cult, however, the one personal Deity venerated had to be represented by some visible emblem : a tool like a sword or a club, a tree, a stone, and above all a picture or a statue, which, once consecrated by the authorized priest, was no longer looked upon as a material thing, but as a visible presence of the personal God.[3]

In Tamilnad, the native country of Sri Ramanuja, where the Agamic cult gained predominance, the thought-pattern was greatly influenced by the life of the people, who mostly dwelt in the open air. They had a great appreciation of the beauty of nature, and developed a direct and personal approach to God as the Lord of nature manifesting himself in its beauty. They called him 'the Lord of the hills', and *Seyon,* the rising Sun.[4] He was not a deity away in the skies, but intimately present to the environment of the daily life of the people. In the mountains, He was the Hunter; in grazing land, the Pastor, the 'Dark-green-one'; in agricultural society, He was honoured as *Vendan,* the king; and on the sea-coast as 'the Coloured One', the Lord of the blue sea.[5] The ancient Tamil poem *Parippadal* shows this experience of God in nature :

> Of the fire, thou art the heat; of the flower, thou art the fragrance;
> Of the stone, thou art the lustre; of the word, thou art the truth.[6]
> In the sun is your ire and your brightness,
> In the moon your mercy and your grace,
> In the cloud is your largesse and your giving;
> In the earth your conserving and your patience.

---

[3] Hindu idol-worship is not merely veneration of images. Once consecrated, the material image or instrument is not considered a material thing, but the Deity himself. The idol is the Deity, but the Deity is not the idol. This is rather analogous to the concept of transubstantiation. As it is consecrated, it may also be desecrated, and then it has no more sacredness. In idol-worship, the Hindu is concentrating attention on another aspect of the material world than the one which is present to us in everyday experience—namely, the presence of the Divine in our midst, the irruption of the Divine into the profane. The two fields are not entirely separated, nor even superimposed on each other, but rather identical, though the spatio-temporal is quite inadequate to comprehend and circumscribe the Divine.

[4] Xavier S. Thani Nayagam, *Nature in Ancient Tamil Poetry* (Tuticorin: Tamil Literature Society, 1952), pp. 67–75.

[5] *Ibid.*

[6] *Parippadal,* III, 63ff., cited by X. S. Thani Nayagam, *op. cit.,* p. 78.

In the flower is your light and fragrance,
In the ocean is your appearance and praise,
In the sky is your form and your voice,
In the air your unfolding and return.[7]

The goals of life

Such a spontaneous and direct approach to reality produced a balanced view of life with equal emphasis placed on its three recognized goals, namely *dharma, artha* and *kâma,* righteousness, wealth and pleasure, which naturally resulted in a fourth, namely *môksha,* liberation from the present state of bondage to a condition of suffering. The *Tirukkural* of Tiruvalluar, recognized as the authentic document of ancient Tamil religious life, systematically explains these three goals of life.

The basis of righteousness is the recognition of God as the source of all things. 'Only those who have clung to the feet of the Lord, who is the sea of righteousness, will be able to sail the other seas. Others cannot.'[8] The greatest penance and renunciation is to walk in right conduct, understanding the true nature of the objects of

---

[7] *Ibid.,* IV, 25ff., *op. cit.,* p. 79. The Saivite devotional writings also show the same understanding of the transcendence and immanence of God in nature. Manikka Vacagar, a poet of the 7th century A.D., writes:
See Him, the First, see Him, the Whole ! . . .
See Him, the Infinite ! See Him, the Ancient One !
See, He extends throughout the wide extended earth
    (*Tiruvacagam,* III, 30–50, trs. G. U. Pope (Oxford : Clarendon Press, 1900), pp. 20–21.)
Appearing like a black vast cloud,
Arising in the hill of Perunturrai blest,
Whilst sacred lightnings flash from every point,
While serpent bright of sensual bondage dies,
While the sore sorrow of the fervent heat hides itself,
While the all-beauteous Hibiscus shines forth,
Swelling in its wrath like our mortal pain,
It sounds forth the mighty grace as a drum.
While flowery *Kânthal* stretches out supplicating hands,
And the tender drops of sweet unfailing grace distil,
While the gleaming torrent swells on every side,
And rises to the highest banks of every lake

....
Meanwhile, the heavenly mighty stream,
Rises and rushes, crowned with bubbles of delight,
Eddies around, dashes against the banks of our embodiment.
    (*Ibid,* III, 66–85, pp. 22–3.)
[8] Tiruvalluar, *Tirukkural,* I, 1. trs. V. R. Ramachandra Dikshita (Madras : Adyar Library, 1949).

sense, and knowing the meaning of birth and liberation. 'That course of conduct that steers clear of every desire, wrath, and offensive speech, is alone *Dharma*.'[9] Acquisition of wealth also is legitimate and necessary. All will despise the poor; riches bring honour. 'The wealth accumulated justly and without sin will confer virtue and happiness.'[10] Similarly the happy union with a wife is not an impediment but a help for a virtuous life.

THE PANCARATRA VIEW OF REALITY

This practical outlook on life slowly developed a deeper under-standing of reality which is reflected in the sectarian writings of the Middle Ages. What is known as the *Pancarâtra Samhita* occupies a special place among these. Ramanuja defends the Pancarâtra literature, though owing to their sectarian character he does not quote frequently from these books. But his predecessor and teacher's teacher Sri Yamunacharya held them in great respect and wrote a special defence of them. They were held in esteem by the *Visishthâdvaita* school in general.[11]

Written in a milieu in which the Vedic and Dravidian world conceptions coexisted, they form a first attempt at a synthesis be-tween the two thought currents. Faithful to the Agamic tradition, the Pancarâtra presented a world pattern of the triple being of God, souls and the material world, but held to the Vedic unity centred in the one Absolute : God.[12] But when the Vedic literature places the emphasis on the transcendental aspects of *sat* and *cit*,

[9] Tirukkural, I, 9; IV, 34 and 35.
[10] *Ibid.*, LXXVI, 752–4.
[11] The name *Pancarâtra* (five nights) is legendary. It means doctrine given in five nights, or instruction given by five forms of the Deity or five gods. Over two hundred of the Pancarâtra treatises are known, of which the majority were composed in Northern India, another section in Southern India, and the rest of uncertain or spurious origin. Each of these treatises is supposed to consist of four *pâdas* or quarters : (i) *jnâna* (knowledge) doctrine; (ii) *yoga*, concentration; (iii) *kriya*, making, including even the construction of temples; and (iv) *carya*, doing which includes social duties, daily rites and festivals. But in each Pancarâtra treatise, one or other of these may predominate. Thus, the *Paramesvara Samhita* follows the well-known division of *Jnâna kânda* and *Kriyâ kânda*, while the *Bharadvaja Samhita* concentrates on moral conduct, especially devotion, or *prapatti*. Cf. F. Otto Schrader, *Introduction to the Pancarâtra and the Ahirbudhnya Samhita* (Madras : Adyar Library, 1916), pp. 22–3.
[12] *Ahirbudhnya Samhita*, ed. M. D. Ramanujacharya and F. Otto Schrader (Madras : Adyar Library 1916), *c.* IV, *sl.* 73–78, pp. 37–8.

reality and consciousness, the Pancarâtra starts from the unitary vision of the personal God and individual human beings bound in the material world, as presented in our everyday experience.[13]

Time and god

However, it was easily realized that the Lord of nature could not have the same condition as that of material nature. This transcendence was conceived first in the duration of existence or time: the higher a being ascends the ladder of existence, the better he comprehends the expanse of time; he holds in his grasp more of the past, and sees farther into the future. Hence the time of *Vishnu* or *Nârâyana,* the Supreme Lord, is infinite,[14] while the world of finite beings has only a limited duration, alternating between long periods of *pralaya* 'dissolution', and *kalpa* 'projection'. This world of finite beings refers to the Supreme as its cause, not in his absolute and intrinsic aspect, but rather in what is termed *Sakti,* his creative force, or *Lakshmi,* which, though identical with him in reality, is in a way eternally distinct from him in the orientation to the world of creatures.[15] Hence, she, *Lakshmi,* has the distinction of days and nights corresponding to the periods of projection and dissolution, comprising millions of human years. Created beings, including Brahma, the deputed Creator, have their limitation in time, though Brahma's single day condenses in itself 432 million human years, and his age is a hundred years constituted of such days.

The creative process

All things are in Vishnyu, identical with him in the time of *pralaya,* or involution. At the end of that period, by a free act of his own will, he rouses up *Lakshmi,* his creative force, from sleep; she manifests herself in dual form, one the *kriyâsakti* or active part, the other an infinitesimal part known as *bhûtisakti,*

[13] F. Otto Schrader, *Introduction to the Pancarâtra,* pp. 6–14.
[14] *Paramatattvanirnayaprakasa Samhita,* I, 3, 43: 'There is no measure to his age.' I, 3, 55: 'He is infinite in time.' Quoted by F. Otto Schrader, 1, c., p. 28.
[15] *Ahirbudhnya Samhita,* XIV, 7–8; VIII, 36; III, 27–8.

'becoming', which evolves into individual beings.[16] Hence, the world is not a part of Vishnu, but of his consort *Lakshmi*, who is in reality identical with him, though eternally distinct from him as a mode or attribute.[17]

This concept of Lakshmi, the feminine creative principle, is an ingenious invention to explain the coexistence of the infinite and supremely perfect God and the limited and transitory creation. Though the *Samhitas* frequently assert the real identity of Vishnu and Lakshmi, their distinction, too, even at the period of *pralaya*, is clearly indicated. They are only, as it were, one principle (*ekam tattvamiva stitau*).[18] Their mutual relation is said to be one of inseparable connection or inherence,[19] of that of a quality and of the qualified,[20] of existence and of that which exists,[21] of I-ness and of I,[22] of moonshine and of moon, of sunshine and of sun.[23] The *kriyâsakti*, or active power of Lakshmi, is said to be identical with *Sudarsana*, the powerful disc weapon of Vishnu, symbol of his effective power; it is independent of space and time and undivided (*nishkala*).[24] On the other hand, the *bhûtisakti*, which appears as creatures, is only an infinitesimal part of the *kriyâsakti*, limited in power and infinitely divided.[25]

This presented a new mode of causality, which cannot be reduced to the efficient, instrumental, and material causality pattern which is found in the Upanishads. The world of beings is not any separate matter, and Vishnu no separate agent. Neither is it a theory of mere transformation. Vishnu does not transform himself into the world. He is transcendent over Lakshmi, whose infinitesimal part manifests itself as the world of beings.

The *Samhita* reacted also against the Upanishadic conception of the Absolute as *nirguna*, attributeless and impersonal, by ascribing to him six positive attributes which became standard in the whole Agamic tradition : *jnâna*, *aisvarya*, *sakti*, *bala*, *vîrya* and *teja*—

[16] *Ibid.*, IV, 78.
[17] *Vishnoh sarvângasampûrna bhavâbhâvânugâminî. Ahirbuhnya Samhita*, III, 24.
[18] *Ibid*, IV, 77–9.
[19] *Avinâbhâva-Samanvayâ. Lakshmi Tantra*, II, 17.
[20] *Dharmâdharmi Svabhâvatah. Ahirbudhnya Samhita*, III, 25.
[21] *Bhavâbhâva svarûpa, Ibid.*, III, 26.
[22] *Ahamta-aham*, III, 42.
[23] *Lakshmi Tantra*, II, 11f.
[24] *Ahirbudhnya Samhita*, III, 43–5.
[25] *Ibid.*, III, 44–5; V, 7–8; LIX, 55–7.

knowledge, lordship, ability, strength, unaffectedness and splendour.[26]

THE BHAGAVATA LITERATURE

The Bhagavata literature marks a step forward in this work of synthesis between the Vedic and non-Vedic currents of thought. The great bulk of writings known as the Mahabharata, the Bhagavad Gîta, in particular, the Bhagavata, and the Purânas in general may be classed together in this respect. Ramanuja defends the positive elements in the Pancarâtra and Pâsupata and other classes of the Bhagavata group, in as much as they all have 'their proof in the Self'.[27] According to him, the *Vedânta Sûtras* of Bâdarâyana criticize them only on account of their erroneous statements about the function of the Lord in creation, and other inaccurate positions held by them.[28]

In all these books there is apparent a definite shift to the side of the Upanishadic philosophy from the popular Agamic conceptions. There is no doubt that these books were mostly written in a milieu where the Vedânta and Sâmkhya-Yoga schools of orthodox Hinduism coexisted with the sectarian *Bhakti* movements. They are mostly irenic in character and never clearly polemic. In concession to the *Bhakti* cults, the personal aspect of God is in the foreground of their world conception.

THE BHAGAVAD GITA

In this whole group, the *Bhagavad Gîta* stands foremost. Ramanuja wrote a commentary on the *Gîta*, and in his *Sri Bhâshya* he quotes frequently from the *Gîta*. Some hundred quotations are cited in support of his doctrine. The *Gîta* is the work of an unknown author, and is in the form of a dialogue on the battle-field between Arjuna, the warrior, and his adviser and charioteer Sri Krishna,

---

[26] *Ibid*, V, 16.

[27] *Sri Bh*, II, ii, 40–43: 'As thus it is settled that the highest Brahman, as known from the Vedânta texts, or Narayana himself, is the promulgator of the entire Pancarâtra, and that this system teaches the nature of Narayana and the proper way of worshipping him, none can disestablish the view that in the Pancarâtra all the other doctrines are comprised.' Trs. George Thibaut (London: Oxford University Press, 1904; Delhi: Motilal Banarsidass, 1962), p. 530. Cf. J. A. B. Van Buitnen, *op. cit.*, on 'the influence of Pancarâtra Agama on Ramanuja', pp. 36–9.

[28] *Sri Bh*, II, ii, 43.

who is an *Avatâr* or incarnation of Vishnu. The document shows first of all its Agamic affiliation, since it shows the futility of Vedic practices,[29] and declares the path of pure knowledge towards salvation as the more arduous one.[30] On the other hand, it clearly shows its dependence on Upanishadic metaphysics, since the absolute reality of the one Supreme Lord is the basis of all its discussions.

Interioristic approach

The whole doctrine of the *Gîta* suggests an interioristic approach to reality. At the moment of giving battle, Arjuna is disturbed in conscience—caught between his duty as a warrior to fight the enemies, the great damages resulting from the battle, and the obligations towards kith and kin who are involved in the war. The whole substance of Krishna's exhortation is that Arjuna is viewing things from a superficial level, the level of sentiments and feelings, and that to get a real estimate of things he has to go beyond them to the depths of his own Self and find the unity of all things in the Supreme Lord of the Universe.[31]

Irenic philosophy

Discussion centres around the basic problems of religious life. What is the meaning of duty? What is the meaning of birth and

[29] *BG*, II, 42–5 : '. . . those who take delight in the word of the Veda . . . which is replete with various ritual acts, aiming at the goal of enjoyment and power . . . are robbed of insight by that. The Vedas have the three Gunas of matter as their scope. . . .' Cf. P. T. Srinivas Iyengar, *op. cit.*, p. 109.

[30] *BG*, VII, 5.

[31] *BG*, II, 11–17 : 'Thou hast mourned those who should not be mourned. . . . Dead and living men, the truly learned do not mourn. . . . Contact with matter causes cold and heat, pleasure and pain; they come and go, and are impermanent; put up with them, Son of Bharata. For whom these contacts do not cause to waver, the man to whom pain and pleasure are alike, the wise, he is fit for immortality. . . . But know that that is indestructible by which all this is pervaded. Destruction of this imperishable one no one can cause.'

BG, II, 25–9 : 'Unmanifest he, Unthinkable he, Unchangeable he is declared to be; therefore knowing him thus, thou shouldst not mourn him. . . .
By a rare chance one may see him,
And by a rare chance likewise may another declare him;
And by a rare chance may another hear of him;
But even having heard of him, no one whatsoever knows him.'

death? What is permanent and ultimately real in all this change, which appears so tragic on the battlefield? What has one to do to attain the Ultimate Reality?

In giving a solution to these questions, the author of the *Gîta* is caught between the different schools surrounding the milieu. He has to reconcile the logic and categories of the Nyâya-Vaiseshika, the *Purusha-Prakriti* (Soul-matter) dualism and evolutionary psychology of the Sâmkhya-Yoga, the transcendental absolutism of the Vedantins and the devotionalism of the *Bhakti* movement. Hence, *Gîta* is partly synthetic and partly syncretic. It combines the dualism and evolutionism of the Sâmkhya-Yoga with the Supreme Brahman of the Vedantins and goes beyond them by conceiving a mysticism centred on the personal God of the Bhaktas. Hence, *Gîta* is generally considered a handbook of Hindu Religion, though among scholars it never lost its sectarian colour. It was accepted only as a part of *smriti,* commentary literature on *Sruti* or Scripture proper, which is known generally as the *Veda*.

The Gîta *world-scheme*

The *Gîta* organizes the hierarchy of beings under the Supreme Lord, who is Brahman embracing all reality. 'I am the *Atman,*' says Krishna to Arjuna, 'that abides in the heart of all beings; I am the beginning and the middle, and the very end, too, of beings.'[32] He is unborn, undying, never ceasing, deathless.[33]

He is the creator of all things. But he does not fashion things directly. He allows *Prakriti*, which is his own *Mâyâ*, the power to produce unreality, to form things by the evolution of its functions of *sattva, rajas*, and *tamas*, the three *gunas* of reflexion, activity and limitation. This evolution helps the individual souls or Purushas, which are also eternal, to attain their final realization of identity with the Supreme.[34]

Though the Supreme Lord is not affected by his own power of *Mâyâ* or *Prakriti*, he still sometimes chooses to take a creature-form. This is called *Avatâr*: whenever right declines and evil is on the increase, he comes down to head the age and restore the balance of good and evil.[35] Though he is born, he is not limited because

[32] *BG,* X, 20.
[33] *BG,* II, 21.
[34] *BG,* IX, 4–14.
[35] *BG,* IV, 6–8.

his consciousness does not suffer any diminution. Though he is constantly active in the world, he is not affected by the limitations of action and its baneful fruits.[36]

The individual souls, on the other hand, though they are pure spirits, are finite and subject to the miseries of birth and death, pain and pleasure, knowledge and ignorance, until they reach their full self-realization and enter the heart of the Lord, which is their final abode. There they realize their absolute dependence on, and unity with, the Lord.

The *Vishnu Purâna*

The *Vishnyu Purânya* is a work of the same class which Ramanuja holds in great esteem as being universally accepted as authoritative, and quotes widely in support of his positions. It also recognizes a unique and supreme ground of all beings, Vasudeva, 'the unchangeable, holy, eternal, supreme Vishnu, of one universal nature, the mighty over all,' who is at the same time Hiranyagarbha (Brahma), the Creator, Hari and Siva, the preserver and the destroyer of the world.[37] This Supreme contained in himself all things :

> He, that Brahman, was all things; comprehending in his own nature the indiscrete and discrete. He then existed in the forms of *Purusha* and *Kâla*. *Purusha* (spirit) is the first form of the Supreme; next proceed two other forms, the discrete and indiscrete; and *Kâla* (time) was the last. These four—*Pradhâna* (primary or crude matter), *Purusha* (spirit), *Vyakta* (visible substance), and *Kâla* (time)—the wise consider to be the pure and supreme condition of Vishnu.[38]

Thus Prahalada, the Daitya prince, protests to his cruel father, Hiranyakasipu, concerning the instructions on political diplomacy imposed on him by the latter : 'It is idle to talk of friend or foe in Govinda, who is the Supreme Atman, Lord of the world, consisting of the world, and who is identical with all beings.'[39] This Supreme Lord, Vishnu, is the universal witness, who, seated in the hearts of all, beholds the good and ill of all. He is the one being 'to whom all return, from whom all proceed; who is all, and in whom all

[36] *BG*, IV, 14.
[37] *VP*, trs. H. H. Wilson (London, 1840), I, i, pp. 7–8.
[38] *Ibid.*, p. 9.
[39] *Ibid.*, c. xix, 36–7, p. 139.

things are (*yatra sarvam*; *yatah sarvam*, *yah sarvam*, *sarva sams-rayah*; *sarvagatvâdanantasya sa evâham avastitah*)'.[40] The coexistence of Vishnu and the world is declared in the paradoxical statement *vyatiriktam na yasyâsti vyatiriktô ghilasya yah* : 'He from whom nothing is distinct; he who is distinct from all.'[41] In the creation of the world he does not acquire anything new. He simply 'sports like a playful boy'.[42]

Thus the whole metaphysical scheme of the Sâmkhya-Yoga is assumed and subordinated to the Absolute of Vedanta, who is revered and adored as the Vishnu, Vasudeva and Govinda of the Vaishnavite *Bhakti* movement.

YAMUNACHARYA'S CONTRIBUTION

More than any one else, Yâmunacharya, Ramanuja's predecessor, as head of the school, prepared the ground for Ramanuja. His life's ambition seems to have been a complete synthesis between the Alvar *Bhakti* tradition and Vedânta metaphysics. The three projects which he is said to have left to his successor to accomplish are symbolic of this main concern : write a commentary on the *Vedânta Sûtras* according to the teaching of his school, a commentary on the *Bhagavad Gîta,* and a comprehensive treatise on the tenets of the school itself. Any authentic Vedantin has to show himself to be in conformity with the *Sûtras* of Bâdarâyana, which was the official text-book of the school; a commentary on those *Sûtras* would be the best way of showing that his school is authentically Vedantic—all the principal Vedânta teachers have written their own commentaries on the *Vedânta Sûtras.* The *Bhagavad Gîta* was already gaining the status of a handbook of Hinduism, and even Advaitins like Sankara were trying to interpret it in an Advaitic sense. Hence it could easily serve as common ground of agreement for all Vedantins, if not for all Hindus. A handbook of the school would give the *Bhakti* movement its own authentic metaphysics. Ramanuja wrote all three.

But the main lines of thought had already been drawn by Yâmuna himself in his *Siddhitraya.* In his *Atma Siddhi* and *Samvid Siddhi* he criticizes the Advaitic theories of the unity of Self, illusoriness of the universe, the concept of *Avidyâ* and the notion of

[40] *Ibid.,* xix, 83–4, p. 142.
[41] *Ibid,* xix, 78.
[42] *Ibid,* ii, 13–16, pp. 11–12.

pure consciousness. With regard to the right approach to reality he proposes, besides Scripture, inference and perception, and also an immediate apperception born of continuous meditation which becomes more and more clear with the intensity of concentration. The individual soul is not pure consciousness as Advaitins would have it, but a substance qualified by the essential property of knowledge. Even though by nature it is without limitation, it is still limited and distinguished by the body which it pervades.[43]

The Supreme Reality or Paramâtman is described as a person, a mighty ocean of all the auspicious qualities (*sakalakalyânagun-amahârnavam*), including the *shadgunas* or the six attributes indicated by the Pancarâtras and many more. On him depend the states and activities of the conscious beings in their three modes as well as of the material world. To explain the coexistence of the Supreme with the finite beings, he added to the Pancarâtra combinations of *kriyâ-vibhuti, aham-ahanta, âtman-sarîra*, the concepts of *amsa* and *amsin* (part and whole), *sesha* and *seshin* (adjunct and principal), possession and possessor, servant and master.[44]

Ramanuja faithfully followed the spirit of synthesis of his predecessor and brought his work to fulfilment.

RAMANUJA, THE SYNTHESIZER

Ramanuja's originality is mainly in his capacity for synthesizing the divergent opinions on a particular problem. Scholars generally admit that he is a faithful interpreter of Indian philosophical tradition in general, and of the *Vedânta Sûtras* of Bâdarâyana in particular,[45] though his views cannot be said to be identical with those of the *Sûtras*. The significant point in Ramanuja's dependence on the Upanishadic doctrine is that, though he quotes the Upanishads[46] in support of his positions, he does not attempt like

---

[43] *Atmasiddhi*, p. 3, quoted by J. A. B. Van Buitnen, *op. cit.*, p. 44.

[44] *Atmasiddhi*, pp. 3–5.

[45] George Thibaut, *The Vedânta Sûtras of Bâdarâyana with the Commentary of Sankara*, Introduction, The Sacred Books of the East Series, Vol. 34 (New York: Dover Publications, 1962), pp. xxiii–xxxi; Arthur Berridale Keith, *The Philosophy of the Vedas,* Harvard Oriental Series, Vols. 31 & 32, pp. 508–9; R. C. Zaehner, *The Comparison of Religions* (Boston: Beacon Press, 1962), p. 119; J. A. B. Van Buitnen, *Ramanuja on the Bhagavadgîta* (S. Gravenhague), Introduction, pp. 4–5.

[46] Against some principal twenty-six texts of the Upanishads and the Gîta adduced by the Advaitins, Ramanuja is able to bring some forty clear texts which uphold the real distinction between Brahman and the individual souls.

Sankara to bring all the Upanishads into a single definite scheme of doctrine. Still, his view suits many of the Upanishadic passages that he cites, and though his views are in many ways difficult to formulate with precision, his interpretation appears at least as a perfect alternative to that of Sankara.[47]

His approach to other systems and schools of Indian thought is conciliatory rather than polemic. Thus he agrees with the *Jaina* school of thought that reality is not a simple entity but a complex system which has to be examined from different angles; the conscious subjects which form the class of living beings, and the non-conscious objects, are the two main sections of this complex system. He also agrees with them that the human self has to rise to a higher level of purity and independence from material things through asceticism. What he objects to in the Jaina system is that they destroy the unity of the universe by denying the Supreme Lord. Besides, the intricate logic of the Jains predicates contradictory attributes to things and makes the multiplicity irreducible to any sort of unity.[48]

While, together with the *Sautrântika* Buddhists, he admits the reality of the external world, he rejects their materialism and joins ranks with the *Yogâchâra* Buddhists to defend the higher reality of knowledge, which is like light which illumines all material things.[49] At the same time, he refutes the Idealism of this latter school which denies the existence of external objects apart from knowledge. According to Ramanuja, this position is contrary to experience and opposed to the nature of knowledge itself, which implies a subject-object distinction.[50]

Similarly he rejects the *Sûnyavâda* or Void Theory of the *Mâdhyamika* Buddhists, showing that their apparently negative assertion contains a positive affirmation of being : 'If you declare "everything is nothing", your declaration is equivalent to the declaration, "everything is being", for your statement can only mean that everything that exists is capable of abiding in a certain condition (which you call "Nothing").'[51]

But the major field of synthesis is between the Sâmkhya dualism

[47] Cf. A. B. Keith, *The Philosophy of the Vedas,* pp. 508–9.

[48] *Sri Bh,* II, ii, 31–5. Cf. F. K. Lazarus, *Ramanuja and Bowne—A Study in Comparative Philosophy* (Bombay: Cetana, 1962), pp. 4–6.

[49] *Sri Bh,* II, ii, 25–9. F. K. Lazarus, *op. cit.,* pp. 7–9.

[50] *Ibid.*

[51] *Sri Bh,* II, ii, 30.

and evolution, and the transcendentalism of Vedânta. Thus Ramanuja admits the subtle condition of matter, *Prakriti*, as a principle of the origination of things, provided it is subordinate to, and dependent upon, the Supreme Brahman.

> We by no means wish to deny unevolved matter and all its effects in themselves, but in so far only as they are maintained not to have their self in the Supreme Person. . . . It is on the ground of just this dependence on the Lord not being acknowledged by the Sâmkhyas that their system is disproved by us.[52]

According to him the Sarîraka Sâstra, or Vedânta, is opposed to the Sâmkhya-Yoga schools only because they do not admit Brahman to be the ultimate self of the principles they postulate as ultimate.[53]

This positive and sympathetic examination of other systems helps Ramanuja to construct his own doctrine with confidence; yet he admits, with a certain amount of humility, the obscure points which defy a clear solution, such as the coexistence of the Infinite Absolute and the finite beings.

CONCLUSION

We have dealt with the background of Ramanuja's philosophy at some length, not because it is necessary to understand his thought, but because it shows how authentically representative he is of the Indian tradition. The system he constructed has behind it a plurality of views and trends, which do not break the unity of outlook in the approach to reality. A clear appreciation of this complex unity in plurality is very important in constructing a system of metaphysics against an Indian background. This is especially true of the Sankara-Ramanuja opposition within the Vedânta school, the Advaita-Visishthâdvaita controversy, which has been now going on for centuries and is even today kept very much alive. We shall discuss the unity underlying their apparently irreconcilable opposition in the next chapter.

[52] *Sri Bh,* I, iv, 3. Cf. I, iv, 8.
[53] *Sr Bh,* II, ii, 43.

CHAPTER IV

RAMANUJA AND SANKARA

The sharpest division within the Vedanta school is between the *Advaita* or non-dualism of Sankara and the *Visishthâdvaita* or qualified non-dualism of Ramanuja, since very few follow extreme dualism; most of the dualist schools align themselves with the position of Ramanuja in their opposition to Advaita, with only minor distinctions and additions. This opposition between Advaita and Visishthâdvaita is clearly brought out by Ramanuja, who devotes a disproportionate part of his commentary on the Brahma Sûtras to a refutation of the Advaitic position. The disagreement derives so much from the basic outlook on reality that the *pûrvapaksha,* or objections, presented by the Advaitin and the theses or *siddhânta* of Ramanuja mostly centre around the first word *athâtah* (which is a compound of two simple words *atha* = then and *atas* = therefore) of the first *Sûtra* of Bâdarâyana.

The *laghupûrvapaksha,* or minor objection, and the *laghu-siddhânta,* or minor thesis, are about the first word 'then' and centre around the approach or methodology towards the study of reality. The word denotes the relation between the *Pûrvamîmâmsa* or *Mîmâmsa* proper, which is ritualistic, and *Uttaramîmâmsa* or Vedânta, which is doctrinal. For Sankara, 'then' of the Sûtra means that the stage of action, asceticism and ritual proposed in *Mîmâmsa* is completely superseded at the stage of knowledge and in no way contributes to the final liberation which is attained solely by knowledge. For Ramanuja, on the other hand, 'then' means that action and knowledge are intimately related as two parts of the same path : what is imperfectly attained through action is perfected by knowledge.

Then comes the major difference on the second member of the compound, 'therefore' on which the *mahâpûrvapaksha,* or major objection, and the *mahâsiddhânta,* or major thesis, concentrate. 'Therefore' indicates the reason for undertaking the path of knowledge, the inquiry into Brahman. According to Sankara, the inquiry is undertaken because true knowledge brings the realization that Brahman is the unique and absolute reality, beside whom everything else is non-real (*anrita*), non-knowledge (*avidyâ*), and illusion (*mâyâ*). For Ramanuja, on the other hand, the value of the inquiry and of knowledge is the realization of the subordination and absolute dependence upon Brahman, the personal Lord, of individual souls and of the material world.

This sharp contrast of positions shows their difference in approach to the problem of reality as well as a certain basic unity. This basic unity in sharp opposition will reveal to us the true genius of Indian thought in its approach to reality.

SANKARA'S METHODOLOGY

Sankara's method of approach to reality is clear from his treatment of the first four *Sûtras* of Bâdarâyana, which together with the introduction, present five avenues of approach, and with the same attitude indicated above in the interpretation of the 'then', deny the finite to attain the Infinite. The five avenues are : (1) our personal consciousness; (2) volitional activity; (3) external experience of things; (4) Scripture; and, finally, (5) reasoning.

The anomaly of conscious experience

Sankara begins his commentary on the Bâdarâyana *Sûtras* with an analysis of the basic anomaly in our consciousness : that we in our experience and thought confuse the spheres of I and Thou, subject and object, opposed to each other as light and darkness; though the Self is the central, changeless point of consciousness, and objects belong to the changing field of non-self, we attribute the qualities of one to the other;[1] we say 'my house', 'my cow', etc., attributing 'I-hood' to material things, and 'I am stout', 'I feel pain', etc., ascribing what is properly of the body to the self. This cross-attribution is so natural to us that it is the presupposition of all our practical knowledge and even of the Veda.[2] Still, from the aspect of reality, the two fields cannot be ascribed the same value. 'Immutability is the true condition of things; for that is indepen-

---

[1] *Ved S Sank Bh,* Introduction. Trs. George Thibaut, *op. cit.,* pp. 3–4.
[2] *Ibid.,* p. 6.

dent of external causes. The true condition of anything is independent of an agent.'[3]

Hence, one is forced to make a choice between the subject and the object, the I and the Thou (or non-I) as real, and reject the other as unreal. Sankara has no doubt that here the 'I' is the field of the real, and the non-I is the area of the non-real.

Finality and desire

Consideration of *jijnâsâ*, desire to know, presents the question from another angle, namely that of our volitional activity. It asks what is the real goal of man. Bondage is essentially ignorance; hence liberation is the attainment of proper knowledge. Internal teleology of nature for attaining liberation in the plenitude of consciousness is the common doctrine of Hindu schools of thought. In Nyâya-Vaiseshika and Sâmkhya-Yoga, this finality is conceived as an impersonal and unconscious force; for Nyâya-Vaiseshika, it is the *adrishtha*,[4] the unseen force grouping the atoms into various things; for Sâmkhya-Yoga the force is immanent in *Prakriti*, which enters into evolution like a dancer to manifest itself before *Purusha* and thus achieve the latter's liberation in *Kaivalya*, or isolation.[5]

But in Vedânta this tendency towards the end is a rational desire for liberation born of the realization of the miseries of the present existence. Hence, Sankara states the object of his commentary on the *Vedânta Sûtras*: 'With a view to freeing one's self from that wrong notion which is the cause of all evil and attaining thereby the knowledge of the absolute unity of the self, the study of the Vedânta texts is begun.'[6]

Thus our volitional activity presents the metaphysical problem under a new aspect: what is the real way of liberation from present suffering? Here again the solution is clear for Sankara:

[3] *Tait Up Sank Bh,* I, II, Cf. II, 8. Anandasrama Sanskrit Series, Vol. 14 (Poona, 1908).

[4] Cf. *Vai S of Kanâda,* V, i, 15; V, ii, 13; V, ii, 17; the movement of the metal to the magnet, the motion of fire upwards and of air sideways, and the egress, etc., of the soul, all caused by the *adrishtha*. Sacred Books of the Hindus, Vol. VI (Allahabad, 1923).

[5] Cf. *Sâm K,* nos. 21, 57, 59, 60, 63. 'As non-intelligent milk functions for the nourishment of the calf, so does the *Prakriti* function for the liberation of *Purusha*' (No. 57), ed. and trs. Har Dutt Sharma (Poona: Oriental Book Agency, 1933).

[6] *Ved S Sank Bh,* Introduction, p. 9.

'Complete comprehension of Brahman is the highest end of man.'[7] Nothing finite, even if it be good works or ritual, can bring final liberation. What originates, what is limited, is subject to change and can be lost. Hence, their possession does not end bondage, but rather serves only to accentuate it, since they bind us more tightly to the world of change.

Experience and reality

Our desire for liberation operates in the field of external experience. Hence, the question arises as to how experience relates us to reality. On the one hand, Sankara defends the validity of our experience in practical life. But it cannot by itself lead us to the knowledge of the real. Brahman, the absolutely real, does not fall within our experience, nor can he be known from *anumâna,* or generalizations from sense experience. But, since he is an existing thing, he cannot be known through our subjective opinions or wishes. The only way to know him as he really is is *anubhava,* realization.[8] The function of our finite knowledge, including that derived from Scripture, is merely pedagogical, to tell us *neti, neti,* 'he is not so, not so'. It is like a teacher who wants to show the student the star *Arundhati,* but first indicates several other stars immediately discernible just to say that they are not what he means, but the one beyond them.[9]

From Scripture to Brahman

Scripture is the only source of information concerning supra-sensible realities.[10] But it also demands the same mode of procedure. For Vedantins generally, Scripture is not the recorded testimony of someone. It is *apaurusheya,* impersonal, the expression of the wisdom of ages. It contains the intuition gained by sages and committed to human speech. So its human mode, the injunctions

---

[7] *Tait Up Sank Bh,* II, 8.

[8] *Ved S Sank Bh,* I, i, 2, pp. 17–18.

[9] *Ved S Sank Bh,* p. 19; I, i, 12, p. 66: 'Just as when a man, desirous of pointing out the star Arundhati to another man, at first points to several stars which are not Arundhati as being Arundhati, while the only star pointed out in the end is the real Arundhati; so here also the Self consisting of bliss is the real Self on account of being the innermost.'

[10] *Ved S Sank Bh,* I, i, 3, p. 21.

and prohibitions, are only the material vehicle by which the know-ledge of the Ultimate Reality is indicated to us. It is like a sign-post; it only points the way. One has to leave the sign-post behind and walk on the way to reach one's destination. Hence, the only meaning of Scripture is to lead us to final Brahma-realization. Therefore, the knowledge of Brahman is the central theme of all the different books of Scripture, and which unites them all like a golden thread.[11]

Reasoning and reality

According to Sankara, reasoning is not a source of information concerning suprasensible reality, but only a 'samanvaya', a co-ordination of the various sources. Though Scripture is absolute wisdom, it is presented in the language of human experience. Hence, at the same time as indicating the nature of the Ultimate Reality, it also contains several injunctions and prohibitions purely in view of practical life, and in a way hides Brahman. Hence, even in Scripture, we need reasoning to understand the real nature of Brahman.[12] This rational approach to Brahman from the empirical statements of Scripture is called lakshana or analogy, which means that Brahman should be understood as the ultimate value and final purpose of all the statements of Scripture, though we have to distinguish between primary statements, which by their very nature refer directly to Brahman, and the secondary statements directly referring to practical life and which have only an indirect reference to Ultimate Reality.[13] Hence, the use of reasoning in the inquiry into reality demands a denial of the empiric aspect and a certain transcendence in subordination to Scripture.[14]

It (Brahman) should first be heard from a teacher, and from the Scriptures, then reflected on through reasoning, and then steadfastly meditated upon. Thus only is It realized—when these means, viz., hearing, reflexion and meditation, have been gone through. When these three are combined, only then is true realiza-tion of the unity of Brahman accomplished.[15]

[11] Ved S Sank Bh, pp. 20–2.
[12] Ved S Sank Bh, I, i, 4, pp. 22–47.
[13] Tait Up Sank Bh, II, 1.
[14] Ved S Sank Bh, II, i, 11, pp. 316–7.
[15] Brih Up Sank Bh, II, iv, 5 (Delhi: Motilal Banarsidass, 1964); trs. Swami Madhavananda (Mayavati, Almora : Advaita Asrama, 1934), p. 360.

But what if a conflict should arise between reasoning and Scripture? Sankara's position is that there cannot be a conflict between the two. If one should appear to occur, reasoning should yield and the difficulty be explained away before the ineffable reality presented by Scripture.[16]

Thus, according to Sankara, the world of reality is presented to us through internal consciousness, desire for liberation, external experience, Scripture and reasoning. But in each the finite and limited has to be superseded and left behind so that the unique Absolute may shine by its own light.

Ramanuja's reaction to Sankara's methodology

Ramanuja agrees with the Advaitins that bondage is ignorance and that knowledge of Brahman is the means for liberation. But his objection is against the Sankarite insistence on pure knowledge without action. Such an abstract knowledge cannot achieve liberation. For,

(1) Mere knowledge can be obtained by a study of the syntactical meaning of the sentences of Scripture, and the application of right logic. But this by itself will not bring discrimination, which alone can put an end to ignorance and bondage.[17]

(2) If knowledge can coexist with non-discrimination and embodiment, it is clear that such pure abstract knowledge is not the liberating factor.

(3) Bondage which consists in innate non-discrimination 'by reason of its accumulation from beginningless time' is too strong to be removed by mere mental conception. It has to be fought on its own level through asceticism. Hence, only that knowledge, 'which is different from the knowledge of the syntactical meaning of sentences, and is imported by words such as *dhyâna*

---

[16] *Ved S Sank Bh,* II, i, 13, p. 318.

[17] *Sri Bh,* I, i, 1, trs. M. Rangâchârya and M. B. Varadaraja Aiyangar (Madras: The Brahmavadin Press, 1899), pp. 15–16. (This edition is referred to hereafter as RVA.) The text of *Sri Bh* is edited by Sri Kanchi P. B. Annangaracharya Swamy in *Sri Bhagavad Râmânuja Granthamâla,* comprising all the nine works of Ramanuja. There are several excellent English translations of *Sri Bh* besides the one by George Thibaut cited above—(This edition is refered to hereafter as T.)—e.g. the translation by R. D. Karmarkar (Poona: University of Poona, Sanskrit and Prakrit Series, 1959 and 1961). (This edition is referred to hereafter as K.)

(meditation), *upâsana* (worship), etc.,' can remove ignorance and bondage. This *dhyâna* concept cuts at the very root of Sankara's methodology. It is not a discarding of the finite and empirical state, but an integration in which a person, faithful to caste-duty and ritual, unites all the means of right knowledge to gain a total and intense realization of the Ultimate Reality.[18]

(4) Ramanuja goes on to adduce a great number of Upanishadic texts in which not mere theoretical knowledge but meditation is prescribed.[19] According to Ramanuja, the distinction between primary texts and secondary texts, those which directly refer to the Absolute Reality and those which only indirectly refer to it, is arbitrary. All texts, even words, primarily and directly refer to Brahman, the ground and substance of all finite things and only secondarily and by participation to things which derive their reality from him.[19*] Ramanuja also adduces the authority of the ancient Acharyas like Tanka and Bodhayana[20] who identify knowledge (*vedanâ*) and worship (*upâsana*) and show the integral unity between action and knowledge.[21]

(5) Ramanuja's most serious objection is against the secondary role ascribed to reasoning in the inquiry into the nature of Reality. For Sankara, reasoning is only the starting point and Scripture is the intuition of sages, which, when realized by the individual, completely supersedes reasoning, and is its own proof and justification. But for Ramanuja, Scripture is verbal testimony, also based on experience and reasoning for its intelligibility. Hence, reasoning is basic, even in the understanding of Scripture. Reasoning is a norm for all other sources of knowledge : 'If logical reasoning refutes something known through some other means of knowledge, that means of knowledge is no longer authoritative.'[22]

---

[18] *Sri Bh* (RVA.), pp. 16–17.

[19] This knowledge is designated as *prajnâ* (*Brih Up*, IV, iv, 21), *dhyâna* (*Mûnd Up*, II, ii, 6), *nichaya* (*Kath Up*, III, 15), *upâsana* (*Brih Up*, I, iv, 15), *sravana, manana* and *nididhyâsa* (*Brih Up*, II, iv, 5).

[19*] *Sri Bh,* II, ii, 17 : 'The terms which are connected with the different moving and non-moving things, and hence denote those things, possess with regard to Brahman a denotative power which is not *"bhakta"*, i.e. secondary or figurative, but primary and direct. . . . Because the denotative power of all words is dependent on the being of Brahman.'

[20] Cf. J. A. B. Van Buitnen, *Ramanuja's Vedarth,* pp. 18–29, about the identity of Ancient Masters Bodhayana, Tanka and others whom Ramanuja adduces as authority.

[21] *Sri Bh,* I, i, 1, pp. 5–20.

[22] *Ibid.,* p. 21.

SANKARA'S VISION OF REALITY

Greater space is devoted by Ramanuja to a discussion of the second member of the first word of Bâdarâyana's first Sûtra, *atah* = therefore. Here in the *mahâpûrvapaksha*, or great objection, Advaitin's position occupies the major part. Sankara's reason for undertaking the study of Vedânta is the need to remove the *avidyâ*, which is at the root of our sense of multiplicity, opposition between I and Thou, subject and object, and to attain the knowledge of Brahman as the self of all.

The key concept of Sankara

There is a certain amount of difference of opinion among scholars concerning the key concept of Sankara's Metaphysics. According to Dr. P. T. Raju, it is the Logic of Non-Contradiction : The question is to decide between things that do really exist and those which only seem to exist. One has to start with the fact that all these things are experienced as existing. Then a criterion is formulated, the criterion of non-contradiction, namely whether the things we experience as existing 'involve a contradiction of their own nature' or not. In this reflective process, the criterion is not merely epistemological but also metaphysical. On applying this criterion, we find that everything finite involves its own negation. Hence, in spite of appearances, the finite should be considered as false existence, and only the infinite which does not involve such contradiction as really existing.[23]

But this interpretation seems to present Sankara's approach as

[23] P. T. Raju, *Idealistic Thought of India* (London: George Allen & Unwin, 1953), p. 124; Cf. A. G. Krishna Warrier, 'Brahman as Value', *The Adyar Library Bulletin,* 25 (1961), p. 483: 'If to be contradictory is to be false, then the categories of the phenomenal world like cause, substance and relations, are false, being contradictory. But what is false implies something non-contradictory. . . . This real basis in Advaita is Brahman whose realization expresses the falsity of the phenomenal world.' But the source of this interpretation may be Bradley as it appears from the ref. 'Ultimate Reality is such that it does not contradict itself—this is an absolute criterion also, for in doubting it, we tacitly assume its validity' (*Appearance and Reality,* p. 139). But, Sankara never says that the finite reality is contradictory. It is our confusion of the spheres of I and Thou, subject and object, that is the source of ignorance.

a rather negative one and too theoretical to account for the positive contribution of his metaphysics.

Some others, like Dr. R. P. Singh and Dr. A. G. Krishna Warrier, try to interpret Sankara's philosophy as a form of Value Philosophy : The world is a variable; its value and significance change with the culture and spiritual insight of the individual who evaluates it.[24] According to A. G. Krishna Warrier the basic question is not whether for the Advaitin the world is an illusion or not, but rather 'To whom is the world real, phenomenal, or illusory?' To the *siddha,* the one who has already attained liberation in this life, there is no world at all by the side of the Absolute. To the 'Advaitic dialectician' and to the *siddha* who returns to the awareness of the plurality, the world may be accountable as illusion. To the worldly-minded man, the world is the sole reality.[25]

The anachronism and incongruity in projecting a twentieth-century European philosophy to interpret the mind of an eighth-century Indian philosopher are apparent in all such rationalizations. But the basic difficulty in this interpretation is that, for Sankara, there does not exist a permanent subject which passes from one level to another, the one who evaluates and profits from the world of finite beings.

According to M. K. Venkatarama Iyer, the keynote of Sankara's Metaphysics is Epistemological Realism : whatever is perceived must be, so far, real. In this evaluation we find three levels of reality : (1) *prâtibhâsika sattâ* or phenomenal reality which is that of our illusions and dreams, having existence only in the mind of the dreamer; (2) *vyâvahârika sattâ* or empiric reality : 'what is

---

[24] R. P. Singh, *The Vedânta of Sankara, A Metaphysics of Value,* Vol. I (Jaipur, 1949), pp. 292–5.

[25] A. G. Krishna Warrier, 'A New Angle on the Problem of Unreality in Advaita,' *Prabuddha Bharata,* LXIX (1964), p. 112. 'Brahman as Value,' *op. cit.,* pp. 477–510. The inspiration for this interpretation, derived from Western contemporary thought, is clear from the frequent reference to books and authors of the Value Philosophy. The key statement is taken from C. E. M. Joad: 'Philosophy is concerned not with phenomena, but with their meaning; not with facts, but with values; not with what is, but with what "ought" to be; not with means, but with ends.' (Cited from *Philosophy for Our Times,* 1940, p. 25.) But 'value' belongs to a context of action, where the end and meaning predominate over means, facts and phenomena. Sankara, on the other hand, was for doing away with action. For him, the way for attaining liberation was not producing anything, but realizing what actually is.

matter of common experience belongs to a higher order of reality';
(3) *Pâramârthika sattâ* or transcendent reality: this is Brahma
consciousness in which the subject-object dualism is transcended;
the world of finite beings belongs to the second level; it is real
for all practical purposes.[26]

But this 'epistemological' interpretation also seems to be too
inadequate to understand the vision of Sankara.

Perhaps, Ramanuja gives the best statement about the basic
position of Sankara: 'Brahman alone, who is pure intelligence and
hostile to all characterizing attributes, is real; all other things than
Him . . . are merely assumed to exist in Him, and are unreal.'[27]
'Unreality is that which, being grounded upon what is perceived,
is liable to be stultified by means of the knowledge of things as
they actually are', like the case of the rope mistaken for a snake.[28]
Pure intelligence or perfect consciousness is the test of reality: anything that shows a defect of intelligence or consciousness is liable
to change its image, and, hence, is unreal.

The Upanishadic background of Sankara's position

In the Upanishads, consciousness or knowledge is the basic note
of real existence. Ramanuja's claim to be in conformity with the
Upanishads made him pay full attention to the texts adduced by
Sankara in support of his position. Ignorance or absence of the
knowledge of Brahman is the cause of embodiment, bondage and
suffering. Hence liberation is knowledge, the knowledge of the
Atman, which is *satyasya satyam*, the Truth of truth.[29] He is 'real
infinite, intelligence',[30] pure knowledge and bliss.[31] Hence He is
the one reality that has to be known,[32] the knowledge of which is
the fulfilment of all desires,[33] and includes the knowledge of all

[26] M. K. Venkatarama Iyer, *Advaita Vedânta* (Bombay: Asia Publishing
House, 1964), pp. 47–9.
[27] *Sri Bh,* I, i, 1, p. 27.
[28] *Ibid.,* p. 30.
[29] *Brih Up,* II, i, 20.
[30] *Tait Up,* II, 1: *satyam jnânam anantam Brahma.*
[31] *Brih Up,* III, ix, 28: *vijnânam ânandam Brahma.*
[32] *Kau Up,* IV, 19.
[33] *Chând Up,* VIII, vii, 12: 'He attains all regions and all desires who
has sought to know the Self and understands it.'

other things :[34] by knowing Brahman, everything else is known;[35] he who knows Brahman becomes Brahman.[36]

Analysis of consciousness

The basic problem for Sankara is what is the ideal or authentic state of consciousness. Only by solving this question can the natural error of our daily conscious experience, in which the spheres of the I and Thou are confused and cross-attributed, be properly resolved. The Ideal state, designated as *svarûpa* and *svabhâva*, is that in which a thing is itself alone unmixed with anything else. Thus in the blowing of a conch, and in music, sound alone and not the individual notes constitute the *svarûpa*.[37] In the various utensils made with clay or gold, clay or gold alone is the *svarûpa*; in the cloth the thread is the *svarûpa* or reality.[38]

When this concept is applied to the field of knowledge, it appears that the time-place circumstances which distinguish the individual acts of knowledge do not belong to its essence.[39] They change and are not always found. Similarly, what distinguishes between waking state, dreaming state, dreamless sleep, and pure consciousness of realization, does not pertain to the essence of knowledge. Only the common factor in these varying states constitutes its ideal condition.[40] This is *cinmâtra*, pure consciousness or sense of 'I'.[41]

This ideal and immutable essence of knowledge should constitute the Absolute Reality, which is therefore of the nature of pure consciousness, *bodharûpa* pure self-awareness, *cidânandaikarûpa*, of the form of knowledge and bliss alone.[42] It is so pure that it does not admit even the subject-object, knower-knowledge-knowable distinctions.[43] Sankara finds the *Taittirîya Upanishad* statement *satyam jnânam anantam Brahma* the best designation of the Absolute Reality, though he will not take it as a definition of Brahman, nor as a list of the attributes of the Absolute, but only a designative

[34] *Mûnd Up*, I, 1 : *sa brahmavidyâm sarvavidyâpratishtham.*
[35] *Chând Up*, VI, i, 1.
[36] *Mûnd Up*, III, ii, 9 : *Brahmaved brahmaiva bhavati.*
[37] *Brih Up Sank Bh*, II, iv, 7, trs. Swami Madhavananda, p. 355.
[38] *G Bh*, II, 16, ed. Dinkar Vishnu Gokhale (Poona, 1950).
[39] *Brih Up Sank Bh*, I, iv, 11, trs. Madhavananda, pp. 364–6.
[40] *Mândy K Sank Bh*, I, 7.
[41] *Brih Up Sank Bh*, II, iv, 9, p. 360.
[42] Sankara, *Atmabodha*, stanza 41.
[43] *Ved S Sank Bh*, Introduction, pp. 5–6.

statement, which points to it as pure consciousness, immutable and infinite; Brahman is *satyam*, the only one who truly is, because He alone is immutable.[44] Immutability is the true condition of reality, since what changes is not itself; Brahman is *jnânam*, fully in itself and shining by itself, and hence also *anatam*, infinite; any limitation will mean imperfection and change.[45]

The World of Mâyâ and Avidyâ

Looking from the side of Brahman—absolute, immutable and infinite consciousness—it is clear that there cannot be anything real outside of or beside it. Hence, everything that falls within our experience should either be reduced to Brahman or relegated to the level of the unreal or illusory. Sankara reduces all that is pure perfection in our conscious experience, such as the sense of I, to Brahman : all this is as light reflected on a piece of glass, the waves and foam projected over the water of the mighty ocean. What is left besides this ultimate reality is merely limitation and determination, namely 'name and form'. 'Although one and the same Self is hidden in all beings . . . yet owing to the gradual rise of excellence of the minds which form the limiting conditions . . . the Self, although eternally unchanging and uniform, reveals itself in a graduated series of beings, and so appears in forms of various dignity and power.'[46]

Sankara's system is called *Advaita,* non-dualism. This is not monism. The negative 'a' only negates the world as a reality added to or beside the Absolute. Hence the world is said to be *mâyâ.* *Mâyâ* is a term which has had different meanings in different contexts in Hindu tradition. Most of these can be reduced to two radical ones, *prâjna,* namely power, knowledge, etc., and *kapata,* deception, mystery, illusion, etc. Advaitic use of *mâyâ* seems to assume both these opposite meanings : on the one hand it is Brahman's light diffusing itself, the power producing illusion, and on the other, the illusory and unreal world beside Brahman, something in itself *anirvacanîya,* mysterious. *Mâyâ* is at best said to be a mystery, a veil around Brahman.[47] Hence it is not false, but

---

[44] *Tait Up Sank Bh,* II, 1.
[45] *Ibid.*
[46] *Ved S Sank Bh,* I, i, 11, p. 63.
[47] Prahbu Dutt Shastri, *The Doctrine of Mâyâ* (London : Luzac & Co., 1911), pp. 7–13.

only non-real (*anrita*), not ignorance but only not knowledge (*avidyâ*).[47*]

RAMANUJA'S CRITICISM OF SANKARA'S POSITION

Ramanuja's general remark about the whole *Mahâpûrvapaksha* is that it is a theory built up with a deceptive and false reasoning, with no concern for religious values, by people 'who have no insight into the nature of words and sentences, into the real purport conveyed by them, and into the procedure of sound argumentation'.[48] He goes on to counter Sankara's conclusions point by point. This criticism of the Advaitic philosophy has been so fundamental a part of his system that his successors have perpetuated his arguments. A few decades after his death, Sri Vedânta Desikar, a prolific writer and a consummate dialectician, reformulated those objections into a book entitled *Sata Dûshanyi*, a hundred counter arguments, while the leaders of the Advaita school answered them with the same vigour.[49] But a good many Advaita scholars have often taken a policy of ignoring the *Visishthâdvaita* objections with the implication that the Ramanuja school is merely proposing a popular religious philosophy fit for the common people, and therefore that their position does not deserve to be handled as metaphysics,[50] which title Sankara's philosophy seems to reserve for itself. The main points of Ramanuja's criticism are the following :

(1) The means of right knowledge do not present to us an attributeless Reality as the Advaitins hold. For these means of right knowledge, perception, inference and Scripture to which the Advaitins constantly appeal 'deal with objects such as possess attributes'. For, anything can be demonstrated only by its specific notes or attributes.[51]

(2) Advaitic definition of consciousness as *svayamprakâsatva*, pure self-illumination, is faulty, 'because perception becomes possible to the knower only in the way of bringing external objects to

---

[47*] *Ved S Sank Bh,* I, i, 10–17.
[48] *Sri Bh,* I, i, 1, p. 53.
[49] S. M. Srinivasa Chari, *Advaita and Visishthâdvaita. A Study based on Vedânta Desika's Satadûshanyi* (London: Asia Publishing House, 1961); Krishna Datta Bharadwaj, *op. cit.,* pp. 76–82.
[50] Cf. R. D. Karmarkar, Introduction to the Trs. of *Sri Bh.*
[51] *Sri Bh,* pp. 54–6.

the light of consciousness'. Consciousness is not mere luminosity, but consciousness of something.[52] Even the aspect of self-luminosity is true only when the subject brings objects into its own consciousness; but this luminosity itself can be an object too, when one experience becomes reviewed in a subsequent reflexion; one man's consciousness can become the object of another's consciousness.[53]

(3) The Sankarite contention adduced in support of the above thesis of the simplicity of consciousness, that perception apprehends only pure existence, is also refuted on the testimony of experience. For 'perception has for its objects only such things as are characterized by generic and other properties'.[54] Ramanuja rejects the Sankarite objection that the general and particular cannot be perceived in the same moment, and that if one has to be perceived in the other, it will lead to an infinite regress. For, 'even if perceptual knowledge lasts only for one moment, yet during that very moment' the generic properties and the distinctions are perceived together. If existence alone were perceived in all things, it would not be possible to distinguish between a jar and a cloth.[55]

(4) But the main Advaitic thesis against which Ramanuja has to marshal his arguments is the absolutization of consciousness, namely the Sankarite notion of consciousness as an unoriginated and attributeless and purely self-subsistent entity. Even eternality, self-illuminating nature and unity are all attributes outside the notion of consciousness itself. All stages of knowledge such as perception, inference and even yogic intuition—known as *jnâna*, *avagati*, and *samvit*—have relation to some object and lead to some practical purpose.[56] To say that there is pure objectless consciousness in deep sleep, intoxication, fainting and other similar physical conditions is an arbitrary assumption. If there were pure experience in these states, there is no reason why such consciousness should not continue at the time of awakening.[57]

(5) The identification of consciousness and conscious subject is a crucial point in the Advaitic absolutization of consciousness :

(*a*) The evident fact against identification is our own experience, in which we find the same subject 'I' is conscious of

[52] *Sri Bh*, p. 55.
[53] *Sri Bh*, pp. 65–77.
[54] *Sri Bh*, p. 60.
[55] *Sri Bh*, pp. 61–4.
[56] *Sri Bh*, p. 61.
[57] *Sri Bh*, pp. 57–9.

different states and acts of consciousness, such as 'I experienced that yesterday', 'I know this', and so on.

(b) The very consciousness 'I know' indicates knowledge as an attribute of the 'I'. The I-entity opposed to the object is the self, and consciousness relates the self to the object.

(c) The one who strives for liberation from the state of bondage, which is ignorance, a limitation of consciousness, acts with the conviction that his now limited consciousness can attain fullness without losing its self-identity. If mere abstract and individuality-less consciousness were the ideal of liberation, there is no reason for me to strive for it, since it will not be 'my' consciousness, and even if I am dead there will remain some such consciousness by itself.

(d) The existence and nature of our special consciousness is so intimately dependent on its relation to the definite subject and to the objects that if it were taken out of this relational context and identified with a subject, consciousness itself would become unintelligible.[58]

For Sankara, the I-Thou opposition is the basis of all false knowledge. For Ramanuja, on the other hand, it is the very essence of knowledge : If consciousness is conceived on the analogy of light, then it is a substance of which luminosity is an attribute. 'If a thing brings to light its own nature as well as other things, it is thereby said to possess luminosity.'[59]

(6) The denial of the reality of particular things is the counterpart of the Advaitic absolutization of consciousness : only those things are real which endure unchanged in all states of consciousness; only pure *cit*, consciousness, is constant like this. But this argument is refuted by Ramanuja on logical grounds : only contradiction between two perceptions makes one of them unreal or illusory, as the rope taken for a snake, and then experienced as rope in the same time-place circumstances. But experience of a thing as existing in one set of time-place circumstances and as non-existing in another context, as is the case in Sankara's four states of consciousness, does not imply any contradiction. Hence the criterion between the real and the unreal is an invalid one.[60]

(7) On the other hand, the Advaitin makes too much of *ajnâna*, non-knowledge, by identifying it with the world of experience; for *ajnâna* by its very nature is only a negation, the antecedent negation of *jnâna*. The Advaitins make it a positive entity, *bhâva rûpa*.

[58] *Sri Bh,* pp. 61–3.
[59] *Sri Bh,* I, i, 1, pp. 79–80.
[60] *Sri Bh,* pp. 64–5.

Ramanuja specially criticizes Sankara's attribution of 'knowership' to *ahamkâra*, egoity, which is merely an evolute of *mâyâ* or *prakriti*; for 'this material principle of *ahamkâra* which constitutes an internal organ is like the body, possessed of non-selfhood'. It belongs to the field of the object. Hence, consciousness, selfhood and knowership cannot be ascribed to it.[61] Only the individual soul, which is of the nature of consciousness, can be the seat of knowership.

(8) This Sankarite identification of individual self in its individuality with the aggregate of the evolutes of *mâyâ* makes the very idea of liberation meaningless, for, in this supposition, liberation should be the end of I-hood. 'Then final release would come to mean the enunciation of the destruction of the Self.' The 'I' is no mere attribute or external adjunct, but the core of the self itself. It is this 'I' that is beset in the present condition with the suffering from the threefold sources of material, living and spiritual levels, and craves to be liberated from it.[62]

(9) Of paramount importance in a metaphysical evaluation is the role ascribed to reason by Sankara and Ramanuja. According to Sankara, in suprasensible matters, when there is a conflict between Scripture and reasoning, the former should be held valid and the latter explained away. But Ramanuja ascribes the pride of place to reasoning; whatever makes perception false and erroneous affects Scripture also. Advaitins, in proving the illusoriness of the world from Scripture, are involved in a vicious circle : Illusoriness of the world of experience is based on Scripture; but Scripture itself can be known only in terms of experience, which is based on ignorance. It is idle to argue that an illusion can give rise to true knowledge, for 'the defectiveness of the foundation of Scripture having once been recognized, the circumstance of its later existence is of no avail. For if a man is afraid of a rope which he mistakes for a snake, his fear does not come to an end because another man, whom he considers to be in error himself, tells him, "This is no snake, do not be afraid!" '[63] Ramanuja's position is clearly stated in these words : 'If logical reasoning refutes something known through some other means of knowledge, that means of knowledge is no longer authoritative.'[64]

[61] *Sri Bh*, pp. 85–6.
[62] *Sri Bh*, pp. 95–6.
[63] *Sri Bh*, pp. 97–100.
[64] *Sri Bh*, p. 100.

COMPLEMENTARITY OF ADVAITA AND VISISHTHADVAITA

The sincerity and conviction with which the Advaitins and Visishthâdvaitins defend their respective positions and face squarely the position of the other side indicates that both of them are right to a great extent and that the apparently irreconcilable opposition between them is mostly owing to a lack of comprehension of the other side's outlook and presuppositions. Once these are understood, it can be seen that their positions are not contradictory but rather complementary.

Their difference of approach

(1) From Experience to Ideal Consciousness : The radical difference is in the use they make of the finite individual conscious experience in the investigation of absolute reality. For Sankara, finite conscious experience is only a stepping-stone to absolute consciousness : Our conscious experience shows a radical anomaly, the I-Thou opposition, the confusion and cross-attribution of what belongs to one field to the other. Hence, the first step towards the understanding of reality as such is to transcend the field of the finite, retaining only what is most basic to it as ideal : consciousness shorn of its time-place conditions. This pure consciousness, *cinmâtra*, is *the* reality from which everything else has to be evaluated.

But, for Ramanuja, the finite conscious experience is valid, and it is through it and in terms of it that everything else is to be evaluated. It is not self-luminosity, pure and simple, but a light that reveals itself and other objects. Hence the subject-object relation is not an antinomy nor an anomaly, but the very nature of consciousness.

(2) Means of Right Knowledge : If we start with Sankara with simple and absolute consciousness as our standard of evaluation, the means of right knowledge, perception, reasoning and Scripture are inadequate means which can only point the finger away from themselves to true knowledge. Their function is rather negative, and purely designative as far as the positive function is concerned. Hence, they have to be transcended and superseded in our striving towards the final stage of *anubhava,* which is realization of consciousness shining by itself.

But, from Ramanuja's point of view, with the emphasis on finite consciousness as the valid ideal, every means of right knowledge is real and brings real knowledge. Though, with regard to supra-sensible matters, Scripture is held to be the authentic source of knowledge, the help of experience and reasoning is indispensable in order to determine its exact meaning. Hence, the ideal and full knowledge for man is not an isolated consciousness shut in itself, but an integration of all the means of right knowledge concentrated in total self-surrender and devotion on the supreme object of knowledge, Brahman.

(3) Attitude towards Scripture: from Sankara's point of view, Scripture is *apaurusheya,* impersonal, the realization of absolute reality committed to writing by the sages in order that the same realization may originate in well-disposed readers. Hence, though it has the defect of the empirical human word, what it suggests and helps to originate is something higher than itself, the Brahma-realization. Scripture does not *impart* knowledge or produce realiza-tion but only helps towards the origination of *anubhava,* which is by its clarity and directness higher than Scripture itself and is its own proof on account of its superior clarity. To one who has attained it, Scripture and all other means of knowledge become superfluous and useless.

For Ramanuja, however, Scripture is a means of knowledge because it is tradition embodying the experience of bygone ages, as well as the word of the personal God who is 'more loving than even a thousand parents'.[65] Here it is the task of the individual to grasp the meaning of what is said in Scripture, and empirical knowledge and reasoning are necessary for this.

(4) Aspects of Reality Emphasized: On account of the difference in point of outlook, the aspects of reality emphasized by the two are also different. If pure consciousness is taken as the ideal reality, Supreme Reality is immutable and infinite truth which does not allow any limitation or distinction within itself. There cannot be anything beside it or additional to it. Hence, everything empirical has to be characterized as *an-ritam, a-vidyâ,* and since it is a denial of reality in terms of consciousness, the only way to characterize it is as *mâyâ,* illusion.

---

[65] *Sri Bh,* I. i. 7. Cf. II, ii, 3: 'The *Sastra* (scripture) is constituted by the aggregate of words called Veda, which is handed on by an endless, unbroken succession of pupils learning from qualified teachers, and raised above all suspicion of imperfections such as spring from mistake and the like.'

On the other hand, from the aspect of individual consciousness, the point of evaluation of Ramanuja, to call the world and individual souls *mâyâ*, illusion, is to deny their very existence and reduce them to mere fancy or dream. The only consistent procedure open for him was to assert the reality of the world and of the individual souls, but also to go beyond them to a deeper level to affirm the absolute and all-comprehensive reality of Brahman, the ground and substance and soul of all things.

Sankara was careful not to assign a locus for the *anrita-avidyâ-mâyâ*. To the question : 'What was the subject of this illusion?' his consistent answer was the counter question : 'Who is asking this question?' In his conceptual system, there is no 'who' to ask such a question; if you have realized the Self, the *mâyâ* no longer exists for you; but if you ask the question, it is evident that you are outside your real Self. The *anrita-avidyâ-mâyâ* complex is just a shadow, a reflexion from Brahman which did not need any locus. But some of the followers of Sankara were not so wise as that. They assigned the locus for illusion as being in Brahman himself, or in the individual self.[66] But the Visishthâdvaitins could easily show that both these alternatives were impossible : to place the illusion in Brahman is to make him bound in worldly existence and tarnish his absolute purity; to place it in the individual self is to absolutize the individual against the Supreme.

For Sankara to allow even a single distinction or attribute in Brahman would be to introduce a contradicition in the Absolute. Ramanuja, on the other hand, from his angle had to affirm that all positive and pure perfections found in the field of experience existed supereminently in Brahman, excluding only the imperfections and limitations. The finite perfection of individual things is not an argument against the absolute perfection and plenitude of the Supreme, but a cogent reason for it.

One who starts, with Sankara, characterizing the individual consciousness as anomalous, and therefore ignorance and illusion, naturally finds the Supreme as pure, immutable and infinite con-

---

[66] Cf. for example P. Sankaranarayana Iyer, Preface to *Sathabhooshani* of S. N. Anantakrishna Sastri (Madras: B. G. Paul & Co., 1956), pp. 10–11: Brahman is the locus of the *ajnâna* for, 'opposition is only between attributive *jnâna* (*dharma bhûtajnâna*) and *ajnâna*, but not between essential *jnâna* (*svarûpabhûtajnâna*) and *ajnâna*'. A. G. Krishna Warrier, *op. cit.*, p. 482 : 'What is *mithyâ*, or false, has the same locus as that of its own absolute negation.'

sciousness, and dares not add anything further to it, but only desires to lose oneself in that ocean of light and bliss in order to find one's own perfection and fullness in it. But once we realize, with Ramanuja, that the individual soul in its inmost core is an absolute in its own right, namely a unique, indissoluble and immortal personality, though limited and dependent, the view of the Supreme Reality also passes beyond the level of 'perfection' (even if it be consciousness) to *the One Who is saccidânanda,* with no consideration of what *comes* from him, or what he *does.* In such an encounter, there is no place for losing oneself; there is no 'where' to be dissolved in, but only an immutable Person who is, as it were, an inextensive point concentrating in his incommunicable and eternal moment all that is.

Nor, in such an encounter, does one start a tea-table talk with the Supreme Person as if he were an equal. Rather, the finite person realizes the infinite gulf that lies between him and the Supreme Lord, recognizes that all that he is and all he has is received, and acknowledges that openness to the Divine Person is the essence of his inalienable personality.

Hence, the basic difference between Sankara and Ramanuja is that the former evaluates reality from the side of Supreme Reality, absolute consciousness, while the latter looks at the Supreme Person from the side of the finite person. It is idle to argue that Sankara's point of vision is a higher and more perfect one, for his basis for taking such an angle is a fiction : he is arguing 'as if' one had already attained Brahma-realization. But this assumption is not a happy one : for, if one has attained that realization, there is no more need for any inquiry; if one pretends to have attained the realizaiton, that itself is a sure sign that he has not attained it.[67] Ramanuja has at least no need of a fiction; he has his feet on firm ground.

The points of agreement

On closer examination, it can be seen that there is more agreement than opposition between the positions of Sankara and

[67] Cf. e.g. *Ken Up,* II, 3 (11):
It is conceived by him by whom It is not conceived of.
He by whom It is conceived of, knows It not.
It is not understood by those who (say they) understand It.
It is understood by those who (say they) understand It not.
(Trs. R. E. Hume, *The Thirteen Principal Upanishads* (Madras: Oxford University Press, 1949), p. 337.

Ramanuja. By presenting two aspects of reality, they complete each other. On all the basic problems of metaphysics their approaches converge, even basically agree.

Both of them agree that the starting point of inquiry into the nature of reality is consciousness. Only by analyzing our conscious experience and sounding its ultimate depths can a true evaluation of all reality be achieved.

Both of them agree that a mere theoretical and conceptual approach to reality is inadequate. What is needed is integral vision in which all the means of right knowledge are integrated and, in a way, transcended. In this, the *anubhava* of Sankara and the *dhyâna* of Ramanuja are in agreement.

For both of them, consciousness is the model and pattern of all reality. Deeper and more basic than being and goodness is *cit*, consciousness, which reveals reality in its own true centre.

For both Sankara and Ramanuja, the way to solve the problem of the one and the many is not to compare them on an equal level and draw parallels between them. No comparison is possible between the all-embracing Absolute and the finite participated. They cannot be placed side by side without implying a contradiction. The only way is to deny the finite on the level of the Infinite and assign it a quite different level, whether it be the *mâyâ* of Sankara or the 'attribute' of Ramanuja.

For both of them, the pattern of causality assigned to the Supreme in producing the world of beings—and for that matter, all causality—is not of the potter-pot type, but rather under the aspects of participation and communication. Causality is not to be dealt with from the part of the cause, but of the effect, and this is not the emergence of new reality from nothing, but the production of name and form, individuality and specific nature.

For both, the highest point of reality is not subsistence or existence, but consciousness which is pure luminosity and transparency.

We shall examine in the next chapter how Ramanuja develops these basic points of metaphysics.

CHAPTER V

CONSCIOUSNESS AND REALITY IN RAMANUJA'S PHILOSOPHY

AVENUES OF APPROACH TO REALITY

From reasoning to reality

Ramanuja, like the other Hindu Acharyas, does not claim originality. They are teachers, and as such interpret the traditional teaching laid down in Scripture. But Ramanuja's importance to metaphysics is that he elaborated the problems from a rational point of view. His main thesis is that even Scripture can be understood only by reasoning, and that if a conflict should arise between the two, reason should be preferred.

The task of reasoning is not to make deductions and generalizations from experience, but to find out the meaning and basic teachings of Scripture, which is handed down from time immemorial, from generation to generation. The most important part of Scripture, according to Ramanuja, is that which sets forth :

the knowledge of the proper form and nature of the individual soul which are different from the body; the proper form and nature of the Supreme Spirit who is the inner Ruler of the soul; the worship of the Supreme Spirit; and the apprehension of Brahman as perfect boundless bliss.[1]

Ramanuja agrees with the Advaitins, and almost all other schools of Hinduism, that the present condition of souls is bondage; it consists essentially in *ajnâna*, or lack of right knowledge. Hence, it has to be removed by a special knowledge of the Ultimate Reality, Brahman, and of finite beings in relation to Him.

Therefore, the nature of right knowledge and the validity of the means for attaining it pertain to one of the basic questions of Indian philosophy. Ramanuja has a singular theory here among

[1] *Vedârth,* no. 3, JABVB, p. 184.

all the Indian thinkers, since he holds the validity of knowledge as such : all knowledge is perception of reality. This is the case even with regard to illusions and dreams![2]

For the Yogacara school of Buddhism, all knowledge is *Atma khyâti*, self-projection, a projection of the purely subjective phenomenon, while the Mâdhyamikas conceive it as *Asat-khyâti*, imagination of the non-existent. The Mîmâmsakas hold the *Akhyâti* view, acording to which knowledge is not the perception of something objective, but the subjective light projected on the object and illumining it; hence, when mother-of-pearl is mistaken for silver, what is perceived is the remembrance of the element of silver wrongly associated with mother-of-pearl. For the Naiyayikas, all knowledge is a combination, the addition of objective categories to the perceiving subject through the relation of inherence or *samavâya*. Hence, all erroneous perception is *Anyathâkhyâti*, the wrong combination of forms. Sankara and the Advaitins consider as valid knowledge only *anubhava*, or realization of the Atman; all other forms of knowledge have only a practical validity and are intrinsically *avidyâ*, non-knowledge, arising out of the superimposition of the field of the subject on the object and *vice versa*. This practical form of knowledge cannot be termed either as real or as unreal; hence, it is *anirvacanîyakhyâti*, undefinable perception.

Against these schools, Ramanuja holds the theory of *Sat-khyâti* : all knowledge is perception of the real.[3] Consciousness is self-revealing and object-revealing. In every instance of knowledge, even in dreams and illusions, there will at least be the first element; at least the knowing subject is manifested.

Scripture

However, as a source of knowledge, reasoning by itself is inadequate. In matters which are beyond our senses, experience and reasoning based on them cannot be final. All that the world of experience, especially the facts of origination, subsistence and dissolution of things, points to is a 'person capable of constructing the entire universe',[4] 'a causal agent, competent to plan and construct the universe and standing towards it in the relation of basis

---

[2] *Sri Bh*, I, i, 1

[3] Srinivasadasa, *Yatîndramatadeepika*, ed. Abhyankar Vasudevasastri (Poona: Anandasrama Sanskrit Series No. 50, 1908), p. 8; *sarvam vijnânam yathârtham*—all knowledge is factual.

[4] *Sri Bh* (T.), I, i, 3, p. 165.

and agent'.[5] But this does not tell us anything about the internal nature of this cause, whether it is identical with the Supreme Being Brahman, nor of the relation of finite beings to the Supreme Being. Even yogic perception, which 'results from the utmost intensification of mental conception', cannot give us knowledge of suprasensible things, because in spite of its being a clear presentation, 'it is still nothing other than the mere remembrance of previously experienced things'.[6]

In these matters, Scripture is the proper source of knowledge. It is the traditional teaching of ages past, as well as the self-manifestation of the Supreme Lord. Individual reasoning can be defective and fallible and may be refuted by someone more clever in logic. But this cannot happen with regard to Scripture :

> The *sâstra* (Scripture) is constituted by the aggregate of words called Veda, which is handed on by an endless and unbroken succession of pupils learning from qualified teachers, and raised above all suspicion of imperfections such as spring from mistake and the like.[7]

Ramanuja also conceives Scripture as a direct and personal communication from Brahman himself, who is 'more loving than even a thousand parents.'[8] What Scripture reveals to us is a 'being who comprehends within himself infinite and altogether unsurpassable excellences, such as omnipotence and so on . . . totally different in character from whatever is cognized by the other means of knowledge'.[9]

Integral vision of reality

But even Scripture should lead to a superior kind of knowledge which is variously indicated by Ramanuja as *dhyâna, upâsana, prapatti* and *bhakti,* each with its own different shade of meaning, but all standing for an integral vision of the whole world of Reality, born of a deep and constant meditation.

Ramanuja explains the general character of this knowledge :

> What we have to understand by knowledge in this connection . . . is a mental energy different in character from the mere

[5] *Ibid.,* p. 170.
[6] *Ibid.*
[7] *Sri Bh* (T.), II, i, 12, p. 426.
[8] *Sri Bh* (T.), I, i, 3, p. 173; I, i, 7, p. 204; II, ii, 3, p. 488.
[9] *Sri Bh* (T.), I, i, 3, p. 173.

cognition of the sense of texts, and more specifically denoted by such terms as *dhyâna* and *upâsana*, i.e., meditation; which is of the nature of remembrance, but in intuitive clearness is not inferior to the clearest presentative thought; which by constant daily practice becomes even more perfect, and being duly continued up to death secures final release.[10]

The need of this integral vision is twofold : the imperfection of our ordinary experience, and the personal character of the object to be known. Things individually presented in our experience easily pass away. Hence, in order to see them in their totality, we have to remember them and, through repeated attempts, connect together our various experiences about the same object. According to Ramanuja, knowledge proceeds from particulars to class concepts, from indeterminate to determinate. Brahman is, in a sense, the totality, comprehending in himself all conscious and material beings. Hence, only by seeing all things as united in him by constant concentration can perfect knowledge of reality be attained. Wholeness is the principal concern in Ramanuja's approaches to the problems of reality.[11]

But the nature of knowledge is determined more especially by Ramanuja's conception of reality itself : for Ramanuja, reality is personal, and supreme reality is the Supreme Person. A person cannot be known by mere inquiry and investigation, but only by the relation of love. Quoting the statement of the *Katha Upanishad* that Brahman cannot be known by much reading nor by thought, nor by hearing, but only by the self-manifestation of Brahman himself, Ramanuja says that the Lord can be approached only through remembrance or re-presentative thought. When one holds before one's mind the most beloved object, the Lord, one becomes oneself beloved to the Lord, and according to *Gîta*, X, 10, the Lord imparts knowledge about himself 'to those who are constantly devoted in worship with love'.[12]

What Ramanuja insists upon is not the substitution of one kind

[10] *Sri Bh* (T.), III, iv, 26, p. 699.

[11] Cf. F. K. Lazarus, *op. cit.*, p. 63 : 'Throughout Ramanuja's various approaches to the problems of Philosophy, there is a concern with wholeness. Not that the whole can ever be known, at least not in its entirety, but it is only as a method that furthers such knowledge that it can lay claim to any validity.'

[12] *Sri Bh*, I, i, 1, pp. 15–16. Cf. Olivier Lacombe, *La doctrine morale et métaphysique de Ramanuja* (Paris, 1938), p. 162.

of knowledge for another, but rather the integration of all the means of right knowledge on the same object. Ramanuja interprets the threefold division of men according to the *Gîta* in terms of knowledge : the ignorant try to reduce all reality to the empirical level and look at everything from a purely worldly motive; those who follow the Scripture in the literal sense remain with their multitude of gods and rituals; while the really wise, the *mahâtmâs*, have their minds fixed on the Supreme, who unifies everything. These last 'know God to be the origin of all beings, the eternal Lord, whose proper form, name and actions are beyond thought and speech'.[13]

Even on the level of *bhakti*, reasoning cannot be dispensed with. To the question of what the need of systematic study of philosophy is if Brahman can be realized through meditation, he answers : 'True, such knowledge arises immediately. But a matter, apprehended in this immediate way, is not raised above doubt and mistake.'[14] To refute contrary opinions, to answer objections and to give clarity to knowledge, reasoning is necessary.

Thus, perfect knowledge for Ramanuja is not objectless (*anubhava*) as for Sankara, but the encounter between an integrated subject and the integrated field of objects, the meeting between the individual soul which properly disposes itself and concentrates all its faculties[15] and the world of reality of which Brahman is the unifying focal point.

ANALYSIS OF CONSCIOUSNESS

This integral vision, characteristic of Ramanuja's theory of knowledge, arises from his conception of consciousness itself, which is the focus of study and pattern for all reality. For him consciousness implies an internal synthesis.

He finds in consciousness a dual aspect : consciousness is both a substance and a *viseshana*, or quality, a knower as well as knowledge. Only a lightsome substance, *teja*, can shine. Thus, light is substance and at the same time a quality. Though lustre is the quality of a lustrous substance, it is not an extraneous and accidental quality like whiteness.

[13] J. A. B. Van Buitnen, *Ramanuja on the Bhagavadgîta* (Summary rendering of the Gîta Bhâshya), pp. 115–8.
[14] *Sri Bh,* I, i, 1, p. 8.
[15] *Ibid.,* p. 17.

. . . In this same manner the Self, which is wholly of the nature
of intelligence, is also characterized by the attribute of intelligence.
Indeed, to possess the character of intelligence (*cidrûpa*) is to be
self-luminous.[16]

Thus, consciousness is a datum which points in two directions.
On the one hand, it is essentially directed to the one who is
conscious : 'Luminosity . . . must necessarily belong to something,
simply because it possesses the character of luminosity. Therefore,
consciousness in itself is not capable of becoming the self.'[17] The
words denoting consciousness—for example, *samvid, anubhûti* and
jnâna—are relative terms as Ramanuja affirms, relying on the
authority of 'those well-versed in word and sense'.[18] 'That intelligent
thing "I" which is proved to itself by the mere fact of its own
existence—that alone is the self.'[19]

Indeed, knowledge is the most basic perfection in the Supreme
Reality, Brahman, and in all knowing subjects. But 'this does not
mean that mere knowledge constitutes the fundamental reality;
knowledge constitutes the essential nature (*svabhâva*) of a knowing
'subject' which alone is the substrate, in the same way as 'the sun,
lamps, and gems are the substrate of light'.[20] Consciousness is
dependent on that substrate as its *viseshana*.

On the other hand, consciousness has, in its turn, a diffusive
and manifestative aspect in as much as it illumines and reveals
objects. As an attribute, it extends even to the body of the knower.
In this respect, the body has a dual function. It is both subject
and object. Carrying on the self-manifestative function of consciousness, it appears as part of the subject; it appears in our awareness like 'I who am a god', 'I who am a man', etc. This co-
ordination of the body with the knower in consciousness 'is explic-
able on account of the fact that the existence of the body is
inseparable from that of the knower, in as much as the only
character of the body consists in its forming a qualification of the
soul'.[21]

On the other hand, the body, with other things, is an object
which knowledge illumines and manifests. For Ramanuja, know-

[16] *Sri Bh,* I, i, 1, p. 80.
[17] *Ibid.* (RVA), p. 82.
[18] *Ibid.*
[19] *Ibid.,* p. 83.
[20] *Sri Bh* (T.), p. 81.
[21] Sri Ramanuja. *Gîta Bhâshya.* XVII, 1.

ledge or consciousness is not a static entity, nor merely a passive reception of forms; it is dynamic in character :

> The essential nature of consciousness or knowledge consists therein that it shines forth, or manifests itself, through its own substrate at the present moment; or (to give another definition) that it is instrumental in proving its own object by its own being.[22]

Consciousness, in a way, diffuses itself like light and makes other things visible.

CONSCIOUSNESS AND REALITY

According to Ramanuja, consciousness is the self-manifestation of Reality and is therefore the pattern for reality itself. In this outlook he is in a certain sense unique, since other philosophers of the Indian tradition gave emphasis to other aspects. Though Sankara also looked at reality from the angle of consciousness, his non-dualist stand was not very helpful in evaluating the reality of finite beings.

Bhâskara, looking at the world of reality in terms of causality, says that the Supreme Being has two aspects, one of cause (*kâranarûpa*) and the other of effect (*kâryarûpa*) in which he transforms himself into the world and things in it, though this latter is temporary and not eternal as the former is. Yâdavaprakâsa held to the doctrine of *Brahmaparinâmavâda*, according to which the Absolute by its own power becomes the Lord and finite beings; absolute is identical with itself, and is not affected by the contingency of the pluralistic world. But Ramanuja questioned precisely this point : if Brahman transformed himself into finite beings, how could they not but tarnish his simplicity and purity?[23]

Mâdhva looks at reality from the aspect of being, and finds a radical difference—in fact a fivefold difference in being itself— namely, between individual self and God, between selves themselves, between matter and God, between matter and matter, and between matter and self. Hence, the only relation that he could establish between the world of finite beings and the Supreme is one of dependence.[24]

---

[22] *Sri Bh* (T.), I, i, 1, p. 48.
[23] Cf. S. Radhakrishnan, *The Brahmasûtra* (New York: Harper & Co., 1960), pp. 39–66.
[24] Cf. B. N. K. Sarma, *The Philosophy of Sri Madhvacharya* (Bombay : Bharatîya Vidyâ Bhavan, 1962), pp. 31–66.

Nimbarka, a philosopher of the thirteenth century, looks at the world of reality from the aspect of essence or nature of things : in this view he finds three irreducible natures, namely the conscious enjoyers, the unconscious objects and the controller of all, Brahman; though all the three are united in the causal nature of the Absolute. Hence, they are by nature identical and distinct at the same time : the *svâbhâvika bhedâbhedavâda*, the theory of natural distinction and non-distinction.[25]

Vallabha of the fifteenth century proceeds by way of inference from the nature of effects, and reaches three forms of Brahman; the supreme impersonal, the personal, and the causal abode of the *avatârs*, and other creations : this third form is the source of the material principle, *Prakriti*, the individual souls, and of all creation and multiplicity.[26]

According to Ramanuja, all these approaches are inadequate : causality can take us from a finite world only to a finite cause; being does not resolve the multiplicity of beings; natures are irreducibly separate and different and cannot explain the unity. Hence, knowledge is the only factor from which reality can be properly studied. It is in our consciousness that all reality presents itself, and in knowledge we are in the midst of the self-luminosity of the real and we understand it from within and not from without. The basis of this attitude of Ramanuja is his theory of knowledge itself, acording to which there is no knowledge without the self-manifestation of reality.[27]

PERSONALITY—THE BASIC REALITY

The bi-polar conception of consciousness as a knower and knowledge, as the one basic and lustrous substance and the shining quality, helps Ramanuja to fix upon personality as the basic value of reality; the Supreme Person is the supreme real :

The one and the same lustrous substance stands both in the form of light and the one possessed of light. Atman, being of the nature

---

[25] Cf. S. Radhakrishnan, *op. cit.,* pp. 78–87, and P. N. Srinivasachari, *The Philosophy of Bhedâbheda* (Madras: The Adyar Library, 1950).

[26] S. Radhakrishnan, *op. cit.,* pp. 88–92.

[27] *Sri Bh* (T.), I, i, 1, pp. 119–29.

of intelligence, has consciousness as quality; having the nature of intelligence is self-luminosity.[28]

Hence the Atman is not mere formless consciousness as the Advaitins would have it, but a knower.[29]

Therefore, what is ultimate is not consciousness nor even happiness, but the One in reference to whom consciousness shines and happiness is joy-giving. That immaterial I-entity which *is* by its own indestructible reality and exists by its own Self is the Atman.[30] To identify consciousness or happiness with this Self is equivalent to concluding from the statement 'Devadatta has a stick', that 'Devadatta is the stick'. If the self were consciousness itself, our awareness would be 'I am consciousness', and not 'I know'.[31] Hence, for Ramanuja the Self is higher than any perfection predicated of him and is the ultimate ground of reference to which all have to be referred.

Svarûpa, Svabhâva *and* Samsthâna

Ramanuja makes a clear distinction in his terminology between *svarûpa, svabhâva* and *samsthâna*. Of these, the most basic is *svarûpa,* the ultimate character of a thing in itself, the proper form and immutable and basic aspect, free from adventitious adjuncts.[32] *Svabhâva* also signifies the essential form, but in the process of being and becoming. *Bhâva* stands for nature as well as what evolves out of it or manifests it.[33] *Samsthâna* is 'the generic structure of an entity by which it can be classified under a group with a class name'.[34] Designations like the Lord and the individual soul, or *purusha,* which are the *dravya,* or substantial category, belong to the *svarûpa* level; perfections like consciousness and bliss, which pertain to the manifestative sphere, pertain to *svabhâva. Samsthâna*

[28] *Ibid., Ekameva tejodravyam prabhâprabhavadrûpenâvatishthate.* (The one and the same lustrous substance stands both in the form of light and the one possessed of light.) *Atmâ cidrûpa eva caitanyaguṇah iti ciddrûpatâ hi svayam prakasata.* (Atman, being of the nature of intelligence, has consciousness as quality; having the nature of intelligence is self-luminosity.)

[29] *Ibid., Atah svayanprakâso ayam atma jnâtaiva na prakâsamâtram.* (Hence, the Atman is not mere formless consciousness, but self-conscious.)

[30] *Ibid.*

[31] *Ibid.*

[32] Cf. J. A. B. Van Buitnen, *Ramanuja's Vedârth,* p. 184, note 20.

[33] Sri Ramanuja, *Gîta Bhâshya,* XVII, 1.

[34] *Sri Bh,* I, i, 1. Cf. Olivier Lacombe, *L'Absolu selon le Védanta* (Paris: Librairie Orientaliste Paul Guthner, 1937), pp. 97–8.

which pertains to the level of individuality is made up of *nâma* and *rûpa*, individual character and specific nature.

Hence, personality is the ultimate, immutable and irreducible category for Ramanuja. Thus, he postulates the existence of a great number of individual *purushas,* or souls. Their plurality is constituted by their eternal *svarûpa.* In *svabhâva* they are all equal, equally of consciousness, but their class distinctions as gods, men and animals are brought about by the addition of external *viseshanas* or attributes, the categories which constitute the *samsthâna.*

The Supreme Person, the Supreme Reality

This hierarchy of values makes the Supreme Person the Supreme Reality. He is the One to whom plenitude of knowledge and bliss has to be ascribed as to the ultimate subject. Even though individual *purushas,* or souls, are persons, they are not absolute entities, but come entirely from the Supreme Lord and are dependent on Him as His modes and attributes, though in their freedom they can either turn to the Lord as their centre and self, or they can turn away from Him to material things and become enslaved to their natural effects of pain and pleasure. Material things have no self or personality, but are perishable and transitory adjuncts. The *svarûpa,* or personality, of the Supreme Atman is 'distinct from all entities other than Himself, since He is absolutely opposed to all evil and comprises solely infinite perfection'.[35]

This transcendence of the Lord above all perfection in pure personality is the main reason why He cannot be known from experience or through generalizations from experience. A person is understood only through personal encounter and personal self-manifestation. Hence, knowledge of Brahman is attained only after the soul understands its own personality, or *svarûpa,* and worships the Supreme Person in devotion.[36] The designation of Brahman in the *Taittirîya Upanishad* as *satyam-jnânam-anantam* is neither a definition of Brahman, nor synonymous with Him, but rather indicates His personality and proper form by pointing out his essential attributes of truth, knowledge and infinity.[37]

[35] *Vedârth,* no. 6, JABVB, p. 187.
[36] *Ibid.,* no. 4, p. 185.
[37] *Ibid.,* no. 24, pp. 198–9.

SUPREME PERSON AND FINITE BEINGS

The principal metaphysical problem for Ramanuja, as for all other Indian thinkers, is the coexistence of, and relation between, Brahman and finite beings. Ramanuja's solution flows from his concept of conscious personality : if Brahman is intelligence as substance, beings are intelligence as *viseshana*, in other words made conscious by Him either as finite knowers or made knowable as objects. If Brahman is pure light like the sun, the beings are his rays. If He is conceived as Atman or soul, they are the body actuated by Him. If He is the intelligent and purposeful agent, they are His instruments; He is the Master and they are His servants. But these various relations constantly appealed to by Ramanuja fall on different levels of thought, namely logical, metaphysical and moral.

The logical level of relations

On the logical level, Ramanuja's key concept in explaining the relation between Brahman and finite beings is *sâmânâdhikaranya*. *Sâmânâdhikaranya* is originally a grammatical term indicating the co-ordination of two or more words in a community of case relation. In Logic, it was accepted as the co-ordination of two or more terms in a judgment. Ramanuja gives it a deeper meaning and defines it as 'the abiding of several things in a common substrate, namely the reference of several terms to one thing, there being a difference of reason for the application'.[38]

This concept of co-ordination provides Ramanuja with a logically reasonable explanation to show how a multiplicity of perfections and beings can be reconciled with an ultimate unity : the very purpose of co-ordination is to indicate 'the unity of a thing distinguished by attributes'.[39] Thus, in the sentence 'The cloth is red', the syntactical connection indicated by 'is' places the cloth in co-ordination with the act of being, while 'red' indicates the inherence of red colour in the cloth. Thus the plurality of predicates ascribed to a thing not only indicates their relation to the thing, but also emphasizes the fact that the substrate is *one* only.[40] It also gives a dynamic aspect to the whole co-ordinate : 'the

[38] *Ibid.*, no. 26, p. 200; *Sri Bh* (T.), I, i, 1, p. 79.
[39] *Sri Bh* (T.), I, i, 13, p. 223.
[40] *Ibid.*, p. 224.

entire sentence finally expresses the connection in which the thing with its attributes stands to the action denoted by the verb.'[41]

When this principle of co-ordination is applied to the *mahâvâkyâs*, or basic statements of Scripture, a correct idea of the structure of the ultimate reality emerges. Thus the *Taittirîya* statement *satyam-jnânam-anantam Brahma* does not indicate an impersonal sea of infinite and immutable consciousness, as the Advaitins interpret it. For these epithets are ascribed to the same subject, Brahman, for different motives. Hence, what is ultimately indicated is the one subject of attribution, the Supreme Person, but as differently characterized by these qualities, whether they be taken in their *mukhyârtha*, primary sense, indicating positive perfections or aspects in the Lord Himself, or *lakshanârtha*, secondary sense, 'denoting modes of being opposed to whatever is contrary to those qualities'.[42]

The same is the case with *Tattvamasi* = 'Thou art that' of the *Chândogya Upanishad*, which is one of the basic Scriptural authorities for the Advaitins, who hold that the statement identifies *Tat* (Brahman) and *tvam* (you, the individual self). But, according to Ramanuja's *sâmânâdhikaranya* theory, both the terms *Tat* and *tvam* refer to Brahman, but under different aspects : *Tat* refers to Him as the Supreme One to whom everything belongs as mode, while *tvam* indicates the same Brahman under the aspect of *Antaryâmin*, inner ruler of the individual soul. Therefore, the *mahâvâkya* means : 'Since you are a mode and manifestation of that Supreme Brahman, he is your inner Ruler without whom you cannot be or act.'[43]

Theory of word-meaning

Ramanuja also has a theory of meaning consistent with his *sâmânâdhikaranya* theory. The question of meaning arises for Hindu thinkers in connection with the interpretation of Scripture, which, dealing with all matters concerning life and reality, presents the words in their authentic use. As for all Vedantins, for Ramanuja also Scripture is *apaurusheya*, impersonal, a beginningless tradition.[44] But this does not mean, as Sankara would have it, that words

---

[41] *Ibid.*
[42] *Sri Bh* (T.), I, i, 1, p. 79; *Vedârth*, no. 24.
[43] *Sri Bh*, pp. 130–1; *Vedârth*, no. 139.
[44] *Vedârth*, no. 139.

are eternal values and individual things mere illusory shadows, and that the individual aspects merely serve to bring home to our mind those eternal values. According to Ramanuja, the generic and individual aspects are combined in things. The denotative power of language does not come from convention, but is intrinsic to it as heat to fire.[45] The relation between word and meaning is that between means and object of cognition.[46]

Ramanuja conceives a parallelism between the emergence of word-meaning from Scripture, which is the word of the Lord, and the emergence of finite things from the Supreme. Individual words in concrete time-place circumstances derive their denotation only on account of the immanence in them of the *jâti*, or generic character. Similarly, individual things have their generic aspect in the modes of Brahman whom they have as Inner Ruler. For this reason, all words primarily and directly designate Brahman who is the substrate, and only secondarily and by participation relate to finite beings.[47] Ramanuja warns us against the general tendency to restrict words drawn from experience or Scripture in the material object indicated; for the material object is only a part of the full significance, which is found only in the Supreme.[48]

Every word denotes a perfection. This denotation cannot terminate in the imperfect thing, which is a limitation of the perfection, but has to find its full significance in the One who is the Master and Lord of all perfections. The complex nature of our predications makes *sâmânâdhikaranya* its basic law : the words which we derive from experience are on the one hand universal and have a trans-spatio-temporal significance. But, however pure they may be, they are so bound up with our conditions and so limited that they cannot be, as such, identified with the Supreme. So, they all have to be referred to the One who is the Absolute, but in an oblique manner, as his attributes and modes.

The structure of reality

Logical co-ordination of terms naturally leads to the consideration of the reality they designate, namely, the structure of things to which they refer. This structure, too, in Ramanuja's philosophy is

---

[45] *Vedârth,* no 137.
[46] *Vedârth,* no. 138.
[47] *Sri Bh* (T.), II, iii, 17, p. 540.
[48] *Vedârth,* no. 21.

governed by his idea of consciousness as a dynamic entity. The
traditional Tamil symbol for God is the sun, which sends out its
rays and illumines all things. Ramanuja faithfully follows the tradition. Light is the essential characteristic of Brahman. But it is not
the light that remains by itself, but which diffuses itself.[49]

However, in studying this diffusion of Brahman's light, Ramanuja, like all other Hindu thinkers, is not concerned principally
with the origin of things, but rather with the state of things:
origin is a matter pertaining to the sphere of time; reality is trans-
temporal. In explaining the structure, Ramanuja draws heavily
from *Vishnu Purâna*, which finds the very meaning of the word
Bhagavat, Lord, in His capacity through his *shadgunas* or six attributes, to reside in the heart of every being.[50]

The Highest Atman, the support and supreme Lord of all,
manifests Himself in the dual forms of *cit* and *acit*, embodied and
unembodied, perishable and imperishable.[51] Commenting upon the
doctrine of Scripture, Ramanuja says that Brahman, having in His
nature not even the semblance of an imperfection or blemish, but
abounding in all auspicious qualities, enjoys the sport of the
origination, sustenance, destruction and entrance within, etc., of
the world.[52] Brahman is like a being 'without form', so that He
can reside in all beings without being affected by the imperfections
of their forms.[53] It is in this sense that all things are said to be an
amsa, a part of the Lord: the entire universe is a self-manifestation
and concretization (*mûrtam*) of Brahman who is of the nature of
knowledge.[54]

Sat *and* Asat

In this context, Ramanuja's concept of *sat*, or being, is important.
For Sankara, *sat* is real, and *asat* unreal; what is existent in all
states of consciousness is *sat*, and what appears only in one or other
state is unreal. But for Ramanuja, all that in any way is, is real.
Hence, *sat* is applicable not only to Brahman, but to the entire

[49] *Sri Bh* (T.), III, ii, 15, p. 611.
[50] *VP*, VI, v, 72–9; *Sri Bh* (T.), I, i, 1, pp. 87–8.
[51] *VP*, I, xxii, 54–5; *Sri Bh, loc. cit.*
[52] *Sri Bh, loc. cit.*
[53] *Sri Bh* (T.), III, ii, 14, p. 611.
[54] *Sri Bh* (K.), I, i, 1. p. 113.

world, intelligent and non-intelligent, since all things do exist. For that very reason, *sat* is not a basic value for Ramanuja, like knowledge and bliss, but is a term which indicates the structure or state of things.

It is in this sense that he interprets *Chândogya Upanishad*, VI, i, 4, *Sad eva somyedam agra âsîd ekam evâdvitîyam*, which is the basic text for the Advaita position. According to him, this text does not assert the unique reality of Brahman and the unreality of other things. It only declares that before creation 'the world was essentially *sat*' (*jagatah sadâtmakatâm*), and that it was not differentiated by structural peculiarities of name and form.[55] It further asserts that all beings have the same unique ground cause (*upâdâna*), namely Brahman, and no other operative or conjunctive cause (*nimittakârana*) distinct from it, like the *prakriti* of the Sâmkhya.[56]

Hence, it is not correct to say that the Lord is pure 'Being' only, for being is only an aspect of the Lord.[57] In the main scriptural contexts where the designation of Brahman as being occurs, like *Chândogya*, VI, i–ii, *Taittirîya*, II, 6, and others, it presents the Lord in the act of creation : Brahman who is *sat* sends forth *sat* and *tyat*, the intelligent and non-intelligent beings, and He Himself enters them as their inner ruler.[58] Therefore, for Ramanuja, *sat* indicates the aspect of the Supreme Person as the originator of all things, as well as the ultimate condition to which all return on their reabsorption.[59]

Thus, on the level of being or nature, Ramanuja sees a co-ordination, or *sâmânâdhikaranya*, of beings : the Lord as Ground Being, the individual souls and the material world as existing things. Here the distinction is not between true and false, real and illusion, but between the permanent and the perishable : *Sattva* (abstract noun from *sat*), existence, means indestructibility, *asattva*, non-existence, means destructibility; the character of the destructible body is *asattva*, non-existence, while that of the imperishable souls is *sattva*.[60]

[55] *Sri Bh* (T.), p. 125; *Vedârth*, no. 16.
[56] *Ibid.*
[57] *Sri Bh* (T.), II, i, 15, pp. 453–61.
[58] *Sri Bh*, I, i, 13.
[59] *Sri Bh*, I, i, 6–10.
[60] Ramanuja's *Gîta Bhâshya*, II, 12; II, 18; *Sri Bh* (T.), II, i, 15, pp. 455–6.

Analogy of reality: metaphysics of attributes and body

The coexistence of the unique Absolute Brahman along with finite beings is a real problem for all thinkers. Does not the reality of the individual souls and of the material world detract from the absolute simplicity and infinite perfection of Brahman? If they are entities independent of Brahman, He is not all reality. But if they are His modes and body, as Ramanuja holds, then do they not tarnish the purity of Brahman by their imperfections? To solve these difficulties, Ramanuja attempts a metaphysical analysis of the reality of attributes and body.

Notion of Viseshana

A *viseshanya*, or attribute, belongs to quite another order of reality than the substance of which it is the quality. Though it is entirely from the substance, it does not change the nature of the substance :

> There is no contradiction between a thing being blue and its being a lotus; not any more than there is between a man and the stick or the ear-rings he wears, or than there is between the colour, taste, smell, etc., of the same thing.[61]

What is essential for an attribute, according to Ramanuja, is that it does not form a part of the essence of its subject, nor does it add something to its essential perfection, but it has its own particular nature distinct from that of the subject and is at the same time entirely dependent upon it. Thus, a walking stick or ear-ring is what it is on account of its function, its use for its owner; it is entirely his and depends upon him. Still, a man does not become more perfect in his humanity for the stick or the ornament. Similarly, we cannot have blue or white without a lotus or something which is blue or white; but a lotus can be blue or white without in any way being affected in its aspect of lotus.

According to Ramanuja, even a substance can be an attribute of another substance, as is clear in the case of the walking stick and the ear-ring. He makes a special use of the analogy of the lamp, flame and light to show how material things and souls are attributes of Brahman : though the flame by itself is a substance,

[61] *Sri Bh,* I, i, 13, p. 221.

it is the attribute of the lamp, and it has in its turn the attribute of light, which again has luminosity as an attribute.[62] Thus, when the souls and the world are said to be attributes or modes of Brahman, the meaning is that they have their proper nature distinct from Brahman, pertaining to a quite distinct order, and hence in no way affecting the intrinsic nature of Brahman, though at the same time entirely dependent upon Him.[63]

The souls and the world, the body of Brahman

The pattern of consciousness suggested another analogy, namely that of the body : on the one hand, the body is an object distinct from the knower, and yet at the same time is also an extension of the knower as part of his self. Brahman is the Supreme Atman or Soul; individual souls are his body. These in turn have material beings for their body.

In order to explain how this body of finite beings in no way affects the purity of Brahman, Ramanuja gives a generic definition to sarira, or body. He makes a clear distinction between deha and sarira, even though both are translated as body. Deha (from root dih) means the composite of elements and hence emphasizes the material aspect of the body. Sariram (srû + iram) emphasizes more the individual and secondary aspect of the body in relation to the soul. He rejects from the notion of sarira aspects which particularly pertain to the deha, namely 'that which causes the enjoyment of the fruit of actions', 'a combination of elements', 'that the life of which depends on the vital breath', and settles on the following definition :

> In ordinary language, the word 'body' is not, like words such as jar, limited in its denotation to things of one definite make or character. . . . Any substance, which a sentient soul is capable of completely controlling and supporting for its own purposes and which stands to the soul in an entirely subordinate relation, is the body of that soul.[64]

The essential and universally verified characteristics of a body according to Ramanuja are : (1) It is supported by the soul; (2) completely controlled by it; (3) subordinated to the soul entirely; and (4) ordered to serve the purpose of the soul. All these points

[62] Sri Bh, I, i, 1, pp. 135–8.
[63] Cf. M. Hirayanna, The Essentials of Indian Philosophy (London, 1951), pp. 179–82.
[64] Sri Bh (T.), II, i, 9, pp. 423–4.

he finds verified in the case of the world and souls in their relation to Brahman :

> In this sense, then, all sentient and non-sentient beings together constitute the body of the Supreme Person, for they are completely controlled and supported by him for his own ends and are absolutely subordinate to him.[65]

According to Ramanuja, all other explanations of the coexistence of Brahman and souls and the world either deny the reality of finite beings, thereby putting the imperfection in Brahman himself (Advaitins), or make Brahman himself subject to modifications (*Bhedâbheda Vâda*), or reduce him to a being among many beings (*Dvaita*),[66] while his own system avoids all such dangers. For, on the one hand, Brahman is absolutely immutable and antagonistic to all evil, while the modes of individual souls and the world belong to a totally different order and are, as it were, an overflow of his superabundant goodness, 'differing in nature from all beings other than Himself, all-knowing, endowed with the power of immediately realizing all His purposes, in eternal possession of all He wishes for, supremely blessed'.[67]

Sesha-Seshi *relation*

This same body-soul relation is designated by Ramanuja in certain places as *sesha seshi bhâva,* principal-accessory relation. The meaning is that the soul is completely controlled by the Lord who assigns to it the purposes to be realized by it.[68] All beings subserve the purpose of the Lord, and hence He in no way depends upon them.[69]

Kârana-Kârya Bhâva *or cause-effect relation*

According to Ramanuja, both the souls and the material world are effects of Brahman but, for Ramanuja, causality is not the production of something out of nothing. He rejects the *asatkârya-vâda* or causation-without-prior-existence-theory of the Nyâya-

[65] *Ibid.*
[66] *Sri Bh* (T.), II, iii, 18, p. 544.
[67] *Sri Bh* (T.), I, iv, 27, pp. 402–3.
[68] *Vedârth,* no. 80.
[69] *Vedârth,* no. 1.

Vaiseshikas. The basic principle is that from nothing nothing comes. The effect cannot add anything new to the cause. Hence the emergence of individual souls and of the material world does not add anything to the reality of Brahman.

On the other hand, he does not admit the *satkâryavâda* prior-existence-theory of the Sâmkhya-Yoga schools, according to which all the effects are accounted for by the auto-evolution of *Prakriti*, the eternal and independent material principle, in the presence of and for the benefit of *Purusha*, the spirit. This would run counter to the basic Vedanta position that the ultimate ground of all reality is one only, namely Brahman.

The key point of Ramanuja's solution to the problem of causality is the shift of emphasis from causality as a relation between two entities, cause and effect, to the view that it is primarily a relation between two states, the prior causal state and the posterior effected state. In both states, the cause remains immutable in the centre. The change is only in the mode : what was in the causal state in Brahman 'in so subtle a condition as to be incapable of receiving designations different from Brahman himself',[70] becomes individualized in the effected state through the evolution of name and form, individuality and specific nature. The only change in this transition that can be assigned to Brahman is that these new entities become referred to Him as His modes and body, and He in turn becomes their soul and internal ruler. So, causality is *Tâdâtmya*, or 'ensoulment'. The reality of causality is not in the cause but in the effect : the material things are transformed in their very nature. With regard to the spiritual beings, the souls, the change is from without. In other words, they become affected by the material things through pain and pleasure according to their own past actions and inclinations.

REALITY ON THE MORAL LEVEL

The highest value in Ramanuja's metaphysics is not being, nor even knowledge, but personality, the Self, which is the ground and subject of consciousness. Brahman is the Supreme Person and the individual souls, too, are persons, or *purushas*, whose essential

[70] *Sri Bh*, I, iv, 27, p. 403. Cf. A. Hohenberger, *Ramanuja—ein Philosoph indischer Gottesmystik*, pp. 64–5; P. N. Srinivasachari, *Ramanuja's Idea of the Finite Self, op. cit.*, pp. 11–13.

nature is consciousness. The characteristic note of the person is freedom. Brahman creates things freely. This aspect of freedom in creation is expressed by saying that Brahman creates out of 'sport', an action which is for no gain but merely for self-expression. Souls, too, are free either to turn to the Lord, the Self of their selves, or to turn to the material things and thus become subjected to their natural effects of pain and pleasure.

On account of this emphasis on personality, Ramanuja's concept of Reality does not stop with mere knowledge of the essence of things, but goes on to elaborate the relation between the three categories of things—God, souls and the material world—on the moral and ascetical planes. Consciousness is the field in which this relation is expressed and realized. In this, he is faithful to the *Bhakti* tradition of the Tamil Alvars and to the ascetic scheme of the *Bhagavad Gîta*.

Brahman, the goal of moral action

The basic moral value is the soul's natural dependence on Brahman as his mode, body, *sesha*, effect and servant; the soul has to live this dependence and realize it in loving devotion.

Bondage

But the evident fact that stands in the way of this ideal life is bondage, the soul's alienation from the Lord through sin, and its attachment to material things.[71] Brahman is the light of the soul; once it has turned away from Him it is in darkness.[72] All actions done in contact with matter, whether good or bad, lead to contraction of consciousness.[73] Action deepens ignorance, and ignorance leads to further action.[74]

Ramanuja accepts the traditional Hindu *Karma-samsâra* theory, according to which all actions, both good and bad, produce in the soul a dynamic residue, or *vâsanâ*, bound to bear fruit in a future life.[75] But, his personalistic approach has introduced a certain modification in the *Karma* theory itself : he does not think it neces-

[71] *Sri Bh* (T.), Introduction, I, ii, p. 256.
[72] *Sri Bh,* I, iii, 18, p. 321.
[73] *Sri Bh,* I, i, 14, p. 232.
[74] *Sri Bh,* I, i, 1, pp. 88–9, 94, 101.
[75] *Sri Bh,* I, iv, 16, p. 378.

sary for all action to end in order to attain liberation. He follows the *Gîta* doctrine that action performed solely for the sake of duty and for the pleasure of the Lord will not cause bondage.

Even in the embodied condition, the core of reality is Brahman Himself, who is the *Antaryâmin,* the internal ruler. Hence, in a certain sense, Brahman Himself is embodied, though He is not affected by the imperfections and changes of matter. The soul becomes subject to pain and pleasure only because it isolates the material things from their natural relation to Brahman the Lord. When we realize that the world is a mode and self-manifestation of Brahman, action becomes positively enjoyable.

The world is a *lîlâ,* sport of the Lord, a plaything given by Him to souls. It is lack of realization of this aspect of the world that makes it an instrument of bondage :

> As long as a boy is not aware that some plaything is meant to amuse him, he does not care for it; when, on the other hand, he apprehends it as being meant to give him delight, the thing becomes very dear to him. In the same way, the world becomes an object of supreme love to him who recognizes it as having Brahman for its Self, and being a mere plaything of Brahman. . . . He who has reached such intuition of Brahman sees nothing apart from Him and feels no pain.[76]

To a sick person, water can be unpleasant and harmful, while to the healthy it is pleasant and useful.

The four goals of human life

Ramanuja insists on totality in moral outlook. A pure spiritualism does not correspond to human condition. Hence, four goals are traditionally indicated for human life, namely acquisition of wealth (*artha*), pleasure (*kâma*), righteousness (*dharma*) and liberation (*môksha*). These are not four alternatives, but normal objectives for a healthy and balanced human life. According to Ramanuja, Scripture itself 'gives rise to the knowledge of the four chief ends of human action'.[77] In spite of the great disparity among these four —two of them temporal and two eternal—he conceives these goals as harmoniously organized in the human life with due consideration for their hierarchy.

[76] *Sri Bh,* I, iii, 7, p. 306.
[77] *Sri Bh,* I, i, 1, p. 48.

Sin

The present bondage is the result of actions in violation of the wishes of the Lord.[78] Therefore it is sin, an estrangement from the Lord. It has 'the disastrous disposition on the part of man, which consists in unfitness for religious works and inclination to commit further sinful actions of the same kind'.[79] It involves also a personal element, namely the displeasure of the Lord.[80]

Liberation

Since sin is basically ignorance, an obscuring of consciousness through material things, liberation should begin with knowledge, 'the yoga of discrimination' given to souls by the Lord in his compassion.[81] But since sin is also disobedience, the soul should turn back to the Lord, dispose itself through ascetic practices and faithful observance of caste duties, and surrender itself totally to the Lord.[82] The whole scheme insists on the establishment of the right order of reality, in which the soul realizes its dependence on the Lord, and loves Him as the personal God, *Nârâyana*, 'who, although residing in the soul, is different from that soul, whom the soul does not know, whose body is the soul, and who directs the soul from within . . . the inner ruler of all beings'.[83]

EVALUATION

In this chapter we have briefly examined Ramanuja's approach to Reality. He starts from conscious experience, analyzing and applying the pattern of consciousness to the world of reality. For him, consciousness is basically a synthesis : between knower and knowledge, between knowledge and knowable attributes, between substance and attributes, between soul and body, principal and accessory, cause and effect. Brahman is the highest point of consciousness, both as the Supreme Knower and as the fullness of knowledge. Other beings are participations from Him. To understand how finite beings can coexist with the Infinite, without

[78] *Sri Bh,* II, ii, 3, p. 488.
[79] *Sri Bh,* IV, i, 13, p. 723.
[80] *Sri Bh,* II, ii, 3, pp. 488–9.
[81] *BG,* X, 10–11.
[82] *Vedârth,* no. 81.
[83] *Ibid.,* no. 4.

implying any imperfection in the latter, Ramanuja makes use of the analogies of attributes, body, accessory, and effect : the attribute which is entirely from the substance does not add anything to its substantiality; the body depends totally on the soul and is controlled by it; it does not add anything to the soul. The accessory is for the principal, and the effect does not add anything to the causal reality. In the same way, the souls and the world can exist in being entirely dependent on Brahman, subject to His will and serving His purpose, without in any way affecting His absolute perfection.

But the conscious subject is the ultimate, immutable reality, both in Brahman and in the individual souls. The personal relation between them is the corner-stone of the whole metaphysics of Ramanuja. Knowledge which constitutes this relation is a personal realization and a total commitment in love and devotion.

The weak points of Ramanuja's system

There are a few obvious weak points in Ramanuja's system :

(1) The insistence on material causality as a fundament obscures the problem of the origin of finite things. There is no proper conception of efficient causality. Ramanuja is unable to understand an absolute beginning of finite beings from the unique efficient cause of all things. So the world of finite beings is explained as being formed of eternal and subtle modes of Brahman.

(2) For the same reason, Ramanuja's theory of tâdâtmya, or 'ensoulment', of things by Brahman is dangerously close to a pantheistic formal or material causality.

(3) Lack of clarity concerning the origin of things also affects the conception of finality. Though material things are said to be perishable and transitory, there is no end of the world. Everything revolves in a cycle : dissolution follows creation, and creation dissolution.

(4) Ramanuja makes use of the common terms attribute, body, part, accessory and the like, in a sense peculiarly his own. Though he makes his opposition to all kinds of pantheism very clear, these terms are liable to be misunderstood and misinterpreted. Since these attributes, modes and parts are said to be eternally existent in Brahman, the accusation of pantheism or panentheism seems rather difficult to avoid.

Positive points in Ramanuja for the reconstruction of a true metaphysics

However, in spite of the above weak points, Ramanuja makes very valuable contributions towards reconstructing a metaphysics according to his mind.

(1) Consciousness presents an advantageous point of view to evaluate the whole field of reality. Here integration, not abstraction, is the right method. Sense experience, psychic phenomena and pure consciousness have to be integrated in a synthesis to see the structure of the world of reality centred around Brahman, the supreme consciousness.

(2) Ramanuja also presents a fruitful approach to the analogy of being : look at things, not in their chronological emergence, but rather in their state of interdependence. In a system of thought which does not recognize creation of things from nothing through the pure efficient causality of God, the only two possible ways of conceiving the world of being are those of Sankara and Ramanuja : either consider the finite beings as mere *mâyâ*, an illusion (existence), alongside the absolute and unique reality, Brahman, or take them as eternally subsisting attributes around Brahman, sustained by Him, without adding any perfection or reality to Him. Here, more than the accurate analysis of the analogies employed, it is rather the total effect of the counterbalancing of descriptions that counts. Ramanuja shows himself a real metaphysician when he approaches the difficult problem with an open mind, taking nothing for granted. He takes the notions of part, attribute, body and accessory in a general sense, so that these concepts counterbalance each other and correct each other's defects.

(3) The most important notion in the philosophy of Ramanuja is that of personality : our knowledge is not complete with the perception of objects, and the understanding of the syntactic meaning of statements. The end of knowledge is not an 'It', but first an 'I', the one who knows, and then finally the 'THOU', the Supreme Person in whom alone I find my fullness and fulfilment.

(4) His approach to causality is also valuable : causality is not the addition of new reality, nor the relation between isolated entities. If looked at from the point of view of the cause, it is an effusion into another without going out of oneself. The reality of causation is in the effect which is dependent on the cause for

what it is and what it has. Looked at from the angle of the metaphysician, it is the relation between two states of things, a prior causal state in which the effects are absent, and a subsequent effected state in which the effects are present, actuated by the cause, which, however, does not undergo any change.

(5) Emphasis on personality gives a new aspect to moral and spiritual values. These are not mere duty, law or practice, but pre-eminently the relation between two persons : the soul in following the laws of its conscious being obeys the Lord and does homage to Him, and surrenders itself totally to Him. He, for His part, in supreme love and compassion reveals Himself to it in intimate communion.

There is no doubt that Ramanuja's metaphysics is more valuable for what it suggests than for what it actually states. We shall try in the second part of this study to develop these suggestions and examine how far they can help us in the reconstruction of a metaphysics from the Indian point of outlook.

PART II

CONSCIOUSNESS
AND METAPHYSICS

CHAPTER VI

NATURE OF CONSCIOUSNESS

The first part of this study has been devoted to examining the Indian tradition in its approach to reality. Down the centuries, it has developed a predilection for consciousness as a point of view for evaluating the world of reality. Sankara, and especially Ramanuja, have perfected the details of this approach. Their basic suppositions and principles provide a sufficient ground to construct a metaphysics from the side of consciousness, distinct from the outlook of objective analysis which has been the traditional procedure of the West. This part of the study will concentrate upon the solutions to the principal problems of metaphysics from the point of view of consciousness. The basic problems occurring in metaphysics are the general approach to reality as such, the coexistence of the Infinite Reality and the finite beings, causality, the structure of reality, and man's own encounter with it. To solve these problems, taking consciousness as the starting point, the nature of consciousness itself has first to be examined.

OBJECTIVE ANALYSIS OF CONSCIOUSNESS

The difficulty in understanding consciousness is that consciousness itself may be looked at from two sides, from that of rational analysis and that of consciousness.

Objective analysis deals with consciousness as a phenomenon and tries to reduce it to universal categories of thought. In this outlook, consciousness stands for self-awareness : not only does one know, but one knows that one knows. The knowing subject perceives not only the table presented to its experience, but also its own perception of it.

Knowing the table means that the table which was so far unperceived now becomes known or perceived. However, this perception is not a mere physical union between the subject and the object. The material object is in some manner raised to the spiritual level of the subject, and the subject, in a way, becomes the object, by actively conforming itself intentionally to the object. Hence, it is a meeting between the subject and the object on the same level of spiritual vitality and of the same objective form; the spiritualized form of the object becomes the form of the subject, and the objective form becomes the self-expression or word of the subject.

It is in this context that the self-perception of the subject has to be understood. The knowing subject is not another object by the side of and superadded to the object. If it were, it would not be known as a subject, but rather as an object, and would be exteriorized and outside itself. Nobody can turn round and take a look at himself. Hence, the self-perception implied in self-awareness is a concomitant phenomenon implied in the act of perceiving the object, and therefore consciousness is not a substance but an action. It belongs to the very structure of intellectual perception. An object *qua* object can be perceived only as opposed to and independent of a counterpart designated as subject. There is no direct perception of the 'I' as a subjective entity. What is actually there is the dynamic construction of the objective reality as something independent in itself, real and intelligible. This active setting up of an object of thought and speech is the directly perceived phenomenon. The subject comes into the arc of perception only to the extent it is involved in this active constitution of the object. Hence, it is neither complete; nor is it of the clarity with which the object presents itself to thought.

On the other hand, this self-perception is the background against which even the object is perceived. Nothing is presented to the mind except as perceived by the knowing subject. This subject is the point of convergence for all perceptions. All acts of knowledge are united in the same awareness : 'I knew that', 'Now I know this', and so on—all unified in the same 'I'.

Critique

However, the basic defect of this objective analysis of consciousness is its inadequacy to deal with self-awareness as such.

(1) The method of objective analysis has, as its basic procedure, the exteriorization and objectifying of things, the analyzation of

them into concepts and then the reconstruction of them into objective schemes and systems. Hence, it cannot deal with a reality which is opposed to these processes and presupposed as the ground of their very possibility.

(2) A second defect is implied in the process itself—namely, the conception of knowledge as a process, an action and a construction; all rational investigation is intended to stimulate and aid this process. This, again, is an assumption carried backwards from the field of experience to the subject. Change and transformation properly belong to the field of material things. They cannot, as such, be transferred to the level of the spirit without affecting the integrity of the latter.

Consciousness Under Conscious Evaluation

The right way, therefore, to understand consciousness is to make use of a procedure, as it were, in reverse gear—in other words, to make use of a method of approach that will be the opposite of what is employed in dealing with objects. The object is constituted in our knowledge through affirmation and construction; consciousness is realized by negation and abstraction. The object is built by addition and synthesis; consciousness is reached through elimination and detachment.

Consciousness as void

This is the reason why all the philosophers who emphasized the subject and adopted an interioristic approach insisted upon the apophatic method. Socratic irony, which closes the discussion in a meaningful ignorance and an eloquent silence, points the finger to this direction. Plotinus and Pseudo-Dionysius, who proceed to the One through the interior unity and beauty of the soul, are declared champions of the method of negation. In India, Buddhist scholars like Nagarjuna and Vedantins like Sankara made use of the same procedure.

The basic idea is this: In order to arrive at consciousness, or rather the conscious subject, all that is constructed by the subject should be eliminated. The subject is presupposed to all action and construction. Hence, to think of the subject in any conceivable manner is to reduce the subject into an object and a projection of the mind.

Here a distinction is generally made between consciousness and the conscious subject. Consciousness appears as the phenomenon of self-awareness. According to the habit of rational analysis, it is easily conceived of as an action, or at least as an aspect or a movement implied in the act of direct affirmation. It may even be conceived as a transitory quality which sometimes is and sometimes is not. An action or quality cannot be in itself, but has to be in some subject. So, whenever we speak of consciousness, we think of a conscious subject, someone who acts or is qualified. But this distinction may be exaggerated if the subject is objectified into a thing, or the quality is conceived in the fashion of an addition to the subject, or the action is imagined as a transition from potency into act. All these, so natural in the procedure of rational analysis, will simply miss the reality of consciousness.

Therefore, Nagarjuna and the Mâdhyamika Buddhists have an element of truth to contribute when they speak of consciousness as *sûnyatâ*, or void. Void does not mean pure negation, or absence of all reality. It only means that the reality does not fit into our mental framework. All we affirm is an object, a construction of the self. Hence, they can never fully represent or reconstruct the self for us. Desire, which is at the root of all outward movement of inquiry, leads us away from the self. Similarly, all the factors conceived as essential to individuality are objective constructions and so cannot reveal the self. Whatever is conceivable belongs to the objective world by that very fact and has to be excluded from the area of consciousness.

The correct method, therefore, is to deny. All that is conceivable may be denied of consciousness. Even then, all will not be denied. What will be left behind is consciousness. It can be called void, since everything conceivable is something illumined by, constructed by, and reflecting consciousness.

To the ordinary way of thought, this *sûnyatâ*, or void conception of consciousness may appear a total negation. But it is not. It is an emphatic affirmation of that which makes everything else understood. The principal drawback of Nagarjuna's *Sûnyavâda*, or Void theory, is that he stops at this point and does not go further to inquire if there is not some positive way of speaking about this consciousness.

Consciousness as self

We may take Sankara's doctrine of consciousness as a more positive approach. His method is to oppose the area of the object with the area of the 'I'. According to him, the two are opposed to each other as night and day, darkness and light. This is not a mere metaphor. Knowledge is the characteristic of the subject and not of the object. The conscious subject illumines things and makes them intelligible. In every respect, the two areas are opposed to each other. The object is divided and composed of parts; the subject is a unity in the consciousness of the 'I'. The object as object does not know; the subject as subject is the principle of knowledge. The object is the field of desire, action and pleasure; the conscious subject appears tranquil, self-consistent and blissful. The object is a thing, exteriorized and constructed; the subject is interiorized in itself, and simple. Objects of our knowledge are intimately bound up with time-space circumstances. Though the conscious spiritual subject may appear actually dependent on objects and bound in time-space limitations, still, these do not actually affect its interior reality. Hence, consciousness is the area of the simple 'I-hood', pure awareness.

Critique

However, Sankara himself recognizes the basic weakness of this view of consciousness: in the present bodily existence, the overlapping of the fields of the conscious subject and of the objective world is an inevitable condition. Sense experience and speech itself necessarily involve a certain objectification of consciousness. There cannot be any meaningful speech, much less a consistent system of metaphysics, without a certain amount of reification of consciousness in objective symbols. The only possible way to construct a metaphysics from the viewpoint of consciousness is to realize the relative aspect of all speech. All concepts and expressions are functional, not merely because they stand for outside objects, but especially because they are symbols of the self and, as such, point to the depth of consciousness itself.

Consciousness as self-manifestation

A positive element contributed by Ramanuja to the understanding of consciousness is valuable here. Consciousness is not a thing, but it is not nothing either; it has its own internal consistency and intelligibility. It is not action in the ordinary sense; but it is not static either; it is a fullness that flows out and manifests itself. It is a light that illumines, and not a lamp hidden under cover. Consciousness is not a quality superadded to any unconscious subject; self-awareness found in conscious acts does not exhaust all consciousness or sound its depths. It only demonstrates an infinitesimal part of the self behind this manifestation.

So, in pure consciousness, one has to recognize an action without change, a self-expression without self-exhaustion, an illumination without self-diminution, a self-manifestation by which the self descends to its own depths at the same time as encountering objects.

LEVELS OF CONSCIOUSNESS

This illuminating and self-manifesting aspect of consciousness is present at several levels in the actual state of the soul-body union in man. External experience evokes the intellectual expression in physical categories of substance, action, attribute, relation, and the like. Thought itself constitutes another level on which the mind moulds logical categories corresponding to things. Psychic experience of thought, action, and limitation indicates a deeper level of empirical consciousness.

These empirical levels do not mean a mere passive reception of forms from things. Even on the level of sense experience, conscious understanding is a construction of the object. Indeed, knowledge does not transform the object. However, it integrates it into a higher level of intelligibility and co-ordination. The object apprehended by the understanding, as presented to the senses, is no longer an isolated thing, but part of a real order, with its proper position and value. This point may be illustrated by an analogy. An engineer, in constructing a bridge, may need stone and cement and a lot of other materials, and depend on the labour of thousands of ordinary workers. But, all the same, he is constructing the ideal plan executed by the architect, and thus investing the stone and mortar and sand with a new order and intelligibility. A rational analysis can reduce the finished bridge to its constitutive elements, discover their proportions, and find out the various factors that went into the construction of the bridge. However, the bridge is not merely the sum total of the materials going into its construction.

It is a 'creation', a work of art. The materials and the unskilled labour of the workers are all co-ordinated and made meaningful by the art itself.

In a way, the materials of inferior quality and inexperienced workmen can hamper the self-expression of the beautiful plan. Even when they are at their best, it is not they who make the bridge, but the ideal which shines out through them.

This analogy may be helpful to understand how consciousness expresses itself on the lower levels of knowledge. When one becomes conscious of the sense experience of a table, one is not acquiring something. A spiritual intelligence has nothing to learn from the material thing itself. The spiritual finite being develops and grows, not by receiving anything from the material object, but by deepening its openness to the superior spiritual reality. In this openness, the encounter with the exterior object is only a moment, and an expression. By the spiritual awareness, the conscious subject is extending and diffusing its selfhood to the object outside—say, the table. The table becomes a part of its conscious world. It is no longer an isolated entity, but a meaningful symbol by which the subject becomes more conscious of its own self. The more crude and objective a thing is, the more opaque it is to the light of consciousness.

However, consciousness appears in its more congenial condition in the transcendental realization of being, truth and goodness in things. These present less of an obstacle to the self-expression of the subject, and approximate to the native condition of consciousness itself.

Plurality of Metaphysics

These different levels of consciousness reveal different modes in which reality can be approached by the conscious subject, and metaphysics conceived. Metaphysics is the science of reality. Hence, it is situated at the meeting point of consciousness and reality. As the conscious mode of approach, so is the aspect of reality attained. Consciousness manifests itself on different levels; so also, it sounds different depths of reality. The level from which one looks out can determine the view of reality too.

The task of philosophy is to discover the most advantageous point of vision that will give the widest view of reality, and also to select the point of emphasis that is most comprehensive of factors. According to Ramanuja, as was explained in the first part, reality should be looked at from a transcendental and integrated point of view, and the emphasis placed on the aspect of encounter implied in human knowledge, namely the meeting with the object which points back to the depth of the self itself in the line of absolute consciousness.

It should be an integrated view, too, since the transcendental outlook does not neglect the other levels, namely the empirical, logical, and psychological, but, rather like the spearhead of a movement, it carries along with it the contributions of the prior stages and in return makes those stages more accurate and puts them in perspective with reality. Similarly, the aspect of personal encounter implied in consciousness does not reject or forget the 'thing side' of reality which emphasizes existence, truth and goodness; it only brings them from the ontic level to the ontological level. In themselves, they are aspects of the thing, as given independently of the knowing subject. Consciousness renders them manifest, discovered and realized.

If we speak in terms of history, various levels and stages of human knowledge, with regard to the apprehension of reality, do not conform to any strict chronological pattern. Even in the earlier periods of philosophy we find flashes of transcendental perception, while, on the other hand, even in modern times we meet with philosophers and schools of philosophy who feel strongly that the empirical and psychological levels of human knowledge have been too much neglected in the past and metaphysical thought cut adrift from its empirical moorings. So, a strictly chronological discussion of stages in the development of thought on reality from the point of view of consciousness cannot be undertaken. This history of philosophy has not been a straight line of progressive evolution. In the spirit of the integral outlook of Ramanuja, we shall here merely outline the main ways in which human knowledge has grappled with reality.

In this approach to reality, consciousness is not a thing or an action, though some schools which identify reality with consciousness explain it in that manner. In general, consciousness is a point of outlook, an open door to the reality of the self on the one hand, and to the world outside on the other.

CHAPTER VII

APPROACH TO REALITY FROM THE EMPIRICAL LEVELS OF CONSCIOUSNESS

CONCENTRIC LEVELS OF APPROACH

A remarkable fact about the Indian approach to reality from consciousness is its capacity to integrate the various levels of thought in the one quest of the real. Even the schools which seem to be engaged in cosmology, logic or psychology, like the Nyâya, Vaiseshika, Sâmkhya and Yoga systems, are concerned with the final attainment of liberation and realization of the ultimate reality. On the other hand, Vedantins, like Sankara and Ramanuja, who concentrate all their inquiry on the study of Atman, give great importance to the *pramânas* or means of right knowledge, which are principally *pratyaksha*, perception, *anumâna*, inference, and *sabda*, verbal testimony. All these belong to the empirical level of consciousness. These means on the empirical level are necessary for an adequate realization of reality even on the transcendental level.

This capacity for integration is a special feature of the approach from consciousness, and is not very evident in the approach through rational analysis. Though both proceed from knowledge to the study of reality, consciousness takes the thing in all its aspects, while rational analysis takes a particular aspect of the phenomenon apart and studies it in isolation. For rational analysis, reality is an object of thought and speech, existing in itself, independently of thought, and has therefore to be examined all by itself and is not to be confused with the subjective impressions of the investigator. Hence, various levels of thought remain distinct, with very little possibility of integrating one to another.

This irreducibility of the levels of thought in rational analysis is reflected in the various systems which follow this particular method of approach. Thus, for the Empiricists, reality is what affects our senses; the impressions left in us may be tabulated, compared and co-ordinated and regularities noted, but they do not permit the affirmation of anything beyond them. For the Logical Positivists, only the experimental sciences attain reality; logic and mathematics are mere mental elaborations and metaphysics, as such, has no useful function to perform in the knowledge of reality. On the other hand, for the Kantian approach, which insists on immutable truth and absolute certainty, forms and categories of thought are the laws of reality, and the things as they are in themselves cannot be attained by knowledge. Even according to the philosophies of Plato and Aristotle, true and universal knowledge is about the absolute and transcendental reality, whether it be ideas, essences or natures; about the individual as such there is no true knowledge.

The approach from consciousness, on the other hand, finds the same consciousness diffusing itself from the higher intellectual faculties of man to the lower powers down to the senses, and finds in the world outside a corresponding diffusion of reality from the absolute to the various levels of the relative.

We shall examine in this chapter how, from the point of view of consciousness, the empirical levels of human knowledge converge on the same world of reality, and lead to its transcendental aspect.

APPROACH TO REALITY THROUGH PERCEPTION

A means of right knowledge acknowledged by all the Indian schools is *pratyaksha* or perception. Its importance is that it is man's basic opening to reality in the present state of bodily existence. Other means of right knowledge are dependent on it. If the validity of sense perception is denied, other means too become doubtful. I shall briefly examine here the nature of perception in as much as it constitutes an avenue of knowledge concerning reality. Its fundamental characteristics will reveal the conscious encounter with reality on the experimental level.

Sense-intellect integration

An important point in the idea of perception from the angle of consciousness is that there is no separation between intellection and sensation. In man, there is no pure sensation that is not accompanied by and permeated with consciousness. Perception is the presentation of reality to the human knowing-subject. Sense experience is a mode of man's encounter with reality. Man is a single being. To be present to his senses is to be present to man himself. Every act of knowledge, even on the sense level, has a certain totality involving the whole of man in confrontation with the whole of reality, for it is not a passive reception of certain material forms, nor a mere modification of a bodily being. Man actively faces the world of reality.

This presentation of the object to the knower is an activity. So, it expresses the basic dynamism of consciousness which is the search for the self, the quest for the stable in the unstable, the choice of the ultimate in spite of the fascination of the superficial. Even on the level of sense experience, it seeks to reduce all things into the general categories of substance, action, attributes and relation. This is a sort of spontaneous evaluation of what is present to the senses into the stable and unstable, essential and non-essential, principal and accessory, active and passive, and so on. For a conscious being, ignorance and confusion constitute anomaly and bondage, knowledge and discernment mean liberation. That is why even the atomist school of the Vaiseshikas indicate discernment of categories as the means of *nisreyasa,* perfect happiness.[1] It is the first lesson in working out one's way through the multiplicity and change of sense experience.

Substance stands for the basic reality, the self of the knower as well as of the known, attributes for the adventitious and transitory. Action symbolizes the dynamic evolution going on in the field of experience through conjunction, disjunction and the cause-effect relation of entities. Attribute, action and relation have meaning only in relation with the immutable substratum which is the substance.

We may take here the Vaiseshika system of Kanada as representative of this mode of approach to reality through perception. According to him, the goal of yoga or contemplation is to obtain a clear discernment of the categories,[2] and realize the *Atman* or Self.[3]

The positive elements implied in this mode of approach have to be clearly discerned. Man's contact with the world brings him face to face with a composite of universal and particular, cause and

[1] *Vai S,* I, i, 4.
[2] *Vai S,* IX, i, 14.
[3] *Vai S,* IX, i, 11.

effect, and such correlatives. A rational analysis can achieve an abstract separation between these opposites and can form clear concepts out of them. But a conscious evaluation demands a facing-up to the complex actuality. The Advaitin advocates the rejection of the particular and effected as unreal, and the acceptance of the universal and the cause as the unique real. Ramanuja's integral approach requires the acceptance of the complex as it is. What is required is man's proper orientation to the universal and the causal as the immutable real, but subordinating to it the transitory particular and effected as accessory.

Continuity

Here one of the positive points rightly emphasized by Ramanuja is continuity. In the world of reality there is no discontinuity. 'The real is known through the real.'[4] The basic defect of all absolute systems, including the Advaita philosophy of Sankara, is the intro-duction into metaphysics of an area of the unreal which is left inexplicable—a sort of borderland of metaphysical residue. Accord-ing to Sankara, the whole world of experience, even including Scripture, belongs to the field of unreality, though it may lead one in some manner to realize the real. But, in fact, reality is one, and whatever exists, whether material or spiritual, temporal or eternal, all belongs in some manner to the real. As Ramanuja rightly points out, a picture of a buffalo as well as the buffalo itself and the similarity between the two all belong to the same world of reality, in spite of the great difference between them. Even conventional signs are not mere fictions, but have their basis on a common understanding of men.

Truth and error

In following objective analysis, truth and error can be found only in the act of affirmation and not in sense perception. However, in following evaluation from the point of view of consciousness, sense perception itself contains truth. For sense perception is not a mere passive experience, but intellectual realization through the sense of the object outside. It implies an active evaluation of reality.

Besides, as Ramanuja rightly affirms against other schools, the

[4] *Sri Bh* (T.), I, i, 1, p. 77.

opposition between truth and error is not an absolute one. Error is not the affirmation of something which is not there, nor a total misapprehension, nor even negation of all truth. Error and illusion contain a partial truth. Even erroneous perception contains an active evaluation, though the immediate object of evaluation may be defective or totally lacking. What is more important than the object in an act of perception is the act itself, which reveals the subject, the source of all act, and the goal of the evaluation, namely the absolute Self, in terms of which the object is evaluated.

Critique

In making use of this mode of approach to reality, the dangers involved in it have to be clearly acknowledged.

(1) Since the sensible world holds a certain fascination for a man with a strong sensitivity, there is the evident temptation to make the approach a closed system of physical categories. This was the radical defect of the Vaiseshika system which was quite materialistic in outlook, containing physical categories of substance, action, relation, and the like, and eternal atoms for principles of reality.

(2) Conceiving substance on the sensible level entails the further danger of reductionism, namely of reducing all realities to the level of subtle material entities. God and individual souls tend to be conceived in the manner of eternal atoms in a universal system of monads.

(3) Continuity of reality, conceived on the level of sense perception, may easily slip into a cosmic pantheism, an error easily succumbed to by those religious schools which exaggerated the affective aspect of worship. For them, the stone and the tree, as well as the crudest expressions of animal passion, were all expressions of the one Divinity.

(4) On this level, there is a great tendency to conceive truth as mere mechanical conformity, rather than the active evaluation of the spirit.

In spite of these dangers, dangers which can be avoided with sufficient care, the approach to reality on the level of sense perception has certain definite advantages for an integral metaphysics:

(1) It avoids the irreducible dichotomy of matter and spirit, body and soul, error and truth, evil and good, which always dogs the

heels of a rational analysis. Even the material world is only a veil cast on the face of the spirit; the body is what it is only by virtue of the soul. Error is no mere negation, but inadequate truth; evil is defective good.

(2) It shows the unity of the world of reality. The stamp of the real is apparent even on the sensible aspect of it. Nothing can be judged totally unreal, negligible or unimportant. Everything is important, being invested with reality by the Ultimate.

(3) It also shows the unity of the human self. Even the lowest conscious action of man involves his self and brings him into encounter with reality.

(4) But the most important aspect of this approach on the sense level is that the unsolved multiplicity of the categories calls for an evaluation on a higher level, namely that of logical thought.

We shall therefore examine here the approach to reality through logical thought or *anumâna*, inference.

To Reality Through Inference

Anumâna, or inference, is a means of right knowledge, generally accepted by the Indian schools. This takes one to a second level in the dialectic approach to reality. Though the Nyâya system has made this logical approach its principal concern, we shall briefly discuss the approach only as accepted by the Vedanta of Ramanuja and integrated into his system of metaphysics.

Logical sphere of reality

Here the radical difference between objective analysis and consciousness is that the opposition between the logical and the ontological that exists in the former does not figure very much in the latter. When reality is conceived as the object of thought and speech, the subject and its categories become a mere framework for measuring and systematizing the forms of the object. On the other hand, when the objective world is looked at from the point of view of consciousness as an extrapolation and manifestation of the Real within oneself, this dichotomy is transcended. Knowledge itself appears as a higher level of reality than the objects themselves.

All the objects outside, the material world and the entities within it, are not an end for thought, but rather something ordered for the self-attainment of the knowing subject. Hence, the means of right knowledge do not enrich the subject by additions from the world below or fill it with information, but rather subordinate the physical world for illumination and organization by the categories of thought. Man's happiness does not consist in acquiring more information, but rather in forming himself by the removal of wrong knowledge and the gaining of a right estimate of reality.

The extraordinary importance ascribed to *tarka,* or argumentation, and its various parts and methods in Indian tradition, may be a result of this predominance of knowledge over objective reality. Even Sankara, who ascribed the pride of place to *anubhava,* or immediate realization of reality, recognized the value of dialectical reasoning as an important aid to Scripture for attaining realization. Ramanuja ascribed a greater importance to reason than to Scripture itself, since the value and meaning of a Scriptural statement can be settled only by *tarka.*

Function of reasoning

Reasoning or logic has a special function in the understanding of reality from the point of view of consciousness. When the Indian logician says : 'Experience is the sole criterion of our acceptance of the reality of external objects',[5] he does not mean an empiricism in the Western sense. Experience is not a passive reception of sensible forms, nor is logic a matrix or framework of mental categories. What is involved in knowledge on the logical level is an active illumination of things by the subject. Knowledge itself is conceived as 'a light that abides in the subject'.[6] It illuminates, comprehends and co-ordinates things below the human self in a meaningful manner in view of the higher reality above the human self. Isolated entities have no meaning in themselves. They have value on the scale of reality only in their reference to the absolute Self. This integration to the order of reality is the function of reasoning.

---

[5] *Nyâyavârtikatâtparyapîtika* (Calcutta Sanskrit Series, 1898), p. 506 : *samvideva hi bhagavati vastupagame nah saranam.*

[6] Cf. A. B. Keith, *Indian Logic and Atomism* (Oxford : Clarendon Press, 1921), p. 42.

Language and reality

This active function of human thought in illumining and organizing the world of finite beings in relation with the ultimate reality gives a special meaning to language itself. In rational analysis, language is the conventional sign for communicating to one mind ideas grasped by another. It has meaning only in the context of social communication.

From the point of view of consciousness, language has a deeper meaning. Speech is a self-expression of the conscious being, rather than a conventional sign to represent the thing outside. It is the meaningful utterance by which the self announces the discovery of the eternal in the temporal, of the necessary in the contingent. I cannot utter 'table' about the thing in front of me unless I have in myself a presentiment of the table as such, the universal and necessary, which is discovered in this material and transitory entity here.

This active self-expression implied in language is the common doctrine of Indian schools, though each school tries to give its own special interpretation for it. The grammarians like Bhartrihari conceived the meaning-bearing aspect of speech as a unique spiritual entity called *sphotha,* hidden in language, while the Mîmâmsakas ascribed it to *âkâmksha,* or self-consistency, of meaningful language. Perhaps the point is best set forth by the Nyâya dictum, '*Artha-prakâso buddhi*',[7] which cannot properly be translated into English. *Buddhi* stands for the knowing self as well as for knowledge in general. Similarly, *artha* indicates the goal and end of human life and action as well as the meaning of speech. Therefore the statement means that the function of the active self-expression of the human spirit in knowledge or language is to reveal its own ideas and, through them, to tend to reality. Ramanuja further clarifies the point when he says that words get their meaning primarily and directly from the Supreme Self and only secondarily and indirectly in their reference to finite things.

The intimate relation between inference and reality is very much emphasized in the *sâmânâdhikaranya* theory of Ramanuja. One thing can be known in conjunction with another only if the two have a certain basic unity. In the Nyâya and Advaita conceptions

---

[7] Cf. K. Kunjunni Raja, *Akânksha: The Main Basis of Syntactic Unity* (Adyar Library Bulletin, 21, 1957). pp. 282–95.

of inference, what is important is the *vyâpti*, or invariable concomitance, in which the *sâdhana* and the *sâdhya*, the proof and the provable, the *vyâpaka* and the *vyâpya*, the principal concomitant and the subordinate concomitant, are united. The relation of unity, according to them, need not be causal or essential. According to Ramanuja, however, the *vyâpya* should be ontologically united with the *vyâpaka* by *tâdâtmya*, or ensoulment, of the finite by the infinite. Thought of reality is no mere logical exercise. If a conclusion, being valid in the ontological order and concerning a finite reality, is to be affirmed, its concomitance with the ultimate ground of reality has to be implicitly admitted.

Critique

(1) The first danger of this level of approach to reality through logical thought is the sort of ontologism involved in it. Concepts, considered apart from things, tend to dissociate themselves from reality and become absolutes.

(2) Ramanuja's theory that words refer primarily and directly to Brahman, and only secondarily to things in our experience, is surely an exaggeration of the function of the word. To refer concepts drawn from experience primarily and directly to the Supreme Being implies an anthropomorphism which stands in the way of a correct understanding of transcendence.

(3) Similarly, Ramanuja's theory of *sâmânâdhikaranya*, according to which Brahman is conceived as the concomitant ground to which all finite beings belong as attributes, involves a certain overgeneralization from human thought to the plane of absolute reality.

(4) Other dangers of a purely logical approach from thought to reality are exemplified in the system of Nyâya thinkers. Since all concepts belong to the same plane, they are unable to explain the intrinsic difference between spirit and matter, knowledge and volition, subsistent and dependent beings. Everything, including Atman and bodies, appears on the same list of things.[8] Even time is absolutized into an eternal substance.[9] Consciousness is conceived as just a quality of the Atman, like desire, aversion, pleasure and pain.[10]

[8] *Ny S*, I, i, 9.
[9] *Ny S*, I, i, 10.
[10] Cf. Swami Satprakasananda, *Methods of Knowledge* (London: George Allen & Unwin, 1965), pp. 168–70.

On the other hand, this level of approach, if properly integrated to others, serves to understand properly certain aspects of reality.

(1) Like the level of sense experience, the logical level also shows that there are no isolated particles of reality. Even thought itself and our logical categories pertain in some manner to the real order.

(2) The co-ordination and concomitance of entities in thought is an active self-expression of the conscious being and, as such, presents an aspect of the unified totality of the world of reality.

(3) This particular level of human thought brings out best the meaning of *abhâva*, or nothingness. On the empirical level, 'nothing' is mere negation, and on the transcendental plane it is mere privation, the defect of some positive entity. On the logical level, nothingness or non-existence appears, in its own title, conceivable and arguable : a finite thing that originates has antecedent non-existence (*prâgabhâva*); something that perishes has consequent non-existence (*pradhvamsâbhâva*). Mutual non-existence (*anyony-âbhâva*) is the affirmation in a particular situation of a thing that is opposed to what is actually there; e.g., if a horse, it cannot be a stone. Absolute non-existence (*atyantâbhâva*) is absolute incompatibility with the order of reality, as are horns on a hare.

But, for an integrated view of reality, this approach through logical thought should be counterbalanced by taking stock of our internal experience as an avenue to reality. We shall therefore discuss next the approach to reality on the level of psychic experience.

FROM INTERNAL EXPERIENCE TO REALITY

The most concrete and most appealing level of knowledge for man is his own internal experience of pleasure and pain, love and hate, light and darkness, satisfaction and discontent. Logical thought, on the one side, and transcendental ideas, on the other, both require a sort of abstraction from immediate experience, while in internal experience one is in immediate contact with concrete reality. Hence, the earliest school of systematic thought in India was *Sâmkhya*, which conducts the inquiry into the nature of reality on the psychological level. Iswara Krishna, whose *Sâmkhya Kârika* is the most authoritative book of the school, states in the first Kârika that the main purpose is the inquiry into the causes of the threefold misery of man and the ways to remove it.[11] This problem of suffering is the outstanding one in Indian philosophical speculation. Even the Vedantins have taken for granted this Sâmkhyan aspect of inquiry into reality, which explains the human existence through principles within man himself. What Ramanuja demands is that the system itself should be subordinated to the Supreme Brahman, who is the sole cause of all things. We shall here briefly examine this Sâmkhyan approach as being typical of the point of view of consciousness on the level of internal experience.

Quest for principles within the system

Sâmkhya wants to explain human experience through principles within man himself. It proceeds with the firm belief in the principle of causality, designated as satkâryavâda : every effect should pre-exist in the cause; nothing comes out of nothing. Hence, all the factors in our experience of pain and suffering, knowledge and ignorance, activity and receptivity, should be reduced to ultimate principles. Only milk can produce curds; anything cannot come out of anything; such the cause, such the effect.[12]

What occurs in our experience is caused, temporal, particular, active, manifold, dependent, mixed with and subordinate to others. These are completely the opposite of what we expect of reality, which is stable, immutable and uncaused. So, we have to postulate, away from our fleeting experience, principles of the opposite nature, namely permanent, eternal, independent, well-balanced and simple.[13]

The spiritual elements of our internal experience, such as I-hood and consciousness of past, present and future, which are independent of time-space conditions, should be referred to an ultimate spiritual principle in us, Purusha, a pure witness unaffected by change. The other three irreducible factors of reflection, activity and limitation, which are, however, by their very nature bound up with material conditions, should be ascribed to an ultimate principle of evolution, Prakriti, with three functions of sattva (reflexion), rajas (action) and tamas (darkness).[14] These three, called gunas, are not

---

[11] Sâm K of Iswara Krishna, ed. cit., Kârika 1.
[12] Sâm K, Kârika 9.
[13] Sâm K, Kârika 10.
[14] Sâm K, Kârika 11–16.

mere qualities but substantial functions of the same basic material principle. *Sattva* represents the ground of thought, appearing as knowledge in mind, and on lower levels as light and lightness (*laghutva*); *rajas* is the root of dynamism and movement; and the reason for limitation, inactivity and unintelligibility of things is *tamas*.[15]

All the faculties of man, his *buddhi, manas,* egoity, internal and external senses, and even the external world of elements which constitutes the object of his knowledge and action, appear in this conception as the interplay of the evolving functions of matter in varying proportions.

Though these two ultimate principles, *Purusha* and *Prakriti,* spirit and matter, are distinct and irreducible to each other, there is still an intimate relation between them : *Purusha* by its intelligent nature is the source of direction and purpose, since it is the only one that can enjoy the evolutions of *Prakriti* and attain the ultimate goal in liberation. On the other hand there is an internal finality in the evolutions of *Prakriti* : but these can be understood only in reference to the liberation of the individual *Purusha* bound in bodily existence.[16]

Critique

What interests us here in this psychological ontology is not so much the particular principles postulated as the general tendency implied in it, which has certain weaknesses as well as strong points to be considered.

(1) The principal drawback of the approach on the level of interior experience is that it tends to make a closed system of the human psyche. Though several individual *Purushas* are admitted, they have no common ground or mutual relation.

(2) The affirmation of three ultimate functions of matter as reflexion, action and limitation, is arbitrary from any metaphysical point of view.

(3) The unity of the human being itself is not properly explained. He appears rather as a sort of questionable peace between spirit and matter. The unity that results is, at best, one of co-ordination.

[15] Cf. A. G. Krishna Warrier, *The Concept of Mukti in Advaita Vedânta* (University of Madras, 1961), pp. 37–41.
[16] *Sâm K,* Kârika 21, 57, 59, 60–3.

On the other hand, certain characteristic notes of the approach to reality from the point of view of consciousness are clearly discernible in this Sâmkhyan conception.

(1) There is no sharp opposition between spirit and matter. Matter is not a pure potency bereft of all positive perfection, but a maternal principle from which all forms of material beings evolve.

(2) If the three *gunas* are taken as illustrative and enumerative, rather than as exclusive, they will show how even the unpredictable and changing aspects of experience may be comprehended within the expanse of consciousness.

(3) The Upanishadic method of parallelism gives the Sâmkhyan approach a cosmic meaning : Man is a microcosm. If his being is properly explained, the whole macrocosm is also explained. The spirit-matter polarity in man can be extended to the cosmic plane too. It is not one of opposition, but of diffusion. The spirit manifests itself in the evolutions of matter.

The Yogic, or ascetic level of knowledge

However, this approach to reality through internal experience is incomplete without taking into account the striving for liberation and transcendence found in the individual consciousness. Hence, another system of thought, practically taken for granted and supposed even by the Vedantins, is the *Yoga* system of Patanjali. We shall briefly indicate here its contribution to the approach to reality on this plane of internal experience, which is acknowledged and approved by Ramanuja.

The *Yoga* is the sister school of the *Sâmkhya,* with the same psychic conception of reality, but with an emphasis on the goal and means of ascetical concentration. *Yoga* as a practice of asceticism is defined by Patanjali as *cittavritti nirodha*,[17] control of the evolution of *citta*, the first evolved state of *Prakriti*, in order to bring it back to its initial state of balance of *gunas*; thereby, that which hides and obscures the reality of *Purusha* is removed, and the realization of its full consciousness attained.[18]

In this approach to reality through Yogic concentration, the final and ideal state of reality and of knowledge is considered to be

[17] *Yog S of Patanjali*, ed. Mandalal Lakshminivas Chang (Ajmeer, 1961), I, 2.
[18] *Yog S*, I, 3.

identical : the Seer remains in his authentic form (*tadâ drashthuh svarûpe avasthânam*).[19] It is also significant that the most noble aspect of *Prakriti* is called *sattva*, the abstract noun from *sat*, being, meaning essence in the literal sense. Knowledge which is the property of *sattva* is the most comprehensive aspect of things; it also includes other qualities such as brightness, lightness, and others.[20] Similarly the opposite of *sattva* is *tamas*, darkness, the hiding and obscuring aspect of matter leading to ignorance.

The present state of bondage is dissipation and alienation from itself and identification with the modifications.[21] Error is false knowledge based on the unauthentic form.[22] So, the whole Yogic effort is directed to withdraw one's attention gradually from the outer layers of existence through thought, meditation, contemplation and concentration, to the pure selfhood of *Purusha*.[23]

This Yogic endeavour leads to an opening up of the closed microcosm of the Sâmkhyan system. Man feels his own inability to transcend ignorance, passion and attachment, and spontaneously stretches out his hand to a being above him, one who is able and willing to help him out of his sad plight. Thus, Yoga postulates an Iswara, God and Lord, though He is conceived as the absolute Being only at a later stage in the history of the school. Iswara is conceived as the ideal *Purusha*, untouched by modifications and limitations,[24] the omniscient creator and teacher.

Once the consciousness of a Supreme Person helping individual souls and dispensing grace to them is reached, the unity of the universe is also realized. Hence, the final state is not merely the cessation of pain and pleasure,[25] nor even mere inactivity, but a blissful, intimate union with the Supreme Person. Vijnâna Bhikshu, a devotionalist commentator of the *Yoga Sûtras* in the 17th century, who could not find any real opposition between Yoga and Vedânta, says that the final and ideal condition of the soul is 'the non-separation of the human itself from the Supreme Self, on the dissolution of the limitations attaching to the former'.[26]

---

[19] *Ibid.* Cf. Vâcaspati's Gloss on I, 2, trs. Rama Prasad (Allahabad : Sacred Books of the Hindus, 1910), pp. 6–7.
[20] *Ibid.*
[21] *Yog S,* I, 4.
[22] *Yog S,* I, 8.
[23] *Yog S,* I, 17.
[24] *Yog S,* I, 24.
[25] *Yog S,* I, 25–7.
[26] *Yog S,* II, 16.

Critique

The Yogic approach to reality shares to a great extent the weaknesses of the *Sâmkhya* indicated above. Besides these :

(1) Its concept of *Prakriti* is less optimistic than that of the *Sâmkhyas*. The evolution of *Prakriti* implies the bondage of the spirit, a deterioration in the condition of reality.

(2) Its *Iswara*, postulated on account of the internal needs of the individual psyche, never reaches the absolute and pure aspect of the Supreme Being conceived on the metaphysical plane.

On the other hand, with Yoga the impersonalism of the lower empirical levels is transcended. Reality is not a mute mass of individual entities; it is principally community of persons, and there is a real dialogue between Iswara and individual *Purushas*.

The evolutions and actions in *Prakriti* are not mere mechanical developments. They have a special meaning for the individual *Purusha* aspiring for liberation, and can be made purposeful and useful if they are recognized as such by man and pursued to their natural goal.

Approach to Reality from 'Sabda'

Another avenue of approach to reality, and one recognized by most of the schools of Indian philosophy, is *sabda*, or Scripture. The importance ascribed to the Word as a source of true knowledge may appear baffling at first sight. Its authority is recognized as absolute with regard to suprasensible realities, since it deals with an area unattainable by other means, namely, perception and inference. But the interesting point is that Scripture is not taken here in the Western sense of revelation from a supreme personal God. It is not verbal testimony in the strict sense of the word. According to the Vedantins in general, *sabda* is impersonal. Sankara conceives it as the beginningless totality of impersonal values, intuited by the sages and committed to tradition by them. Though Ramanuja conceives *sabda* to a certain extent as a personal communication from the Lord, he also admits the eternal *apaurusheyatva*, authorless nature of it. The necessary note of an orthodox Hindu system is the acceptance of the authority of *sabda* or the *Veda*, consisting of the *Vedas*, *Brâhmanas*, *Aranyakas* and the *Upanishads* as a *pramâna*, or means of right knowledge.

What interests us here is its metaphysical value. It is not verbal testimony, but a philosophy of the Word developed by the Grammarians in ancient times, and later implicitly accepted by all the schools, and specialized in by the Mîmâmsakas as the basis of their ritualism. We shall briefly explain it in as much as it constitutes an authentic approach to reality from the point of view of consciousness and, as such, can be integrated into metaphysics.

In antiquity, at the beginning of philosophical thought in India, the grammarian was the philosopher and grammar was called *vedânâm vedâh*, the Veda of the Vedas, for it made the Veda itself understood.

The merit of this approach to reality through the word is that it shows the first steps in metaphysical transcendence. The grammarian's work is a *samskâra*, processing of speech. The *vyâkrita vâk*, or processed speech, shows up not only what is discordant with the general rule and what is in agreement with it, but also what is peculiar to an individual and what is proper to a word as such. Thus the word 'cow' uttered by different persons may differ from person to person in pitch, volume, intonation, etc., may be pleasant or harsh, may express different attitudes to the cow, and yet always means the same quadruped in our mind, and indicates a definite universal structure of animal form. Thus, we proceed from the crude external form, or *prâkrita dhwani*, to the word itself, which is represented by the *vyâkrita dhwani*, and from there to the meaning mentally conceived by the speaker and the listener, and then finally to the universal reality indicated.

In the immediate processing, the grammarian's work is purely logical : he distinguishes *jâti* and *vyakti* (genus and individual), coinherence (*sâmânâdhikaranya*) and inseparable connection (*samavâya*), the substantial and instrumental causes (*kârana* and *hetu*), substance (*dravya*), qualities (*guna*) and relation (*sambandha*), parts and the whole (*avayava* and *avayavi*), and so on.[27] But he does not stop there. He spontaneously proceeds to the notion of the word as such. The word as such is not restricted to a particular place or a particular time. It is beyond time and place, is non-relational and featureless.

The grammarian-philosopher could easily apply to his word the Upanishadic description of Brahman as *asabdam, asparsam,*

[27] Prabhat Chandra Chakravarti, *The Philosophy of Sanskrit Grammar* (University of Calcutta, 1930), pp. 34–44.

arûpam, avyayam, not bound by empirical speech, untouched, formless and imperishable.[28] This was precisely what Bhartrihari did. For him, the word was itself absolute and ineffable. Neither written word nor even Scripture could express all that is implied in the word itself. Hence, its interpretation through discussion, tradition and inference creates a variety of theories about the supreme reality. As eternal subsistent word, reality is pure existence, comprising all time and transcending all time. It has no beginning or end, birth or death. Hence it is pure authentic being itself. This was how Bhartrihari absolutized the word as the reality.[29]

This philosophy of the word developed by the grammarians was readily accepted by the orthodox Hindu and applied to the *Veda*, or the sacred writings of tradition, which were held in great esteem.

Another significant point in the philosophy of the word, a philosophy so appealing to Indian tradition, was the identification between word and consciousness. The word, by its very nature, is meaningful and self-revealing. Even in its crudest expression on the empirical level, it indicates a meaning of the speaker. In our own individual self, the word is meaningful. The word in itself is a meaning-bearing symbol which stands for the basic reality of the things it signifies.[30]

Critique

This approach to reality, commonly accepted by Indian metaphysical systems, has its drawbacks too.

(1) The most important weakness of the approach is typified in the philosophy of the Mîmâmsaka school, according to which *sabda* is the sum total of universal values, independent of everything. Hence, it does not show any interest in a God-creator, either as the source of the wisdom of Scripture or as the cause of the world. Once the absoluteness of the impersonal eternal values is recognized, a Creator would only contradict those values. Thus, the approach through *sabda* on account of the abstract character of the word can become a closed system which ignores the personal aspect of God and several other aspects of reality.

[28] *Kath Up,* III, 15.
[29] Gaurinath Sastri, *The Philosophy of Word and Meaning. Some Indian Approaches with Special Reference to the Philosophy of Bhartrihari* (Calcutta: Sanskrit College, 1959), pp. 1–3.
[30] *Ibid.,* pp. 4–6.

(2) A second weakness is the blind acceptance of Scripture itself by Indian thinkers. When the abstract idea of the word is identified with the written word, namely the books of the Hindu tradition, one fails to examine critically the value and authority of these books. Those who assume that these books contain the intuition of sages have no reliable means of proving that those sages really had an authentic intuition and that they faithfully transmitted it down the long centuries of Indian tradition. Neither Sankara nor Ramanuja gives a clear justification for the authority of the Scripture to which they appeal in the solution of every problem.

But the positive value of this approach to reality through the word is that it indicates an easy method of metaphysical transcendence which is very valuable in the study of reality itself. In the analysis of the phenomenon of speech, man's own self is in a way reflected. Hence, it also has a personal importance.

Conclusion

In this chapter we have examined the various approaches to reality on the empirical level : perception deals with things in terms of physical categories; inference elaborates experience through categories of thought. Analysis of internal experience into psychological categories deals with reality on the individual level. *Sabda* tries to rise from individual speech and traditional lore to the absolute and transcendent aspect of speech itself.

The weak points

(1) The principal weakness in all these approaches is their tendency to become closed and autonomous systems which absolutize one or other aspect of reality. (2) They all suffer from the fault of reductionism and tend to bring down the higher realities of God and the spiritual souls to their own particular categories, the physical substances, logical categories, individual psyche or even the mere abstract *sabda* of the grammarians.

Positive contribution

But a study of reality from the point of view of consciousness cannot afford to ignore them, since they have their positive contributions to be reckoned with.

(1) Each one of them brings out a special aspect of reality which is not properly explained in the other approaches.

(2) The positive contributions of these approaches are recognized and integrated into their metaphysical systems by Sankara and Ramanuja. Hence, to discuss their transcendental approach to reality without taking into account the details they suppose will be to miss their integral attitude to reality.

(3) The positive values of these approaches show that the correct attitude in metaphysics is not an exclusive preference for a particular mode of outlook or attachment to a single system, but a comprehensive and conciliatory approach which, like the bee, gathers honey from many flowers. This conciliatory attitude creates the mental background for understanding the convergence of transcendental approaches on the metaphysical plane, which will be the topic of the next chapter.

CHAPTER VIII

TRANSCENDENTAL APPROACH
TO REALITY

Scope and method of procedure

We have, above, discussed the approach to reality from the point of view of consciousness on the empirical level. However, the empirical level does not deal with reality as such, but only under particular aspects, physical, logical, psychological and linguistic. Though all these indicate the one reality, they still do not ask what reality is in itself. This question can be dealt with only on the transcendental level, where the basic dimensions of reality are existence, truth and such other notions which characterize everything indicated as real. Hence, I shall discuss here how reality as such is attained from the point of view of consciousness on the transcendental level.

In the present bodily existence of man, he has no direct intuition of reality as such. The complexity of the world of reality, therefore, requires a synthetic approach. I shall expose briefly the *Sûnyavâda*, or Void-theory, of Nagarjuna and the Advaita of Sankara as two possible extremes, in order to explore the feasibility of a synthetic view on the lines suggested by Ramanuja.

On this transcendental level, too, rational analysis and consciousness proceed in opposite directions. Rational analysis examines reality as something presented to thought and speech, an object. It is being, because it *is* independently of thought, exists in itself. All transcendental notes flow from this presentation of being as objective to the human mind. Consciousness, however, does not take reality as purely objective, but directs the attention to one's own self as the core of reality. The problem is: what is the ultimately real in this self?

110

Three ways

When one tries to reach the real on the level of pure consciousness, three main ways present themselves. One can concentrate
one's attention on the complexity and imperfection still left on the
level of our experience of the transcendental qualities of reality,
I-hood, truth, bliss and being, and can try to eliminate everything
that is imperfect, complex and therefore in any way conceivable
by our mind. This is the line of thought followed by Buddhists in
general, especially by the metaphysical school of Nagarjuna.

A second possibility is to proceed with the view that complexity
and imperfection are accidental to consciousness and to fix the
attention on absolute and limitless selfhood as ideal reality. Sankara
opts for this way.

Ramanuja accepts a third course which admits that a certain
duality and complexity is intrinsic to consciousness as a perfection,
and concentrates on the person who is the ground and subject of
consciousness as ultimate and ideal reality.

This threefold approach is a direct contrast to the three steps of
rational analysis, namely *ana-lysis, kata-lysis* and *para-lysis*—ways
of affirmation, negation and supereminence : all the perfections
found in finite beings have to be affirmed by way of ascent in a
Supreme Being, but their limited modes and imperfections have
to be denied about Him, and finally the supereminent way in which
all perfections are in Him indicated. But because we proceed from
consciousness, the order has to be reversed so that the first step
comes last, and the negative step comes first. Consciousness, by its
very nature, is the affirmation of the self as the source and unifying
centre of all perfections, and the Supreme Reality is the Self of
the self. In order to affirm the transcendent Self, one has to start
eliminating all the empirical layers of conscious selves which capture
and focus one's attention in mundane life. The second step is an
affirmation of the supereminent and transcendent reality of the
Absolute. Once the immutable and absolute reality of God is
affirmed, a third step is called forth to affirm the existence of the
finite beings along with Him, without, however, in any way affecting His absolute transcendence and purity. Though this last step
is, in reality, similar to the first step of rational analysis, it is not
an ascent but rather a descent, not an *ana-lysis* but a *kata-basis*.

The positions of Nagarjuna, Sankara and Ramanuja roughly

represent these three steps. Hence, they are not exclusive of each other, but rather complementary. We shall briefly examine these three positions and indicate how each opens out to the others.

REALITY AS 'SUNYATA'

The negative approach to reality is found in the *Neti-Neti* doctrine of the Upanishads :

> That *Atman* is not this, it is not that (*neti, neti*). It is unseizable, for it is not seized. It is indestructible, for it is not destroyed. It is unattached, for it does not attach itself. It is unbound. It does not tremble. It is not injured.[1]

But it became the central point of the Buddhist religious outlook.

I do not intend to give a historical study of the Buddhist negative philosophy. Supposing the excellent studies on the topic by Stcherbatsky[2] and T. V. R. Murthy[3] and others, I shall merely indicate the principal points of this negative approach in as much as they are relevant to metaphysics.

Buddhist opposition to all philosophical positive notions of reality rose first from practical considerations, as a reaction to the overtly theoretical religion of the Brahmins. The principal problem is man's misery and suffering, a mortal sickness from which release is sought. One who is wounded with a poisoned arrow should not bother about the caste or clan of the one who shot the arrow, the nature of the bow from which it was shot, or the material out of which it was made, but only about how it can be taken out and the wound healed. Concrete existence, with all its complexities, is the poisoned arrow in question. Hence, according to Buddha, all questions about reality and existence are irrelevant. What matters is misery, its origin, and its cessation, because 'this does profit, has to do with the fundamentals of religion, and tends to aversion, absence of passion, cessation, quiesence, knowledge, supreme wisdom, and *Nirvâna*.'[4]

---

[1] *Brih Up,* III, ix, 26; IV, ii, 4; IV, iv, 22.
[2] Th. Stcherbatsky, *The Conception of Buddhist Nirvâna* (Leningrad, 1927).
[3] T. V. R. Murthy, *The Central Philosophy of Buddhism* (London, 1955).
[4] *Majjhima Nikâya,* Sutta 63, *Buddhism in Translation,* trs. Henry Clarke Warren (Cambridge: Harvard University Press, 1953), pp. 117–22.

Conscious self as a composite

However, the philosophy underlying this negative attitude is a conception of self as a composite of experiential factors. Consciousness is described to be like a watchman taking his seat at the cross-roads, watching all that comes from the four sides. Whatever form a man beholds, whatever sound he hears, odour he smells, taste he tastes, tangible thing he touches, 'whatever idea he is conscious of with the mind, of that he is conscious with the consciousness'. Here, consciousness is taken as an act, rather than as a stable reality : 'Consciousness is the act of being conscious.'[5] This is said to be the sixfold consciousness, on which *Karma* depends, and which has to be resolved in order that liberation may be attained.

Inadequacy of logic

Nagarjuna and others, who tried to provide a philosophical basis for this general outlook, emphasized the inadequacy of human affirmation and logic to attain true reality. For the Brahmins, imbued with the philosophy of the Upanishads, every affirmation implied the affirmation of the Atman, who is the Self of all. But the Buddhists showed that the claim was unwarranted. Whatever form an affirmation may take, it implied, according to Nagarjuna, a certain contradiction : it attains only an aspect of reality, and yet it absolutizes that aspect as the whole and immutable reality.

Something can be stated in four ways : it is; it is not; it is and it is not; it neither is nor is not. This is considered as an exhaustive enumeration. But the emphasis is not placed on the exhaustive nature of the enumeration, as the critics of the Buddhist doctrine often seem to take for granted. Nor is it necessarily a denial of the principle of the excluded middle. What is meant is this : when something is affirmed to exist, an impression is given that reality is a thing like other things which fall within our experience. For example, when it is said that the soul exists, it is liable to be conceived as an exteriorized and extrapolated thing. Existence is something which originates, and hence is a composite. On the other hand, if it is said not to exist, the impression is given that it is nothingness. A composite of 'is' and 'is not' in a statement will imply that reality is a simple composite of two halves, existence

[5] *Milindapanha*, 62[8], H. C. Warren, *op. cit.*, p. 182.

and non-existence, on the same level. 'Neither is nor is not' implies, in spite of what it intends to state, that there is some other category besides existence and non-existence, but on the same plane, applicable to reality. Hence, the conclusion is that reality, as such, cannot be affirmed in terms of empirical existence.

Limitation of causality

According to Nagarjuna, the principle of causality cannot take us beyond the empirical sphere either. On the one hand, finite things require only finite causes for their production. Hence, however much the chain of causes can be extended, it may not be possible to get out of the sphere of the finite. Even if an 'Infinite Cause' is affirmed, both terms of this designation, 'infinite' and 'cause', are drawn from the field of experience, and are therefore intrinsically and inextricably bound up with finite things. When I say 'infinite', I am not grasping anything actually infinite, but only putting a negative tag on a vivid finite thing in my imagination. I can never conceive the Infinite. By affirming the Infinite, I am just looking into a void, a *sûnyatâ*, by removing from sight all that can in some way be conceived.

With 'cause', the case is more difficult. What I call cause is either some matter from which something is made like clay formed into pot, or someone who acts on something else, as the potter on clay, or the shape and form which make a thing, or the model or goal or gain from which the agent acts. But all these cases involve intrinsic imperfection and outside dependence. I can deny from an agent like a potter the factors of his dependence : he does not need clay; he need not sweat and labour. Still, to postulate causality, he must have at least an effect, and the effect *qua* effect is on the same level as the cause; they are correlative terms. This means that causality is necessarily bound up with duality, and therefore cannot be applied to the unique and absolute reality. If the cause affirmed is not a correlate of the effect to which it points, causality does not serve any purpose.

This is the intrinsic difficulty of the arguments used by the Nyâya philosophers and others to prove the existence of God : they try to postulate the Supreme Reality from things which originate. According to Nagarjuna, everything that has a dependent origination (*pratîtyabhâva*), including our words, belongs to the field of intrinsic unreality, *sûnyatâ*,[6] though it is not nothing, but practically real and useful.[7] But the real cannot be deduced by generalization from the unreal.

Sûnyatâ also stands for the ultimate reality, since we cannot form any positive idea about it. The consciousness which transcends the world cannot come within the sphere of conscious experience which constitutes the world of rebirth.[8] This absolute consciousness is also designated by the positive term *prâjnâ*, intuition, as distinct from *vijnâna*. *Vijnâna* is knowledge in terms of positive perfections, while *prâjnâ* is realization in a momentary flash by the negation of all that *vijnâna* stands for. Hence, *prâjnâ* cannot be expressed in terms of *vijnâna*. In *vijnâna*, which is a system of concepts, contradiction is the basic law, while in *prâjnâ*, the principle of contradiction is not even applicable.

The *prâjnâ* is attained, not by analysis and ascent, but by elimination and withdrawal. One should isolate oneself from the exterior spheres of consciousness, from sensual pleasures, demeritorious traits, cross the spheres of reasoning and reflexion and even happiness, completely overpower all perceptions of form, even of infinite consciousness and of nothingness. Thus, 'through having completely overpassed the realm of neither perception nor yet nonperception, (one) arrives at the cessation of perception and sensation; and before the clear vision of wisdom all one's depravity wastes away'.[9] Since the oneness *prâjnâ* points to is not abstracted from the many on which *vijnâna* depends, it is not a numeric identity, nor a pantheistic unity.[10]

Critique

We have to remark, first of all, that most of the criticism made against the Buddhist position by the Vedantins and Nyâya logicians arises from a misunderstanding of their real outlook. *Sûnyavâda* is

---

[6] Nagarjuna says: 'That which has been produced through causes and conditions we call *sûnyatâ*.' *Mûla-mâdhyamika Kârika*, XXIV, 18, cited by N. K. Devaraja, *An Introduction to Sankara's Theory of Knowledge* (Delhi, 1962), p. 141.

[7] *Vigrahavyâvartani, sl.* 23–8.

[8] *Visuddhi Mâgga, c.* XVIII, *Buddhism in Translation,* p. 184.

[9] *Majjhima Nikâya*, Sutta 26, *Buddhism in Translation,* pp. 347–9.

[10] Cf. Daisetz Taitaro Suzuki, 'Reason and Intuition in Buddhism', *Essays in East–West Philosophy,* ed. Charles A. Moore (Honolulu, 1951), pp. 17–48.

no mere logical ingenuity, nor absolute nihilism. It does not deny all reality. Nor does it proceed by a denial of the principle of the excluded middle. All that it challenges is the possibility of passing from the finite world to a positive conception of the absolute. Hence, the whole philosophy gets a negative outlook for all practical considerations.

But the principle difficulty with this way of approach is that it cannot produce any metaphysics which is useful for the ordinary man. Once the final *prâjnâ* is attained, metaphysics itself becomes useless.

The positive contribution of this negative stage is the idea of transcendence itself, which is the corner-stone of all metaphysics.

(1) The absolute and the conditioned cannot be placed side by side. Absolute Reality can in no way be conceived, but only affirmed. Something comprehended by our conception cannot be absolute. On the level on which Absolute Reality *is*, the finite beings of our experience and all that come within our consciousness in definite form and figure *are not*.

(2) Our conscious experience can therefore be an obstacle in the right understanding of the Real, on account of our inclination to translate and generalize our experience of the finite world as the form of the Absolute. This will only distort the Real.

(3) This also emphasizes the meaningfulness of the negative or apophatic method in philosophy. Socratic irony, which refused to be satisfied with generalizations from daily experience, opened the way to deeper analyses and more comprehensive solutions. The Plotinian negative characterizations of the One, and the apophatic method of pseudo-Dionysius, paved the way to a deeper understanding of Reality in Western tradition. Augustine's negative experience of reality at Ostia is more constructive than all he has contributed towards the building up of the City of God. Nagarjuna's *sûnyatâ*, void, is a real *pûrnam*, a plenitude, and his meaningful silence an eloquent eulogy on Reality. His principal fault is that he stopped at the negativity of silence.

REALITY AS 'CINMATRA'

The second step on the transcendental way to reality from the point of view of consciousness is an absolute affirmation : the affirmation of the Absolute Self as the plenitude of all reality, infinite and immutable. Metaphysics cannot end in silence. Silence of the finite implies in itself the plenitude of the Real.

On this point, Sankara is the principal guide in the Indian tradition, though he too has the Upanishads as the principal source. The same Upanishads which affirmed non-being, *asat*, as the beginning of things,[11] also affirm the unique *Sat*, the One without a second, the *Atman*, as the sole reality, in knowing which everything else is known.[12] We shall briefly explain this positive step in the light of Sankara's philosophy.

Sankara has no difficulty in admitting and assuming all the basic arguments of *Sûnyavâda*—namely, that the Absolute cannot be attained by way of causality from the finite world, and that the world of our experience, dependent and relative, is unreal. But when we look into our own self-consciousness, we realize that the time-place conditions which make it relative and dependent are not essential to consciousness as such; consciousness as such is a spiritual reality independent of material conditions. What is essential to something should be found in it in all conditions. The sense of 'I' is not bound to any particular time or place. It, by itself, is what makes all time-place conditions intelligible.

It is interesting to note that all Vedantins appeal to the state of dreamless sleep as an indication of the ideal state of consciousness : in a sleeping man, the self is not destroyed, it exists; yet it is not affected by any time-place conditions. But the ideal condition of consciousness is beyond sleep, the fourth state in pure *cit* remaining by itself.

That the ideal reality is not in our field of experience but beyond it, deep within our own selves, is clear to Sankara by the anomalies in our experience itself :

(1) Though the subject and object, the 'I' and the 'Thou', are irreducibly opposed to each other like light and darkness, we easily attribute the properties and characteristics of one to the other : we add selfhood by the designation 'my' on material things —my property, my body, and so on—and *vice versa* attribute material and bodily properties to the self, saying 'I am heavy', 'I am sad', and the like. Since the I-Thou opposition is evident, this ordinary cross-predication of attributes should be considered an

---

[11] *Tait Up*, II, vi, 7; *Chând Up*, II, xix, 1; *Brih Up*, I, 2.
[12] *Chând Up*, VI, ii, 1; *Kath Up*, II, ii, 12; *Svet Up*, VI, 12; *Ait Up*, I, i, 1.

anomaly and error, and pure selfhood or consciousness should be taken as constituting the area of the Real.[13]

(2) Even within the field of our self-consciousness, we can distinguish several concentric circles or levels, with each of which one can identify oneself, and from each of which one can withdraw oneself by rejecting all identification with it. Thus, on the one hand, I can say 'my food', 'my life', 'my feelings', 'my knowledge', and 'my happiness', or I can choose to repudiate food, life, feelings, particular knowledge and particular happiness, and still remain my own self. Hence, it is clear that there are depths of reality beyond all these particular levels in pure selfhood which it would be contradictory to deny.[14]

(3) In our knowledge itself, we have to distinguish between our desires, opinions and true knowledge of reality : our desires and opinions are free, can be changed, argued out, and so on. But, with regard to reality, we cannot have it as we wish, or entertain mere opinions about it. For example, I cannot say about a post : 'It is a man or something else'. I attain reality only when, through *anubhava* (a sort of becoming one with it), I say 'It is a post'. So, in the case of Supreme Reality, opinions and options are not admitted. We have to become one with it in the depth of our consciousness. Everything else, even Scripture, only leads to the final realization of Reality.[15]

(4) All that is produced and acquired is limited, and therefore bound to perish. Hence, knowledge of reality, truth, cannot be produced. On the other hand, a produced knowledge cannot contain the real. We can, therefore, only realize the Real, discover what is already in our deepest centre. The attempt to *obtain* a 'true' knowledge of the Real is a contradiction in terms. Hence, the approach to reality can only be to realize what is already in us, pure *cit*, immutable existence and infinite bliss.[16]

Though the Real cannot be perceived by any of the senses and other means, still there is the negative procedure which cannot end in pure negation : the void is positive. Deny all the attributes we can, and there will still be existence left. If non-existence is affirmed about the Real, it will imply the non-existence of the

---

[13] *Br S Sank Bh,* Introduction.
[14] *Tait Up Sank Bh,* III.
[15] *Br S Sank Bh,* I, i, 2.
[16] *Tait Up Sank Bh,* II, 1.

knower himself. Therefore, true intellect (*sad buddhi*) affirms existence.[17]

But even this consciousness and existence, *cit* and *sat,* cannot be taken as a definition of the Supreme Reality, nor are they synonymous with it; they only designate the Real. Since these notions, by their very nature, exclude limitation and imperfection, they have to be verified in their primary sense in the Absolute selfhood, and only in a secondary sense in finite things. In comparison with the Absolute, everything else is unreal, mere *mâyâ,* illusion, and *avidyâ,* negation of knowledge.

Critique: weakness of the approach

The radical inadequacy of using this approach to reality to constitute a metaphysics is that it is too abstract to give sufficient intelligibility to all the sections of reality. It places the absolute on a level so remote and so sublime that human knowledge can approach it only through *neti, neti,* not-so, not-so. To add anything beyond and besides *sat* and *cit* would tarnish the purity of the Absolute.

On the other hand, it reduces the world of finite beings to a level of unreality. There is nothing much more to be said about a thing which one has labelled 'illusion'. The spheres of the Real and the unreal are so much opposed to each other that there is no possibility of passing from one to the other.

Importance of the step

However, if Sankara's position is taken as a step to the understanding of reality, it is meaningful and necessary. It places in a clear light the transcendence of the Supreme over all finite beings, and at the same time shows His intimate immanence in them as the ground of their reality. Any number of finite beings cannot deduct from or add to the Infinite Reality. Beside Him they are '*mâyâ*', they cannot exist or be understood except in relation with Him. All that is intelligence and perfection in beings is rooted in the Supreme, like a prototypic reflexion.

[17] *Kath Up Sank Bh,* VI, 12.

REALITY AS PERSONAL ENCOUNTER

Once the reality of finite beings is denied, and the absolute and immutable reality of the Supreme affirmed, a third step of integration is needed to understand the positive value of finite beings. Any absolutization of the finite is excluded by the first step of negation; any synthesis between the finite and Infinite on the level of entitative perfection is excluded by the second step of absolute affirmation. However, the finite cannot be neglected or denied as a mere nothing, nor relegated to the void of Nagarjuna or the vague *mâyâ* of Sankara. Hence, the question arises as to whether a coexistence of the Absolute and the finite, other than on the level of perfections, is possible. Ramanuja provides the answer by his concept of personality. I shall indicate briefly in this chapter the general outline of this synthesis, reserving for the following chapters a more complete study of the details of this integral approach to reality.

The merit of this third step is that the emphasis here is not on impersonal perfections, but on the one who is, who knows, and who loves. Person as the ultimate reality shows, on the one hand, how a multitude of perfections can be predicated about the Supreme Being without impairing His simplicity and infinity, and, on the other, how the finite can be a person without becoming a rival to the Supreme.

Consciousness as self-consciousness

Here again, the procedure is from consciousness. All consciousness is self-consciousness. Only in being conscious of myself am I conscious of others. Only what is luminous in itself illuminates others. Whatever the level of knowledge, there must be one who knows. Man is conscious because he knows other things, and knowing them he knows himself. He is the symbol of the unity and self-consistency of reality itself.

The very idea of liberation suggests that Self is the greatest value in nature. Unless there is someone to be liberated, all ascetic effort towards liberation is meaningless. An impersonal consciousness is a purposeless nonsense for a goal.

All the material and spiritual goods in the world require some person to enjoy them. Man is indeed a person. But if he examines his personality, he comes to the knowledge of the Supreme Person : the fact that man finds himself dependent upon and subject to material things shows his limitation. Hence, he is not the absolute Self. He has not produced the things he knows and enjoys, so he is forced to look for the source from which the origination, etc., of the world proceed. Material things which are unconscious are not their own selves; they are only modes and manifestations of a cosmic self, the Supreme Person. In relation to him, even the human person is only a mode and participation, though a conscious one.

The Supreme Person, the Supreme Real

The true knowledge of reality, therefore, is recognition of the Supreme Person as the core and centre of all reality. Everything is a manifestation from Him. He cannot be defined by any perfection, even by *satyam-jnânam-anantam*, the truth-knowledge-and-infinity formula of the Upanishad. All perfections pertain to his *svabhâva*, his self-manifestation. For the perfections we attribute to Him are drawn from the finite world of our experience, which is only an external manifestation of the Real. Everything is He, and has to be referred back to Him as its ultimate Self. Yet nothing can be identified with Him. All imperfection and limitation have to be denied to Him as incompatible with His self. But all perfections, even the least ones, have to be referred to Him first and foremost, as to their ultimate and authentic ground, and only secondarily to the finite subjects in which they appear. All created entities, including celestial beings and men, are only the manifestation of an infinitesimal part of his pure being. Yet man, too, as a conscious being, is a person and can address himself to the Supreme Person who is full of love and compassion for his creatures.

Person, the point of integration

This personalist outlook has the capacity to integrate and reconcile with itself the other metaphysical approaches. There is no doubt that the subsistent perfection of the Supreme Person is ineffable as Sankara and Nagarjuna rightly emphasized. But the One who subsists in that perfection is some One. In general, we may say that the person is a metaphysical point of reference which need not be identified with its perfections; it can be with infinite perfections as in Brahman, or be with any number of limitations and imperfections as in man. The Sâmkhya-Yoga principles of *Purusha* and *Prakriti* as ultimate constitutive principles in individual beings, and the Nyâya-Vaiseshika categories as constitutive of the world, all postulate a supreme ground of all reality, namely the Supreme Lord. Hence, the Person as the counterpart of consciousness is the co-ordinating point of all metaphysics.

PARALLELISM BETWEEN WESTERN AND INDIAN PHILOSOPHIES

In this slow evolution from objective knowledge to the discovery of the Person as the ultimate ground of reality, there is a certain parallelism between the two great world traditions of Philosophy.

Greek Philosophy started with the knowledge of material elements, being, intelligence and goodness, concentrating attention on nature. Modern Philosophy shifted the emphasis from the thought about nature to the subject of thought. The emphasis on personality introduced by Christian philosophy has finally gained ground in contemporary Existentialism, in which the aspect of Existence as Being-with-Others forms the core of metaphysical thought. Reason slowly moved from the 'It' of the Greeks to the 'Ego' of Descartes, and finally to the 'We' of contemporary thought.

In Indian Philosophy, objective and analytic Reason was replaced by Consciousness, the root of self-awareness. But here also, Consciousness has shifted its point of emphasis from the objective categories of the Vaiseshikas through the Logic of Nyâya and the Psychology of the Sâmkhya-Yoga to the *Sûnya* of Nagarjuna and the *Atman*, Self, of Sankara. Ramanuja further moved it to the 'We' of the devotional encounter between man and the Supreme Person.

Hence, these two traditions are complementary, rather than contradictory. But the main problem arising out of a conception of reality in terms of consciousness and person is that of the coexistence between the Infinite and the finite, the all-perfect and the imperfect. Does not the encounter between the human person and the Supreme Person affect adversely the transcendence of God? This will be the point for discussion in the next chapter.

CHAPTER IX

THE SEARCH FOR THE ONE FROM THE POINT OF VIEW OF CONSCIOUSNESS

GENERAL INTRODUCTION

In the three preceding chapters I have briefly outlined the nature of consciousness and the various approaches from it to reality. It remains to see how reality is attained in a comprehensive synthesis according to these approaches, especially on the transcendental level.

This survey of reality, according to the Vedantic tradition, is done in four steps, indicated by the first four *sûtras* of the *Bâdarâyana Sûtras,* the official text-book of the school. These four sûtras constitute a certain compact unity, and are therefore designated by the common title of *'Catussûtrî'* extensively commented upon by the *Achâryas,* or teachers, as a comprehensive view of metaphysics. In our discussion below, we shall follow the same scheme.

The first sûtra, *athâto Brahmajijnâsâ,* 'Then, therefore, the inquiry into Brahman', shows an approach to the Supreme Reality from the human desire for liberation through right knowledge, and in its light evaluates the world of finite beings. The second sûtra, *janmâdyasya yatah,* 'That from which the origin, etc.', is a discussion on Causality from the point of view of consciousness.

The third sûtra, *sâstrayonitvât,* 'Since Scripture is the source', concentrates the attention on the central doctrine of the Upanishads and attempts a definition of the Supreme Reality as existence, consciousness and infinity, and in its light discusses the reality of finite beings. The fourth sûtra, *tattu samanvayât,* 'And that on account of the connection', presents the Ultimate Reality as the highest goal of man, and studies the metaphysical conclusions involved in the God-man encounter.

This gives us the principal problems of metaphysics : the problem of the One and the many—namely, the existence of the Supreme

123

Being and the analogy of being, the problem of causality, the problem of the transcendental properties of being, and finally the notion of personality and the inter-personal relation, including moral values.

The scope of this chapter

In this chapter, I shall, in the spirit of the first sûtra, discuss how the Supreme Reality is known through consciousness. This will present a synthesis of the main positive elements that contribute to an understanding of the One from the angle of consciousness.

ATHATO BRAHMAJIJNASA : THE QUEST FOR THE ONE

From the standpoint of consciousness, the discussion of the problem of the One and the many starts with the discovery of the One. In rational analysis, the many is taken for granted as the datum and the ontological inquiry concentrates on the discovery of a point of unity. In the approach from consciousness, the basic unity experienced in our self is the datum. Still, the existence of the One is not taken for granted; it has to be consciously discovered. It has to be located in the centre of human life itself. Hence, we shall discuss first how the One is discovered in the immediate reality of concrete human experience, in the vivid desire for liberation from pain and ignorance and for knowledge.

Atha: This first word of the first sûtra of Badarayana is an inceptive and auspicious particle which cannot properly be translated into English. It stands for the whole background of a discussion. Here it stands, according to commentators, for the relation between practical human behaviour constituted of moral principles, ritual and asceticism, and the *jijnâsa* or desire for knowledge. The meaning of the expression is that inquiry into the nature of reality does not start in the abstract. The beginning of philosophy is in suffering, in the painful worldly existence from which man seeks liberation. Philosophical investigation is not an idle pastime, but something flowing out of concrete human existence beset with need and anxiety.

Therefore, the beginning of the inquiry must be in a certain ordering of human life itself. The sundry details of daily life are organized through morality and ritual. Moral laws bring in the demarcation between right and wrong, freedom and obligation, duty and liberality, and other pairs of opposites.

Ritual, to which one is normally introduced according to tradition, adds another aspect to man's encounter with concrete reality. In ritual, things are symbolized and indicate the integration of the material world to a higher order of things and to a deeper value than what appears on the outside. The temple is the symbol of the universe, and its tower rising in the middle stands for the link of aspiration that binds earth with heaven, ordinary everyday existence with transcendental values. Sacrifice is symbolic of man's total surrender to God, and the ancient Hindu altar, built over a golden effigy of the sacrificer lying with face turned upwards, was supposed to carry the vital breath of the golden man, along with his offering, heavenwards.

Ascetical practices, too, prepare the mind for the inquiry into truth. The aim of asceticism is not bodily death or dissolution of the material body. *Tapas*, the Sanskrit word for religious austerities, literally means heat or intensification of energy. Through austerities, one is supposed to gather up and concentrate all one's dissipated energy into one's authentic centre.

Thus, moral living, ritual and austerity, which are the necessary preparation for inquiry into Brahman, indicate an initial unification of the conscious self before the search for the ultimate One is undertaken. They show that philosophy is an integral part of human life and that it should start with a practical integration and orientation of life itself.

One is reminded of the *pratike* of Platonic and Plotinian asceticism, with the purifying virtues of prudence, justice, temperance and fortitude, which steady the mind for contemplation. However, there is a certain difference : the cardinal virtues of Platonic thought balance man within himself and towards others, in order that he may take a look upwards; moral life, ritual and asceticism of the Indian tradition direct his gaze inwards to his deepest centre.

Atas : *the reason for* Jijnâsâ

The reason for an intense desire to know Brahman is in this preliminary preparation through moral life, ritual and asceticism. They create the desire in two ways. In a positive way, they manifest the internal dynamism of human existence. External composite unity achieved through right living is only a sign of a deeper unity of simplicity. Every organized thing is for someone who can profit by it. The external organization of actions, things and circumstances points to a self for whose ulterior goal all these serve as means. Hence, they do not find their full meaning until that supreme goal of the self is discovered.

But the more important function of this preparatory stage is a negative one, namely to show the non-finality of the world of experience. What is immediately achieved by the actions of men is finite and perishable. However much a finite being may acquire and add to its being, it will always remain finite. The meaning of life, therefore, cannot be in acting, effecting, achieving and acquiring, but rather in searching, knowing and being. It cannot be a looking out, but rather a looking into the deepest centre of one's reality.

Action and achievement are limited and restricted on every side, while the enthusiasm behind it, the dynamism of the self, remains almost unlimited. Energy of the human spirit expended in external activity gets dissipated and lost, while, when turned inwards, it becomes focused on the unique centre of the self. The only field where man's dynamic outlook gets infinite scope is knowledge, delving deeper and deeper into the ground of his own reality.

The Jnâna of Jijnâsâ, or the knowledge of desire

What opens the door to the fulfilment of the desire for knowledge of the Ultimate Reality is a knowledge of the desire itself. Desire for knowledge and knowledge of desire are so intimately related from the point of view of consciousness that they may be said to be identical, though referring to different aspects and with different implications. Consciousness is not pure abstract knowledge, but embraces the whole human self in its dynamic self-evaluation. A proper understanding of the desire as the basic dimension of finite consciousness can yield the knowledge that the desire is directed to and defined by. This is the reason why Hindu *Achâryas* like Sankara and Ramanuja place great emphasis on an intense desire (*mumukshutva*) as a precondition for true knowledge and realization of the Ultimate Reality.

This desire is not for any particular object but for all reality, and therefore for reality as such. Nothing finite can satisfy it. Every passion, attachment, and petty interest will only impede and dampen this desire. Hence, 'liberation', proposed as the goal of spiritual endeavour in Hindu tradition, is not a negative word. Once the external obstacles created by passion and self-interest and sin are removed, the human spirit, with all its force, tends towards its deepest and authentic centre, which is the Ultimate Reality. It is a setting-free of the conscious self to follow the weight of its own being. This is why the Sâmkhya-Yoga schools speak of liberation as *kaivalya*, isolation; when the spirit finds itself in its authentic selfhood, freed from the confusing outgrowth of the material and limiting environment, it discovers in itself the greatest force drawing it to the ultimate depth of its reality in the One.

Hence, this desire is not an act, but a state or condition. It is the dynamic condition of the limited, yet conscious, reality which tends to transcend the limits and to be all that it can be. Now, for a conscious being, to be is to know. Therefore, desire to know is the basic dimension of the conscious being.

Brahmajijnâsâ, *desire to know Brahman*

Desire to know is the desire to know Brahman, God, the Ultimate Reality. There is no other knowable in which consciousness can find its plenitude and transcend all limits. Finding itself as a reflexion of the Ultimate is, for the finite self, the end of its journey.

To know oneself as a reflexion of the Absolute does not do away with the frontiers between the finite and the Infinite. But it does show that the Absolute is not an alien, a simple other, a mere 'Thou' for the finite self. What the finite is, the Absolute is in a fuller sense, in a more authentic way. Hence, the Absolute is the Self of the finite self, so the finite can speak of the Ultimate as its own fullness.

The desire of the finite self extends into infinity; it will be satisfied only when it finds that there is nothing more to be received. But it cannot, by any amount of addition or achievement, reach such a plenitude. Its one possibility of fulfilling its desire is to surrender itself totally to the supreme Good, so that it can call that good its own good. However, this total surrender is not achieved in any material or physical way, but only by knowledge or consciousness. So, the desire to know involves by itself this total surrender to the Ultimate in consciousness; the greater the desire, the greater the knowledge.

'BRAHMAJNANA' : KNOWLEDGE OF GOD

There are two ways of knowing God—positive rational inquiry and conscious realization. Of these, the first, which is the principal one in the approach through objective analysis, is only a negative step in the point of view of consciousness.

Rational argumentation

Rational arguments proposed to prove the existence of God have their universal validity. (1) This well-organized world with its infinite details requires a Supreme Creator, who is the author of all finite things and is therefore outside the world of finite reality. (2) When we proceed up the scale of beings, according to increasing spirituality and decreasing dependence on time-space conditions and materiality, we have to postulate a pure, spiritual, self-subsistent and absolutely independent being beyond all others. (3) Since this beautiful and well-arranged world, with all its intelligent and non-intelligent beings, is perfectly organized, there must be a goal and purpose for it, and one who guides its course to the realization of his own aims.

The arguments will surely show that no being within the world system, no finite being, can explain the world. The world is not self-explanatory. This line of argumentation goes well against the closed cosmology of the Vaiseshika and Sâmkhya philosophers, as well as against the negative philosophy of the Buddhists. But there its value ends. For others who generally admit the existence of the Supreme Being, these arguments do not provide any positive knowledge about the nature of the Ultimate Reality. The transcendent reality of God cannot be understood by any generalization from everyday experience of the finite world.

The approach through consciousness

The positive approach to God from consciousness takes the finite consciousness in its symbolic or designative value as pointing to the transcendent. This transcendental designation implied in the finite is indicated by the theory of meanings advocated by the Vedantic scholars. According to Sankara, all the pure perfections designated by words like truth, goodness, bliss, and the like, have their primary denotation in Brahman, while other words refer to him by their *gaunârtha*, or indirect or analogical sense. Ramanuja, on the other hand, holds that every word has its primary denotation in God, since it is a symbol of reality, and only secondarily refers to finite objects. But what is important in both these theories is that, from the point of view of consciousness, every finite presented to our conscious experience is a function of the Infinite and has full meaning only in reference to it.

However, this reference in consciousness to the Ultimate has different aspects, all of which serve as points of metaphysical transcendence from the finite to the Infinite. Limitation points to absolute greatness; change calls for stability; reflected light points the finger to the ultimate source of light; and above all, all forms of consciousness refer back to an ultimate Self beneath.

Param Brahma[1] : *the Supreme Great*

The very term Brahman, applied to the Supreme Being, is indicative of the transcendental reference implied in consciousness. Brahman means 'that which is great'. As Ramanuja rightly remarks, though there are many things which have the characteristic of greatness, it 'primarily denotes that which has greatness of essential nature'[2] and only secondarily and in a derivative sense those things which are relatively great.

Finiteness and limitation are, by their very nature, restrictions put on consciousness : limited perfection is not in its own self, but extrapolated out of its authentic centre. Limitation is, therefore, a point of reference that reflects the perfection framed in it back to the authentic self of consciousness as the truly great and ultimately real. All finiteness in conscious experience is a phenomenon which calls the attention to the really and essentially great, Brahman.

This same idea is expressed in the Upanishadic designation of Brahman as *Pûrnam*, plenitude, of which the integrity and totality

---

[1] *Tait Up,* II, 12.
[2] *Sri Bh,* I, i, 1.

of the world is only a reflexion.[3] Sankara emphasizes this same aspect by characterizing Brahman as *bhûman*, fullness, as comprehensive of the essential characteristics of God.[4]

Param Tattvam[5] : *the immutable ground*

Change is another sign leading to an ultimate and immutable ground of stability. What changes its form is not true to itself. It is *anrita*, untrue. Hence, a self, subject to change and variation, readily realizes that it is not in its authentic ground. Change manifests the dynamism involved in the finite reality tending to transcend the limitations imposed upon it, in order to attain stability and immutability. This dynamism can be understood only as the centripetal force of all participated reality, responding to the self-consistency of the Ultimate Real, which draws all to itself.

Param Jyotih[6] : *supreme light*

This Self, the centre of all reality, is best indicated by the analogy of light. All reflected light and diffused rays turn our attention to the source from which they proceed. Light in a non-luminous substance has no sufficient intelligibility, unless it is referred to a source which is luminous. So also, man is not pure consciousness, but only a subject that has received consciousness; he knows sometimes, but at times he is ignorant and in darkness. Hence, his consciousness is not its own light, but reflected from a deeper source. This point is clearly set forth by the Upanishadic text which compares Brahman to the supreme light :

> The sun shines not there, nor the moon and stars,
> These lightnings shine not, much less this (earthly) fire :
> After Him, as He shines, doth everything shine,
> This whole world is illumined with His light.[7]

This solemn statement is given in reply to a question about Brahman, as to whether he shines by himself, or shines in reflexion. Every limited light shines by the light of Brahman; but Brahman himself is not illumined by any.

---

[3] *Brih Up*, V, 1.
[4] *Ken Up Sank Bh*, II, 1; *Br S Sank Bh*, III, ii, 21.
[5] *Chând Up*, VI, ii, 1.
[6] *Chând Up*, VIII, iii, 4.
[7] *Kath Up*, V, 15; *Mûnd Up*, II, ii, 10; *Svet Up*, VI, 14.

This analogy of light is important, because it embraces not only the individual conscious sphere of the knower, but the whole objective world as well. The material things that appear in consciousness have no intelligibility or light of their own. They are made intelligible. Nor is the intelligibility simply supplied by the knower. He is conscious that he had not the knowledge of the things in question, and that now he comes to know them. The knower and the known are suffused by the same light from a transcendental source. The universality of truth and conviction vouches for the transcendental aspect of this source of light. Hence, this ultimate source of consciousness is named the *Param Jyotih*, the Supreme Light. He is the Truth of all truth, *satyasya satyam*.

Paramâtma *and* Sarvâtma: *Supreme and Universal Self*

From consciousness, what leads most directly to an understanding of the One is the anomaly of the conscious self itself. The self appears as the immutable and common ground of all experiences, and also as opposed to the objective world outside. On closer examination, this ground of stability, light and unity appears to be beset with change, ignorance and conflict. Still, the need for unity and stability in consciousness is not resolved. Hence, spontaneously, the awareness of the finite self indicates a Self beyond, an ultimate self, *Paramâtman*. This Self of the self is also the point of unity and immutable and universal truth for all that is intelligible. The Self of the individual self, therefore, is also the universal Self, the self of all, the *Sarvâtma*.

There are several other ways in which consciousness opens out to the One. The limited knowledge calls to boundless consciousness as its source and centre. The sense of dependence, or *pâratantrya*, discovered as the condition of the finite conscious being, points the finger to one who is absolutely free, *svatantra*.

The nature of the ascent

But, in all these procedures, from finite consciousness to the supreme Consciousness, the basic idea is the same : Deep calls to the Deep; the shallow depth of the finite self calls to the profound depth of the absolute Self. It is not an intuition in any sense of the term. The knowledge of God here is mediate and indirect, never proper or direct. On the other hand, it is not syllogistic reasoning either. One does not start with pre-established premises in order to deduce from them the existence of the Ultimate.

The procedure may in some manner be compared to the way in which the intellect moves from the perception of sensible qualities of a thing to its intelligible essence. It is not the sum total of the sensations that produces the knowledge of the essence. The intellect that evaluates the work of the senses spontaneously rises to the understanding of the essence. Similarly, the realization of the limitations and anomalies within the finite consciousness spontaneously leads to the One beyond. It may be called spontaneous deduction or deductive designation of the Ultimate from the finite.

The Infinite in the heart of the finite

However, it is not merely the quest for an ideal to unify the multiplicity of experience, as the Platonic quest for the ideal appears to be. For Plato and Plotinus, the limited perfections in the beings of our experience were the problem. The limited perfections were the anomalies which contained in themselves their own contradiction, unless they had behind them an absolute perfection in which they participated. But, the Indian thinkers did not take things as they are in themselves, but only in their symbolic reference to the knowledge of reality as such. Hence, they were not very much preoccupied with the origin and intelligibility of things in themselves.

For the same reason, Brahman is not postulated as the efficient cause of things. When their very reality was in question, nobody bothered much about how they originated or who produced them.

Approach from consciousness is preoccupied with the thinking subject itself: the One that will resolve the contradictions in my own self. I am conscious, yet I am ignorant; I reside in myself, yet I am not happy, not possessing myself fully. I am active and autotelic, seeking my own good, yet my desires go out of me extending toward something beyond. The One postulated as the Self of my self is the central point in which all the complexities and perplexities of my personal existence are resolved. He is infinite consciousness of which my own knowledge is only a reflexion. He is the plenitude of bliss in which alone I can find my perfect happiness. He is the dynamic centre of my existence which draws my whole being by an internal and centripetal force. My desire to be fully myself is realized by surrendering myself to this unifying centre.

THE TWO APPROACHES : A COMPARISON

From what has been said, the fundamental differences in the approach to the One from objective analysis and consciousness can thus be summarized :

(1) In objective analysis, desire to know, means of knowledge and knowledge itself are clearly distinguished, but in consciousness, these are all taken in their totality : the very desire to know involves a certain knowledge of the absolute, and is therefore a basic means of knowledge.

(2) In rational analysis, the reality and integrity of the finite being has to be assumed in order to prove from it the existence of God. God is postulated as a condition for the logical intelligibility of the finite. He is not in any way involved in the finite. The atheist can know the world of finite beings in the same way as any convinced theist. On the other hand, from the point of view of consciousness, the finite thing itself is a problem. It may be an illusion, a mere phenomenon, and yet it serves as a symbol of the beyond. My own finite self is a bottomless and unintelligible abyss, and my intellectual quest a self-contradictory tendency, unless there is an ultimate and infinite Self, the ground of all. From the angle of consciousness, only this symbolic and designative value of the finite is taken into account, and its entitative aspect is not emphasized.

(3) Rational analysis is concerned with the origin, activity, existence, transcendental perfections and finality of the finite being, from which it looks at the Ultimate Reality. The value of the arguments rests on the metaphysical validity of the premises built upon these aspects. Consciousness, on the other hand, takes the finite as a phenomenon, rather than as an entity, as a mere state of being than as an immutable condition. Hence, it is not concerned with the origin of things or their activity. The phenomenal world should be considered only as a projection from the absolute; its origin and progress have no absolute meaning. It is a mere stepping-stone, a point of reference to affirm the Absolute Reality. Even a mere illusion can serve the purpose in this transcendence.

(4) In rational analysis, causal relation is the link that leads one

from the finite to the Infinite. In the approach from consciousness, causal relation has very little importance in the knowledge of God. It is important only in evaluating the finite in relation with the Infinite. What points the finger to the Ultimate is the manifestedness of the Supreme Self in the finite conscious self.

Even so, the question still remains as to how the finite is accommodated with the Infinite.

CHAPTER X

MANY FROM THE POINT
OF VIEW OF CONSCIOUSNESS

The scope of this chapter

In the problem of the One and the many, the more difficult to explain from the viewpoint of consciousness is the many. We shall discuss in this chapter how the multitude of finite beings can exist with the absolute reality of the One, without in any way affecting its absolute simplicity and infinite perfection. The best way to understand the solution from the angle of consciousness is to contrast it with the answer according to objective analysis. So I shall briefly explain the analogy of being as conceived in the Western tradition, taking St Thomas as a representative, before proceeding to examine the question according to the Indian approach. However, we shall not attempt a historical study of St Thomas's ideas, but rather, profiting by the excellent studies already made on his doctrine of analogy by Father George P. Klubertanz, S.J., and others, only summarize their conclusions here.

THE ANALOGY OF BEING

The problem

When reality is presented to the scrutiny of reason, what unites the great variety of things constituting the real world is *being*: they *are*. They are independent of the mind, existing in themselves, but not all in the same way. Though existing, they are not existence, but only existents, some in themselves—which we call substance—some in others, and therefore designated as accidents. Some come into existence and are capable of passing out of existence, while being itself denotes only the perfection of existing. Being is not, and cannot, be applied to all these in the same way. There is only a general unity among them. The difference is

135

deeper than unity. The doctrine of the Analogy of Being tries to express this idea of unity in diversity.

The meaning of analogy

Analogy has different meanings in language. In ordinary speech, analogy is reasoning by example. However, analogy is not the same as simile; simile stresses the common factors, while analogy places the emphasis on the basic difference. In Science, analogy is a tentative suggestion towards the discovery of a general rule from individual cases. In Mathematics, analogy is the identity of ratios, or proportion.

In Philosophy, however, analogy occupies the border area between logic and metaphysics. In logic, it stands for the application of the same term to different things for reasons partly the same but partly different; there is a certain unity of meaning with a radical diversity. A word can be univocal—namely, when it has the same meaning when applied to several things—or multivocal, if it has different meanings. This multivocality can be merely accidental —as when we use 'Board' for a flat piece of material as well as for a committee of people—or intentional, when it constitutes analogy. Univocal terms have clear and consistent meaning in themselves and can, therefore, be defined. Analogous terms do not have a single meaning in themselves. The two things indicated by the same term have a certain unity or community, but with a fundamental difference. Hence, the term cannot be forced to become determinate without destroying its community.

The metaphysical analogy

The metaphysical aspect of analogy is best expressed by what Klubertanz calls 'the analogy of participation' of the beings in the Being.[1] The basic fact in this is, according to St Thomas, that 'the very act of existing is common to all',[2] and all, in a way, communicate in the same act. This community of beings in the same

---

[1] George P. Klubertanz, S.J., *St Thomas Aquinas on Analogy. A Textual Analysis and Systematic Synthesis* (Chicago: Loyola University Press, 1960), p. 140.

[2] *Summa Theologica,* I, q4, a3; *De Veritate,* q5, a9, ad7; *De Potentia,* q3, a1; *Contra Gentiles,* I, c. 42; III, c. 66.

perfection of existing is only a partial aspect of their participation from the one subsistent supreme being.

St Thomas explains this analogy of participation thus : 'Everything can be called "good" and "being" from the first being, which is good and being by its essence, in as much as everything participates in it after the manner and measure of a particular likeness, though remotely and deficiently.'[3] Similarly, truth, whether it be human truth or divine truth, is analogous, because it has an intrinsic similarity in all subjects, on account of the participation of all truth in the one subsistent divine truth.[4]

Intelligence and analogy

This Thomistic doctrine of analogy is very significant, even from the point of view of consciousness, because the participation on which it is based is most significantly understood in intellectual thought. Human knowledge itself is a participation in the divine intellectual light. Man, by virtue of this light, is able to know all things, and has *omne ens* for object. In the multiplicity of the *omne ens*, by the very dynamism of his participated intelligence he tries to discover the unity.[5] Here his own finitude and the multiplicity of knowers like himself is the immediate problem. An intellect, fully in act to all being, should be infinite, and can be only one. This means that if an intellect is finite, it is only potential.

The analogy of participation appears to correspond directly to this potentiality of the human intellect : in every act, the intellect opens out itself to being as being, all being, infinite being. This infinite being corresponding to the simple and single existent potency should be simple, single and existent, otherwise the tendency of the intellect will be meaningless and contradictory. This infinite object corresponding to the basic orientation of the intellect is God,[6] the subsistent intelligence. But man has no intuition of the infinite intelligible. He proceeds through finite things, asking what they are, and whether they are, to the final discovery of the source and plenitude of all actuality. In this, he is carrying on the discovery of the analogy of participation, evaluating the particular

[3] *Summa Theologica*, I, q6, a4c; Cf. *De Potentia*, q7, a7, ad3.

[4] *Summa Theologica*, I, q16, a6; Klubertanz, *op. cit.*, p. 143.

[5] *De Veritate*, q2, a2; *Summa Theologica*, I, q55,, a3c; q79, a4c; *et ad* 1 and 5.

[6] *Contra Gentiles*, I, c43, 10.

facts in reference to the absolute and existent norm of fact and truth, sharing in which everything is being and true.

The being and intelligence in finite beings are not additional to or outside of the reality of the Supreme Being, but entirely dependent on Him, as illumination in reference to the rays of light.[7] The very actuality of the finite beings is the resemblance to the pure act of God,[8] and by the very reason of participation they are many.[9]

ANALOGY OF BEING FROM THE VIEWPOINT OF CONSCIOUSNESS

In contrast to this Thomistic approach to the problem of the many, with its strong emphasis on the unity of all in the One, we turn now to the Indian approach where the core of the solution is in the intrinsic weakness of the many : the many is too unreal to be a challenge to the reality and absolute simplicity of the One. We shall make a brief synthesis of the various elements contributed by Indian thinkers on this central point of metaphysics.

The problem

Here, the problem is not how a certain unity can be found in the many—the unity is the first and most easily realized fact—but how to account for the multiplicity itself, which appears as the anomaly, an alienation of reality from its authentic unity. The ultimate ground of reality, stability and identity is the unity of the Self. The non-self contradicts this basic condition of reality, and so calls for an explanation.

The method

A useful method in this approach to reality from the side of consciousness is a synthetic one, namely that of parallelism between the individual self and the universal Self, God. As the individual self is the centre of consciousness and reality for the body and the senses, so the ultimate Self is the centre of consciousness and reality for all beings on the cosmic level.

[7] *Summa Theologica,* I, *q*8, *a*1.
[8] *Quodlibet,* XII, *a*5*c*.
[9] *Summa Theologica,* I, *q*75, *a*5, *ad*1; *Contra Gentiles,* II, *c*58, no 'Adhuc'; *De Potentia, q*7, *a*1, *ad*10; *De Veritate, q*2, *a*7, *ad*3.

This synthetic or parallel method is generally made use of in the Indian philosophical tradition. In the Upanishads, the cosmic deities of Fire, Air and Sun are symbols of the human faculties of sight, hearing and intellect.[10] The cosmic and individual spheres are considered two sides of the same reality : 'He who is here in a person, and he who is yonder in the sun—he is one', says the *Taittirîya Upanishad*.[11] It is by solving the problem in one's own individual consciousness that a solution on the cosmic level can be discerned.

The problem of the many is one confronted on the various levels of human consciousness, especially logical, psychological and transcendental. Hence, it calls for a solution on these various levels, in order to constitute an integral metaphysics.

Solution on the logical level

The first movement in philosophical thought is to achieve an adjustment of one's own ideas. Ideas are representative of things, and it is only in and through them that one has access to things. Ignorance is confusion and division, and knowledge is clarity and unity. Logic faces the things outside as its object and tries to understand it by analyzing it into mental categories. Hence, the problem of the many here appears under two aspects. There is first of all a subject-object duality, and secondly the internal plurality of the object itself. The first duality is resolved by the active function of the thinking subject which illumines and manifests the object as its own self-expression. The objective multiplicity is resolved by recognizing the centrality of substance in all reality.

The thinking subject faces the world as its own field of operation. Truth is a quality of the spirit, by which it illumines the world of multiplicity and makes it meaningful. Even sense experience is not a passive reception of forms, but an active encounter in which the spirit illumines the object.

Hence, the world of multiplicity, compared with the spirit, is primarily a point of reference. It is not a 'thing', opposed to and absolutely independent of the spirit. It is rather a function, a veil cast on the spirit. We do not think of a veil as a thing but only about its function. On the one hand, it hides what is within, and

[10] *Kath Up Sank Bh*, I, i, 26.
[11] *Tait Up*, II, iv, 1; Cf. *Kath Up*, II, i, 10–13.

at the same time it also means that something precious is within it. Similarly, the crude material world of finite beings surrounding us is a veil. It hides the light of the One Self which is in all and illumines all. At the same time, all the intelligibility which seeps through these beings points the finger towards the intelligibility of the Self. All the light perceived in them emanates, not from them, but from the spiritual Self.

All the same, the world of multiplicity constitutes a challenge to the one reality of the Self by appearing as another absolute opposed to it. Once this false absolute is dissolved and resolved into its ultimate elements, it will not appear as a rival, but only as a sign-post for directing and concentrating attention on the One.

But the world of plurality is not a pure negation. It has a practical value, in as much as it helps the finite knower—through the medium of its converging points of diffused reality—to direct back his attention to the source of all reality. In this way, it is not absolutely affirmed, but only indicated as points of reference, namely as substance, quality, action, relation, and so on, which by their conceptual determinations show that they are not in any way absolute. They turn the attention of the attentive student to the centre of consciousness, which alone provides unity and intelligibility to all these. This is the reason why even schools like that of the Vaiseshikas and Naiyâikas, which appeared to take a purely logical approach to reality, were able to propose the knowledge of the Atman as their goal, and to indicate meditation, concentration and self-control as means towards it.

The psychological polarity

The one-many relation which appears on the logical plane as Self *versus* a substance-quality-action-relation composite, assumes on the psychological level the aspect of a soul-body polarity. The individual spiritual self is the symbol of the absolute Self in the microcosm of the individual, and the body is the sum total of the multiplicity of beings. Pure spirit is the datum, and the evolving composite of faculties, senses, sense objects, and material elements is the problem. The body has no light or consciousness of itself, nor activity, yet it grows and acts and, in a way, shares in the consciousness of the spirit.

The solution to this dual and anomalous aspect of the body is to trace all the light, activity, unity and finality manifested in the body back to the spirit as their ultimate source. But the spirit, as pure consciousness, cannot in any way be said to be intrinsically involved in or depend upon this material evolution. Its role is that of the *sâkshin*, witness. The body's communion with the spirit, receiving the latter's light and actuality, sets its dynamic self-manifestation in process. The farther the evolutes move away from the spirit, the less do they participate in the light of the spirit.

An important point to be noted here is the parallelism between man's psychic realm and the cosmic order of beings. In rational analysis, the two orders look totally different. In the macrocosm, God, the absolute reality, creates the finite beings which have their proper natures, activities and goals. On the other hand, in the microcosm of the human being, all action, unity and finality is ascribed to the spiritual form, and its coprinciple is conceived as a pure potency. In the approach from consciousness, there is a certain parallel between the two orders. The coprinciple of the spiritual soul is not a pure potency, but the maternal principle of all psychic activity, with its own special faculties, directions and goals; even the faculties of knowledge appear on the side of this maternal principle. We shall see below how this soul-body relation helps us to understand the God-world relation.

BEING AND BEINGS ON THE METAPHYSICAL PLANE

The negative aspect of the world of beings

When we pass from the level of experience to the transcendental plane of being, truth and goodness, our consciousness first presents a negative view of the world of beings. It is the field of the non-I, something opposed to the I. It is easier to say what it is not, than to positively evaluate what it is. Hence, Nagarjuna's concept of *sûnya*, void, is an easy and plausible explanation of the world of multiplicity in relation with the reality of the unsoundable depths of the I.

Our consciousness is the meeting point between two worlds: the 'I' that knows and the 'Thou' that is being known. At first, the 'I' alone may appear the authentically real, and the 'Thou' as something diametrically opposed to it, as darkness is to light. Hence, according to Sankara, the world of beings is raised to the status of reality by our superimposing our I-hood on the Thou;

it is the world of illusion, fleeting like a shadow. The many constituting it is nothing : *neha nânâ asti kincana,* said Sankara : they are all covered with falsehood.[12]

But on closer examination we can find that this adverse judgment of Nagarjuna and Sankara on the world of finite beings is not correct. One has to admit that this superimposition of I-hood on the world of objects is the natural procedure of human knowledge, without which our daily experience and normal course of life itself would be impossible. What is important for metaphysics is that self-consciousness, at the same time as it reveals, on the one side, the area of the real, in the immutable and deep realms of the 'I', on the other side, also illumines with consciousness the world of finite beings.

Even according to Sankara, this reflexion of consciousness on the world of finite beings brings out several positive elements :

(1) The practical validity of our experience should be taken for granted, since it is the basic supposition of all philosophical enquiry. The world should be accepted as it is, with its definite and organized nature.[13]

(2) On the other hand, the world cannot be absolutized into an independent principle beside God, like the *Prakriti* of the Sâmkhyas. Its only ground is God.[14] It is organized and supported by Him.[15] Hence it has a certain intelligibility in itself.[16]

(3) The only problem is to assign it a place in the world of reality in comparison with God, the absolute reality, the pure subsistent consciousness. It cannot be asserted to be *sat,* being, in the sense in which God is *sat,* nor can it be merely *asat,* non-being. It is not non-existent, nor totally unreal. It therefore has to be designated as *anirvacanîya,* something defying *nirvacana,* or definition, in respect of reality and unreality, according to Sankara.

St Augustine has expressed this point very clearly in a significant text in his *Enarrationes in Psalmos* :

> Indeed, He exists in such a way that, in comparison with Him, the things that He has made are not. When not compared with Him, they are, for they are from Him; but when compared with

[12] *Chând Up Sank Bh,* VIII, iii, 2.
[13] *Brih Up Sank Bh,* IV, iv, 6.
[14] *Ved S Sank Bh,* II, ii, 28.
[15] *Chând Up Sank Bh,* VI, ii, 3.
[16] *Ved S Sank Bh,* II, ii, 1; I, i, 2.

Him, they are not, for truly to *be* is to *be* immutably, and this He alone is. He is *is* (Est enim est), just as the good of goods is good.[17]

(4) The position of finite beings in the order of reality may be indicated by various analogies drawn from the field of experience : if the real is pure consciousness similar to the waking state, the world of finite beings is a dream; if reality is immutable and stable, the changeable world of multiplicity is *mâyâ*, the illusions produced by a magician. Taking reality as true knowledge, then the world is untrue and non-knowledge. The world is a kind of shadow cast around the Supreme Being, but not in Him.

THE INFINITE CONSCIOUSNESS AND THE FINITE

But if we go beyond the above considerations based on the ontological value of beings, and focus on the value of consciousness as such, the position of the finite reality is best realized in the encounter of the finite consciousness with the infinite Self. As Ramanuja rightly points out, the individual consciousness serves as a bridge between the pure and infinite consciousness of God on the one side, and the unconscious world of multiplicity on the other.

Self-awareness shows that one's individual self is beset with all kinds of limitations, related to the body; it is not pure consciousness but only a knower; knowledge is only an accident and not a substance. This consciousness helps one to ascend to the pure consciousness of the supreme Self, God, on the one side; on the other side, the soul's relation to the world manifested in the same consciousness provides a pattern for understanding the relation of the world of finite beings, including individual souls, to God. The analogies used by Ramanuja to clarify this point are very helpful in understanding the analogy of being from the angle of consciousness.

Conscious substance and attributes

The first pattern derived from self-consciousness to understand the God-world relation is that of *viseshya* and *viseshana*, substance and attribute : the knower is *viseshya* and knowledge is *viseshana*. Though these terms are translated as substance and attribute, a possible misunderstanding has to be avoided : substance

---

[17] *Enarrationes in Psalmos,* 134, 4, *t.*IV, 1494–5, trs. Vernon J. Bourke, *Augustine's View of Reality* (Villanova University, 1964), p. 141.

is that which is in itself, and an attribute or accident something in another. Substance is so called, not only because it subsists, but also because it stands under the accidents and is modified by them, though it supports them as the subject. With regard to natural accidents like quantity and quality which result from the union of matter and form, the substance is even a sort of efficient cause. Still, what stands out in the relation of a substance to the accident is the passive aspect of being modified by an accidental form.

But in the consciousness of ourselves as knowing substances and of our knowledge as an accident, knowledge is the word that flows out of the fullness of consciousness, which in no way thereby suffers a change or modification. The finite knower does undergo change in acquiring knowledge, but this is only in the preparatory stage; knowledge itself is an active self-expression in which the knower, as such, is not a patient.

This is precisely the difference between the logical and transcendental levels. In the former, ideas are considered representative of things, acquired from them and dependent on them. On the transcendental level, ideas are taken as the self-expression of the knower.

Hence, when, from the aspect of consciousness, the world of finite beings is said to be an attribute of God, no imperfection, limitation or modification of God is implied. God is pure consciousness. The world of beings is a word emanating from Him, a word which implies no change or modification in Him.

However, the word itself is subject to modifications according to the level of its expression and the composition of factors implied in it. What is common is communion. Every word is in some manner an emanation from the knower. All creatures in some manner have their actuality from God.

The farther the word gets from its source, the less it participates in consciousness. In the conscious mind, the word is conscious; out of it, it is unconscious and is merely intelligible. In the mind, it is simple. But, in the word of mouth, it is a composite of sound, pitch, tone and several other factors. In the written word and in all sign-language, the composition and complexity go on increasing. In the mind, the word is a pure symbol. But outside it gets reified into things. In the same manner, the world, as a word of God, has its varying degrees of composition and complexity. In the human person, it is conscious and simple; in material things, it is complex and only intelligible. In the soul, it is immortal; in material things, it is perishable.

In this approach from the angle of consciousness, the word is not taken as an element of the act of affirmation of the human intellect in its orientation towards infinite truth, but rather as the word emanating from the Divine Knower. The word of the human knower is a mere pattern and a symbol to understand the relation of finite things to the Divine word.

Soul and body

The place of the human body in consciousness is another fruitful analogy in aiding comprehension of the relation of the world of beings to Supreme consciousness. Here again, two functions of the body have to be clearly distinguished. The body with the sense-organs and faculties has a necessary function in the soul's attaining consciousness of things. But this needful help from the side of the body belongs only to a preparatory stage of knowledge. Consciousness which is spiritual cannot be said to depend intrinsically on the body. The relevant function of the body with regard to consciousness is in the expressive and manifestative aspects. The body is, as it were, a continuation of our self to give expression to our ideas, to communicate them to others through signs and symbols. Yet the body as such does not enter fully into consciousness. To a great extent, it is impervious to consciousness, and can even be treated as an object. In this way, several levels of approximation to the soul may be distinguished in the body, as the internal and external sense-organs, the organs of action and the non-sentient parts of the body.

This figure of the body shows how the world of individual souls and material things proceeding from Supreme Consciousness as words shares, in a way, in the plenitude of Brahman's consciousness and diffuses it in its own proper modes, without in any way affecting the purity and transcendence of God. This diffusion goes in concentric circles, the conscious beings coming closest to God and crude material things forming the outermost circle.

Transcendent immanence

This analogy of the soul's immanence in the body also indicates the way in which Supreme Consciousness, remaining immutable and transcendent in itself, pervades and fills everything. Looked at from the angle of consciousness, the spiritual soul is not merely the form of body, but transcends it. The life and sentiency of the body can thus be conceived as an overflow from the pure consciousness and spirituality of the soul. If the soul could be taken for a pure spirit, it would show how Brahman makes all things exist and be intelligible.

Here, it has to be borne in mind that the soul's essential ordination to matter as the substantial form, and the transcendental relation to the individual body as well as the dependence on it, are factors that stand out in a rational examination which proceeds from formal objects to actions, and from actions to the subjects which they specify. Hence, in a rational approach to metaphysics, the analogy of the soul actuating the body may be rather misleading to explain God's immanence in His creatures. But in an approach from the side of consciousness, the spirituality and transcendence of the soul over the material body predominate, and dependence itself is found to be secondary and almost accidental.

This is the reason why the Upanishads love to show the immanence of Brahman in all things as their inner soul and ruler, and at the same time emphasize his transcendence.

The soul-God encounter

The soul's relation to material things is not merely a pattern to be applied on the cosmic level. It also shows how the conscious human being, standing between the material world and God, can break and go beyond the pattern itself. The diffusive and, as it were, centrifugal character of human consciousness is an important point in this respect : man tends to go out of himself and seek the fullness of his consciousness. But in going out to the material things, he becomes a slave to them and suffers a diminution of consciousness. This is an indication that his conscious tendency has to be directed in the opposite direction, to the core of consciousness, the Supreme Consciousness. This shows that man has a unique place in the realm of finite reality. He is not a passive element of it but, as the most active and most noble part of it, he can even turn its current of diffusion, directing it back to the source and fount of all consciousness. The world of material things has no selfhood. It is not being in the full sense of the term, but mere ex-sistence, an extrapolation of reality. It is man's task, through asceticism and ritual, to bring material things back to the centre of all reality. Without man, creation is mute and dumb. His ritual touch makes it eloquent.

The world of material things cannot face God or address Him, but man can. He can bring the whole creation into a meaningful encounter with God. However, he does not face God as an equal, but as the ray of light reflected back and returning to the Sun, as the slave facing the Master, as the loving devotee surrendering himself to the Lord. We shall discuss this person-to-person aspect of reality in another chapter.

CONCLUSION

The differences between the two approaches in evaluating the reality of finite beings are clear :

(1) In the rational analytic approach, which proceeds taking the world of multiplicity as the datum, the problem of the One predominates. The search is to find a certain point of unity among the many. The approach from consciousness takes the unity of absolute consciousness for granted, and tries to solve the problem of the many seeking to reconcile the multiplicity with the unique reality of the Supreme.

(2) Reason proceeds organizing the multiplicity through the analogies of proportionality and attribution to the notion of participation and communion. Mere analogy can only end up in a logical unity. Participation alone fails to do justice to the multiplicity. Hence, only a synthesis between analogy and participation can properly account for unity in multiplicity. From the angle of consciousness, categories of experience and thought and their analogy serve rather a negative function, namely to show that the world of multiplicity does not constitute a challenge to the One. The world of experience and thought has only a practical and derived reality compared with the absolute of pure consciousness.

(3) In both approaches, it is the transcendental aspect of knowledge that brings out the positive value of finite reality. In the rational approach, the act of affirmation reveals the world of finite beings to be constituted as real and true, and so guaranteed by a supreme norm of truth and fact. The same act of affirmation, by its synthetic character, discovers the complexity and composition at

various levels of the finite being : the contrast between the radical finality of the intellect tending to infinite being and its proportionality limited to finite material quiddity reveals the distinction between essence and existence in the world of reality. The synthesis between sense and intellect found in every judgment shows the composition in the heart of the concrete material object itself.

However, the approach from consciousness takes finite consciousness itself as a pattern to measure the world of finite beings. The emergence of the finite word from the fullness of the conscious self shows how finite beings, proceeding as finite words from the supreme consciousness of God, imply no limitation or imperfection in Him. The grades and compositions implied in the human word are symbols of the grades and compositions in being itself. The actuation of the body by the spiritual soul, looked at from the angle of consciousness, shows the transcendent immanence of God in His creation.

(4) The most basic difference between the two approaches is that the one from reason tries to conceptualize the relation between the world of finite beings and God and determine the exact meaning of terms like analogy, participation, communion and the like. The procedure from consciousness, on the other hand, tries to gain some understanding of the ineffable relation through known patterns, analogies and complementary pairs like waking state *vs.* dream, reality *vs.* illusion, conscious subject *vs.* word, the soul *vs.* body, and the like.

It is futile to ask which approach is the better. Reason delights in neat distinctions and clear-cut concepts and definitions regarding even the most subtle and ineffable realities. Consciousness, on the other hand, loves mystery and strives to gain some understanding of its depths through analogies, figures and patterns. Hence, the two are complementary. But a crucial question in the understanding of reality is that of causality, which will be discussed in the next chapter.

CHAPTER XI

JANMADYASYA YATAH
CONSCIOUSNESS AND CAUSALITY

Causality is a basic notion of metaphysics. In it, Western and Indian approaches complement each other in sounding the depths of reality. As we have shown in the last chapter, the problem centres around the One in a rational analysis, while from the angle of consciousness, the many is problematic. The universe of 'being', as analyzed by reason, requires an investigation of the ultimate causes for its full intelligibility, while consciousness, which takes the reality of the One as the starting point, has to reconcile the many with the One through the link of causality.

The scope of this chapter

In this chapter, I shall first briefly indicate how the problem of causality is discussed from the side of objective analysis and then, against its background, examine the approach to the problem from the point of view of consciousness. In studying the Western tradition of rational analysis in this subject, I shall follow St Thomas as one typical representative and summarize his position.

RATIONAL ANALYSIS OF CAUSALITY

Causality is so fundamental to the approach through objective analysis that to know is said to be to know through causes. Cause is called the *'finis ad quem consideratio scientiae pertingit'*,[1] the very goal of scientific investigation. A thing is considered known only when all the causes from the immediate to the ultimate ones are known,[2] for the investigation of reality, presented to thought as its object, proceeds by asking first what it is, and secondly why

[1] *In Metaphysic. Aristot.*, I, 1, 1.
[2] *In Physic. I,* lect. 1, *n.5.*

it is. The *what* explores the internal structure and principles of a thing, while the *why* seeks the external factors that brought it into existence.

Both the questions imply an inquiry into causes. Cause means something that contributes in some manner to the being and reality of the effect.[3] It is something on which a thing depends, either in actual being, or in the process of becoming.[4] According to this consideration, four causes are indicated for a thing : formal, material, efficient and final.[5] The first two answer the question of what a thing is or what is responsible for a thing being such and such, and the last two why a thing should be, rather than not be.

Internal causes

To the question of what is responsible for a thing being such and such, the answer is its own form. Form makes it what it is. A statue is what it is, not principally and primarily on account of the bronze or marble out of which it is made, but rather on account of the form or figure imprinted on it. The 'suchness' of the thing is a composite structure. Thus, the tree before me is such and such, and acts in such and such a manner, because it belongs to such a class of trees and has its particular nature; it has a certain unity, integrity and consistency of its own. Yet it does not show all the perfections such a tree could have, nor does it exclude there being other trees of the same nature; it does not exhaust the perfection of its specific nature. This tension between perfection and imperfection, unity and multiplicity, stability and activity, shows that the finite being before us is not simple, but constituted of at least two basic principles. The principle that makes it perfect, united and consistent is called the formal cause, while limitation and multiplicity are ascribed to a receptive and potential principle, designated as the material cause.

Thus, the formal cause makes something into such a being—a tree, or man or cow—while the reason why there are many trees or men or cows, and why they are limited, and why should the form of tree, etc., be so, is received in and determined by a potential

[3] *In Metaphysic. V*, 1, n.751.
[4] *Summa Theologica*, I, q104, a1c.
[5] *Summa Theologica*, I, q3, a8c; q105, a5c.

subject, the material cause. The causality of the form is indicated by St Thomas in the terse statement: *Forma dat esse*, the form gives being. It is the principle of activity, finality, unity and of all other perfections in the thing. But in finite and material beings, the form does not exist by itself, but only as received in a subject, individualized and concretized by it. The material cause, which is the receptive principle, is the source of limitation and distinction.

This question about suchness can be asked on several levels, and on all of them the formal and material principles will also appear. This is true to a certain extent even about the perfection of existence: if it is asked what is responsible for a thing being existent, the answer is existence as a quasi-form, with regard to which the whole essence, the composite of matter and form, is the receptive and determining principle.[6] What is responsible for a thing being green is the formal cause of green colour, and the material subject is the material cause.[7] The first perfection on every level is the form through which a thing has being and suchness.[8]

External causes: efficient cause

To the question of why this finite being, which is not existence pure and simple and therefore not existing by its own title, comes to be, the answer cannot be found within the thing itself. It does not provide the reason for its own existence. This is true, not only of the moment when it comes to be, but also of its continued existence. It is not existence, but only something that has received existence. So, there must be outside it a principle capable of conferring existence, or at least positively contributing towards its existence. This principle which positively contributes to the existence of another thing is called efficient cause.

The reality of the change and the new being are in the produced effect, yet its emergence into existence is dependent on that from which it has received the new being. Hence, it is a communication of being; it is a bringing out or effecting of something new. Therefore it is called *efficient* cause.

[6] *In Sent. I, d8, q1, a2, ad2.*
[7] *In Sent. I, d17, q1, a1.*
[8] *De Veritate, q1, a1, ad3.* Cf. *q21, a4, ad6; q27, a1, ad3; Contra Gentiles, I, c27; II, cc54–68.*

The final cause

However, the efficient activity is not aimless. If the agent is intelligent, he intends to achieve something definite by his action. Even without this, the activity itself should have a definite goal, to be an act. This goal, in a way, makes the activity what it is and specifies the act and the effect. Hence, this end or goal is something which contributes to the being of the effect. It is, therefore, called the final cause.

Transcendental causality

Though the notion of causality is drawn from our finite experience, it has implications that point to the transcendental order. Here the general principle is enunciated by St Thomas : 'Whatever is found in anything by participation must be caused in it by that to which it belongs essentially, as iron becomes heated by fire.'[9] This principle is applied to finite existence : all finite beings by their very nature are not existence, but have only participated existence. If they were existence, they should be all existence and should have always existed and be imperishable, immutable and infinite. But this is not the case. Their participated existence can, therefore, be understood only by reference to a cause which is subsistent, pure and infinite existence : 'All beings other than God are not their own being, but are beings by participation, and therefore . . . are caused by one First Being, who possesses being most perfectly.'[10]

This basic postulate of the transcendental cause is elaborated into the five ways for arriving at the existence of God, taking five different aspects of the finite thing confronting us as starting points. Change, which shows that a certain perfection is acquired or lost, should have as its ultimate ground of intelligibility a changeless source from which all perfections are received. Dependent activity in beings points the finger to a pure, independent, efficient act. Existence that comes to be and can cease to be has its ultimate intelligibility only in a necessary existence. Graded and limited perfections require infinite perfection as their supreme ideal. Order and beauty found in nature have to be reduced to a subsistent

[9] *Summa Theologica,* I, q44, a1c.
[10] *Ibid.*

supreme intelligence as their source. In all these arguments, the transcendence of subsistent existence and first cause is implied.

Critique

This analytic approach to causality has several positive contributions towards the understanding of reality as a whole, as well as certain drawbacks as a method.

Positive contributions

(1) The basic intuition of this analytic approach is that of the transcendence of the First Cause. There is no possibility of confusing the cause with the effect. Subsistent existence, though all-comprehensive, stands beyond all finite existents.

(2) It places the emphasis on the transcendental efficient cause as the most basic one among all causes. Only existence that is all by itself can account for the existence of finite beings. That which is not by itself cannot act by itself. Hence, all finite beings derive their being and activity from the supreme subsistent form of existence.[11]

The causes are therefore listed by St Thomas in ascending order of importance; matter, which does not act, but is a subject that receives the effect of action, is at the bottom of the scale; end, agent and form are the principles of action. But even the agent acts only by virtue of his form.[12] Existence is the most common feature that embraces all things, the first and most intimate reality of all effects; so it has to be referred to God, the subsistent existence, as His proper effect.[13]

(3) The emphasis on subsistent existence as the source of all things shows also that this First Cause is the efficient cause of all things. The proper causality of transcendent existence is to effect things and place them out of their finite causes with their own individual existences.

(4) This pre-eminence of existence also shows the intimate immanence of the First Cause in all the effects and their actions. God not only produces things, provides them with their natural

---

[11] *Quodlibet*, X, q3, a6.
[12] *Summa Theologica*, I, q105, a5c.
[13] *De Potentia*, q3, a7.

powers and continually conserves them in existence, but also moves and applies their powers to their proper activities.[14] He is the immediate and proper cause of the new existence conferred by the activity. Since existence is the most basic reality in a thing, He is more intimately and immediately present in the least action of the finite beings than they are themselves.[15]

There is no doubt about the validity of this causal explanation which refers all things in their most intimate reality as effects to the First Cause. It clearly shows the transcendence of God above all things and His unique reality, as well as showing his intimate immanence in all reality.

Inadequacy

But the principal point to be considered here is how far this notion of causality helps us to understand the world of reality. This means how far the world can lead us to understand the supreme Reality, on the one hand, and on the other, how far the world of experience is real in terms of the ultimate reality. These two aims can be achieved only to the extent that we manage to bridge the gulf between the world and God. The inadequacy of the analytical approach to causality is in its inability to bridge the gap.

(1) A general complaint against the analytic approach to the problem of causality is that it conceptualizes existence and detaches it from the world of actuality. The transcendental cause is postulated as the necessary requisite for the intelligibility of the finite being. However, in actual experience, the finite being as a datum appears to have a completeness and intelligibility of its own. The whole philosophical interpretation of the relation to a transcendental cause appears as a logical exercise superimposed on the world of experience. Philosophy pretends to provide meaning to the world; but what is presented by the conceptual analysis of causality looks very much like a meaning without a world.

(2) The procedure starts by recognizing as a basis the reality of the world. Hence, the supreme cause, postulated on account of it, appears as something beside the world, correlative to it, outside it, additional to it, and real on the same level with it. This

[14] *Ibid.*, and cf. *Summa Theologica*, I, q104, aa1–2.
[15] *Contra Gentiles*, III, c71, no. 5.

creates a sort of God-world dichotomy, making the world into something outside and additional to God. On the one hand, this seems to deny the infinite reality and transcendence of God, and on the other, the analytic concept of transcendence seems to deny all real immanence of the subsistent Existence in finite beings.

(3) The preponderance of the formal cause may be primarily responsible for this difference in perspective. The Platonic forms or ideas did not get involved in the individual things which were mere imitations and inadequate approximations to them. Even the Aristotelian and Thomistic concept of Act-potency-polarity appears a logical postulate which cannot, as such, be applied to the actually existing thing. Though it is easy to admit that Peter is not all humanity, but only an individual subject that shares in humanity, it becomes difficult to understand how the ideal and pure act of human nature becomes this individual human soul in Peter, or how Peter's soul is really related to that ideal. This remains a natural mystery, especially with regard to existence— in other words, how the subsistent Existence remaining unaffected and immutable in itself can make all finite beings exist.

(4) All the examples of causality drawn from experience, for example the marble-figure, sculptor-statue and like analogies, are so intimately bound up with the limited aspect of experience that they cannot be transferred to the ontological level without purifying them of their limitations. Once these limitations are removed, what remains is merely a relation of dependence of the effect on the cause.

But the mere relation of dependence does not help us to understand the one from the other : the figure of the statue does not affect the nature of the marble, nor does the quality of the marble tell us much about the figure that may be carved out on it. The statue does not give us an adequate knowledge of the human being who fashioned it, nor does it in any way share in his vital nature.

Even the spiritual examples of teacher and taught, learner and knowledge, do not help us any better. These, in fact, only widen the gulf between the cause and the effect. The best example St Thomas gives us to understand the divine immanence in finite beings is that of light illuminating the air.

The basic difficulty here is the cause-effect duality itself implied in the analytic approach. A knowledge of the cause may not give any idea of the effect; an understanding of the effect cannot provide us with a sufficient knowledge of the intrinsic nature of the cause, nor of the immanence of the one in the other, nor of the transcendence.

The approach to causality from the angle of consciousness tries to transcend this dichotomy. We shall examine below how far the cause-effect relation in this approach helps us to understand the world of reality.

CAUSALITY FROM THE POINT OF VIEW OF CONSCIOUSNESS

When one proceeds from the side of consciousness—in other words from the unity discovered in consciousness—to examine the meaning and relevance of multiplicity, causality has a slightly different metaphysical connotation. It is no longer the anxious search for the One, but rather the leisurely explanation, with a rather pedagogical emphasis, of how the world of multiplicity does not offend the absolute unity, but is harmonized with it. Causality is the central point on which a philosophy according to rational analysis depends, but for an evaluation of reality based on consciousness, causality is so secondary that several systems like that of the Buddhists could simply ignore it. It amounts to determining how important our phenomenal world is. Even if one were to deny the whole phenomenal world as an illusion or as a mere aggregate of phenomenal elements, one would not thereby become nihilist in the metaphysical sense.

On the other hand, for a complete metaphysics, even according to the approach from consciousness, causality is vital, since it constitutes the ontology of the finite. Besides, in the Indian tradition, the inquiry into the nature of Brahman has reached a kind of saturation, leaving very little scope for further fruitful discovery, so that the world of causality, the world of finite effects, constitutes the main field that presents an indefinite scope for investigation. Time and space, individual and person, activity and progress, moral life and social evolution, and everything that demands the immediate attention of man, all proceed according to the laws of causality. This is also the area for a fruitful dialogue between philosophy and science.

Starting point of causal investigation

When the *Vedânta Sûtras* state *janmâdyasya yatah*, 'that from which the origin and the rest', as the second step in their investigation into reality, they are not proposing a proof for the existence of God from causality. The text itself is taken from *Taittirîya Upanishad* III, 1, where it is proposed by Varuna to teach his son Bhrigu Varuni how to conceive Brahman in relation to the world of experience. For man standing with the transcendent Brahman on the one side as his ultimate Self, and the material universe on the other side of him, causality provides a comprehensive and unified view of reality.

The world of reality is constituted of Brahman and the world of finite beings. But they are not two absolutes. Brahman is the ultimate and unique reality, the cause 'from which these beings are born, that by which when born they live, that into which they enter at their death'.[16] These beings do not point to a transcendent form or idea which they imitate, but rather to an ultimate substance from which they emanate and which they manifest. To understand this causal outlook on the world of reality, we have first to examine the general notion of causality itself, and then see how it is applied to the world of beings.

(a) General notion of causality

The notion of causality that underlies the approach to reality in terms of consciousness places the emphasis on the material or substantial cause, rather than on the formal cause. The reality of the effect is not outside of, or additional to, the reality of the cause, but rather is an overflow and emanation from the plenitude of the substance of the cause. The individuality of the effect, its proper form, only contributes limitation and determination to what is of the cause. Hence, the substantial cause in a sense combines in itself aspects of the material, efficient and final causes.

The Upâdâna Kârana or material cause

In the outlook from the unity of consciousness, the basic source of things is known as the *upâdâna kârana*, or material cause. On account of the purely passive and receptive role assigned to the material cause in Western tradition, starting especially with

---

[16] *Tait Up*, III, 1.

Aristotle, the term is totally inadequate to designate the *upâdâna kârana,* or ground cause, of Indian tradition.

It is interesting to note that both Indian and Greek philosophers in the beginning of philosophical thought, when looking for a word to name the basic reality of things, adopted words with similar meaning from the pre-philosophic language, namely the Greek *hyle,* a trunk without branches, and the Sanskrit *âtman,* the body without limbs or the reflexive 'self'. But *hyle* came to designate 'the matter out of which' something is made, while *âtman* stood for the spiritual self and ground of reality. *Atman* is the *upâdâna kârana,* the unique and all comprehensive ground of all things, a truly maternal principle. It is not a matter to be modified, determined and perfected by a form, but the immutable fullness which merely manifests its richness in the various forms that proceed from it.

Substance, or *sattâ,* also has a different significance in this connection : in an analytic approach, a substance is that which is in itself, the subject and support of accidents, and in turn perfected by them. It merely indicates the ground structure of reality in relation to accidents which modify and perfect it in diverse secondary ways. But, looked at from the angle of consciousness, *sattâ* is the ultimate ground of concrete existence. All the multifarious accidents and forms do not modify or perfect it, but only show forth and manifest what exists in the fullness of the substance. By that very reason, they are also a sort of veil, since they do not manifest all that the substance implies.[17]

The terms *svabhâva* and *svarûpa* also indicate aspects of the *upâdâna kârana.* If, for the Greeks, the form stood for the whole essence as its active part, the matter or ground constitutes the essence in the Indian outlook. Of the two terms, *svabhâva,* with its derivation from the root *bhû,* to become, indicates the dynamic aspect of the substantial or ground cause. It tends to manifest itself in particular forms and acts. *Svarûpa,* meaning proper form, stands for the immutable personal self of a conscious being which is the ground of all its actions.

Existence also does not appear as a mere form, but as the ground and source of reality. Though the Sanskrit *asti* (= is) belongs to the same parental root as the Greek *esti, sat* (= being) does not, however, stand for a mere object of thought, idea or form, but has a strong existential meaning and indicates that which is in itself.

[17] Cf. Olivier Lacombe, *L'Absolu selon le Védanta,* pp. 53–4.

Satyam (= true) is immutable nature, and *sattva* (= reality) means that which is imperishable and immutable.

All these various expressions designating the cause indicate the primacy of the material cause above other causes.

Tâdâtmya

The dynamic aspect of this material cause is indicated by the term *tâdâtmya*, used by both Sankara and Ramanuja. This means that the cause forms the self, or *âtman*, of the effect, or rather that the effect which is presented to our experience has *tat*, that, the cause, as its self and ground.

Here the popular examples are the milk and curds, gold and gold ornaments, seed and tree, clay and utensils made out of clay, etc. Though these examples may sound very similar to the marble-statue example, there is a radical difference. In the marble-statue example, the form of the statue, which makes it what it is, is more important than the marble, while in the pairs cited above the first member has the preponderant importance. What is important in the ornament is that it is made out of gold. Even in the utensils, according to Sankara, the real knowledge, or *sadbuddhi*, is to understand the clay out of which they are made; their shapes and forms do undergo change. What remains immutable is the clay.[18]

The Formal Cause—When the emphasis is placed on the material cause, the function of the formal cause becomes rather secondary. With an immutable substantial ground as the core of reality, all particular forms are only a veil that hides and refracts reality. They are only names and forms, individuality and specific nature, which do not add any further reality to the material cause, but only particularize and define it.

Efficient and Final Causes are implied in the material cause itself, which is the substantial ground of reality. An active substance, by reason of its own fullness, manifests itself in the effects. It is also its own goal and end. Its actions are not for adding anything to itself from the outside, but for manifesting what is implied in its own deepest self. Hence, what is achieved in the effects is a spontaneous self-expression, which is a certain return to the cause itself. The dictum 'cause as cause does not receive' is especially applicable to the material or substantial cause.

[18]   *G Bh,* II, 16.

(b) *Application of causality to the world of reality*

From the standpoint of consciousness, the material and formal causes define the whole metaphysical field : the material or substantial cause stands for the Supreme Reality, which manifests itself in the multiplicity of the finite world. These finite beings do not add any further reality to the Ultimate other than the name and form, individuality and specific nature which constitute them. Hence, the world of beings may be designated as *prakriti, mâyâ,* or body. *Prakriti* receives its light and movement on account of the presence of *Purusha; Mâyâ* or illusion comes entirely from the magician who conjures it up by his magical powers. The body is entirely dependent on the soul and is, as it were, its extension and instrument.

This approach in two ways transcends the dichotomy of cause and effect on the transcendental level between God and the world. On the one hand, it can take the cause at the critical moment when it is set to break forth into the multitude of effects, and on the other, it views the procession of effects itself, according to the pattern of the emanation of the word from the conscious self. The former method is emphasized by Sankara, while Ramanuja prefers the second.

Reality as one without a second

Brahman, the ultimate cause, is that from which all beings originate. Hence, they do not add anything to Him. They are *not,* when compared to Him. They are all from Him, but they do not detract anything from Him. Therefore, the best way to understand the Ultimate Reality is to have, for a moment, the multitude of beings in all their variety and richness before our mind, and the next moment proceed beyond them, denying them all, to a moment before their procession; take the Absolute in its infinite plenitude at the critical point when it tends to break forth and diffuse itself into the multitude of beings. That moment of non-distinction gives us a better insight into the uniqueness and fullness of the Supreme than the conceptual distinction between the One and the many in cause-effect relation.

But, this non-distinction is not the passive *apeiron* of the Greeks, but the active *sat,* the existence which is in itself and by itself.

There is only one Reality, and all distinction and diversity in which the One is conceived a member or a partner are false superimpositions. This is not a negative outlook, but a vision of convergence of all that is presented in our experience, but in the reverse order. Hence, *janmâdyasya yatah* means that Brahman is that one Absolute in which all this multitude of beings and their richness were pent up, in which they have actual subsistence, and into which they will all return as their goal and final good. They are all denied only in order that one may envision their fullness concentrated in the One.

Reality as creativity

The other method to conceive the cause-effect unity, the method which Ramanuja prefers, emphasizes the immanence of the Cause in the effects even after their procession as their innermost reality. Here, the basic principle is that once the absolute unity of all reality is admitted, all the multiplicity and creativity will only make us understand better that internal fullness of the One, and will not in any way deny that unity. In this outlook, emphasis is placed on the dynamic aspect of the One. All causality is *tâdâtmya*, ensoulment of the effect by the cause. All causality in the ontological order is the Supreme Brahman becoming the *âtman* or soul of the beings characterized by name and form, individuality and specific nature.

This approach to causality is supported by the statements of the Upanishads. *Chândogya Upanishad* says:

> In the beginning this was being alone, one only without a second. It thought, May I be many. . . . That divinity thought, "Well, let me enter into these three divinities by means of this living self and let me then develop names and forms'.[19]
> All this is ensouled by Him. Hence, that (world) is real, He being the Atman.[20]

This is the reason why, in the Upanishad, Uddalaka tells his son that by knowing Brahman everything else is known.[21]

---

[19] *Chând Up,* VI, ii, 2; iii, 2.
[20] *Chând Up,* VI, viii, 7: *aitadâtmyam sarvam idam tat satyam sa âtma.* Sankara takes the *tat* to refer to the Atman.
[21] *Chând Up,* VI, i, 2.

The efficient activiy of the Sâkshin

How the One can pass out into the multitude of beings without undergoing any change is specially brought out by the idea of *sâkshin,* or witness. The Supreme Being enters his creatures as their inner ruler and witness. The efficiency of consciousness is not in the mode of any physical endeavour that brings change in the agent, but rather witnessing, in other words knowing and willing. No other efficiency is conceivable in a being who is pure consciousness; to ascribe any other activity to Him will be mere anthropomorphism.

The *sâkshin,* or witness concept, is a pregnant one. The *sâkshin* is not an inquisitive intruder, nor an inactive onlooker. Witnessing implies knowing and willing without any involvement or dependence on the factors of the change. All change and transformation take place, not in the cause, but in the effect. Still, the efficiency comes from the conscious will of the *sâkshin.* Hence, Brahman is both the ultimate ground and efficient principle of the universe of beings. He is the sole cause, who produces all things by His will and desire, as Ramanuja states.[22]

Origination by word

However, the nature of this immanent efficiency, which in no way affects the transcendence of the cause, is best set forth by the traditional statement, *'vâcârambhanam vikâra',* all change is introduced in creation through *vâc,* the word. All procession of beings from the Supreme Being who is pure consciousness can come only through an intellectual emanation, symbolized by the word. It can be conceived as the magic word of the juggler that conjures up things, or as the expressed will and desire of an all-powerful God who creates castles and chariots by his command. But the best way will be to conceive it in the fashion of the thought or spoken word which emanates from the fully conscious self, yet never equals or fully translates the internal knowledge. The word does not add anything new to the internal consciousness, but is only an inadequate manifestation. Through the word, the self becomes a witness, a *sâkshin.* The world is the word of God. All that is in it is super-

---

[22] *Vedârth,* no. 14.

eminently in God, yet it is the word of God and His self-manifestation.

In the conscious self *versus* word combination, there is no strict cause-effect dichotomy. The conscious self manifests himself in the word, and can be known only through his word. On the other hand, the word in itself has no independent reality; it is the word of the one who utters it and bears witness to him. Similarly, the world has full intelligibility and meaning only as the word of God.

The finite being certainly has its entitative reality, the specific nature and individuality, but these do not constitute it into an absolute. All its being and reality are received. The specific nature and individuality serve only as a point of reference, a sort of reflector, which manifests the meaning and intelligibility shared from God. It is God's self-manifestation. God can be known only through his word, the word of finite beings.

This immanence of the cause in the effect is brought out also by the familiar analogy of light. The Upanishad says :

> The sun shines not there, nor the moon and stars,
> These lightnings shine not, much less this (earthly) fire !
> After Him, as He shines, does everything shine.
> This whole world is illumined with His light.[23]

Light itself is often used as a synonym for *caitanya* or consciousness. Creation is a mere reflection of the light of Brahman. He illumines all, but is not illumined by them. Their light turns our gaze to the light of Brahman as their real source.

Final causality

Looked at from the angle of consciousness, final causality loses its aspect of purpose in the agent, which is the very source of order and beauty. Efficiency for a conscious agent is not for increasing his consciousness. External activity, and all the effects thereby produced, cannot add anything to the internal consciousness. Much less has the Supreme Consciousness anything to gain through its efficient activity. His only goal is Himself, His self-manifestation, which by its very nature returns to Himself. Hence, in Him, material, efficient and final causality are identified as in a single principle. Sankara, who ascribes to the qualified Brahman a proper

---

[23] *Kath Up*, V, 15. Cf. *Mūnd Up*, II, ii, 10; *Svet Up*, VI, 14.

efficient causality, admits that plan and purpose have to be supposed in intelligent agents. But he finds Brahman's purpose in
creation *anirvacanîya*, indefinable. According to both Sankara and
Ramanuja, the only purpose assignable to the all-perfect Supreme
Brahman is *lîlâ*, mere sport, the free and spontaneous self-expression.[24]

Ramanuja adds a new element by stating that the things of the
finite world are produced by Brahman as playthings, not for Himself, but for the enjoyment and education of souls. Though Brahman
Himself has no personal purpose, the world has a purpose : to cater
to the enjoyment, education and final liberation of souls.

Finality is something that expresses itself in the structure and
order of the effect, rather than in the desire of the cause. The very
diversity of conditions and states in the world of finite beings
arises from an internal finality and dynamism, which produce
certain tendencies and reactions leading to a new order of things.
The Karma theory is only a naive expression of this internal
teleology in nature. The metaphysical element in this facile moral
theory is that the world of finite beings, as a self-manifestation of
the Supreme Reality, contains in itself a dynamism and purpose to
reduce the conscious beings back to their origin. The finality in
the world is not superimposed from the outside.

Hence, the conception of the Sâmkhyas, in assigning an internal
finality to the evolutions of *Prakriti* for the self-realization of
Purusha, has a valid insight behind it. But their fault is that they
isolate all finality in the individual self without a cosmic view of
reality. The non-intelligent *Prakriti* cannot be conceived as purposeful if it is isolated from the Supreme Intelligence from which all
order and beauty derive as participations.

The four ends of life

This concept of internal finality in finite beings integrates the
finite order as moments of a universal order. Even material wealth
and pleasure are not anomalies or exceptions, but meaningful in
the light of consciousness : material wealth is something to be
acquired, possessed and used by man; *Artha*, or wealth, is a legitimate goal of human life. *Kâma*, or bodily pleasures, indicate the

---

[24] Cf. Sankara's and Ramanuja's Commentaries on the Brahma Sûtras,
I, i, 32–4; II, iii, 41 and 42.

harmony of the body in unison with the spirit. Only selfish isolation of these pleasures from the harmony of the spirit makes them evil. Both *Artha* and *Kâma* are comprised by, and integrated into, a higher goal of human life, namely *Dharma*, which puts the individual in agreement with the cosmic *Rita*, or harmony. By the very nature of *dharma* as an all-comprising harmony, differences of obligations and duties arise according to the conditions and states of particulars. *Môksha*, liberation, the fourth goal of human life, is the full flowering of *dharma*.

Conclusion

The two approaches to the problem of causality do differ in their metaphysical preoccupations :

(1) In the Western conception, Causality is the relation of the finite effect to the causes of its efficiency, form, receptivity, order and beauty, all traced to one Ultimate Cause of all reality. Looked at from the Indian point of view, Causality is the supreme, one, immutable consciousness diffusing itself in limited and individualized beings, rational and irrational.

(2) From the point of view of rational analysis, formal causality predominates and matter is merely the passive and receptive principle. But in terms of consciousness, material cause is the substantial and maternal principle to which form adds only limitation and determination.

(3) God, as the transcendent efficient cause of all things, is realized best from a rational analysis of the finite effect, while the causal inquiry from the side of consciousness shows Him immanent in the heart of every being, though affected by none of their imperfections.

(4) From the rational point of view, every secondary cause and created agent is a *movens motum*, a sort of instrument of the First Cause disposing for and communicating new being. On the other hand, from the angle of consciousness, every finite agent is a reflector shining by the light of the supreme consciousness, partly hiding it and partly manifesting it.

(5) According to rational analysis, every agent acts for an end, and the end influences the action through the efficient cause, in being known and willed by him; action is the execution of the blue-print which the intelligent agent has drawn up for himself

before the action. Hence, the First Efficient Cause is also the Final End. But in terms of consciousness, the end is not in the efficient cause but in the effect : the agent *qua* agent is fullness of perfection and does not need any goal to be attained. Finality is in the internal dynamism of the limited form that seeks to transcend the limits and reach its plenitude.

(6) In rational inquiry, the quest for the cause is the search for Reality itself, and is therefore the central point of rational metaphysics. But for one starting with the awareness of pure consciousness, the real, as such, does not appear problematic. For him, causality is an attempt to explain the finite phenomenal world, and so is of secondary importance.

Thus, the two views of causality approach the problem from different angles and complement each other to give us a full idea of the coexistence of the finite and the Infinite. But causality is not an isolated point in this respect. The difference appears in almost all categories of metaphysics.

CHAPTER XII

SHASTRAYONITVAT—THE UPANISHADIC SYNTHESIS

The scope of this chapter

We have so far examined the discovery of the Ultimate Reality as well as the problem of the coexistence of the finite beings along with the Supreme, from the point of view of consciousness. But an approach from the angle of consciousness is not satisfied with a mere discovery or a theoretical description of reality. It endeavours to obtain a deeper realization of reality by concentrating upon it all the available means of knowledge. That is why Ramanuja insists on *dhyâna* and *upâsana*, concentration and devotional meditation, in which the mind constantly dwells upon the ultimate object as the comprehensive means for knowledge of Brahman. This is the principal scope of the Upanishads which, with a pedagogical approach, constantly strive to direct the mind to a deeper and more comprehensive understanding of reality, especially of Ultimate Reality.

The need for such integral knowledge of reality is emphasized by the third *sûtra* of Bâdarâyana, *shâstrayônitvât*. It means that *Sâstra*, or Scripture, is the *yoni*, or womb, of the knowledge concerning Brahman, the supreme reality. We shall discuss in this chapter the principal ways in which the Upanishads try to attain a deeper and more comprehensive understanding of reality.

The Vedantins generally admit the *apaurusheyatva*, or authorlessness, of Scripture. It is simply wisdom, the record of the direct experience which the sages had of reality in general and of the Ultimate Reality in particular. In this sense, Sankara calls it a sort of *pratyaksha*, direct experience.[1] Such a direct experience cannot

[1] *Br S Sank Bh*, I, iii, 28; III, ii, 24.

be challenged by, or tested with, any other means of knowledge.[2] The self alone is the witness to it.[3]

However, what interests us here is not that direct experience itself, but the ways proposed by Scripture for attaining a deeper realization of the Ultimate Reality. An approach that avoids rational analysis of data can proceed in two ways towards understanding its object : it can institute methods of meditation, by which attention is concentrated on a particular subject, or it can try to embody the comprehensive view of the matter in pithy and pregnant statements. The Upanishads, the philosophical portion of Hindu Scripture, make use of both these methods to deepen the realization of reality. On the one hand, making use of the phenomenal world as the starting point, they propose three meditations to attain an integral vision of reality. On the other hand, taking the Absolute as the starting point, they make four great statements, or *mahâvâkyâni*, which represent four steps of metaphysical investigation.

The first method of meditation, called *Dahara vidyâ*, centres on the presence of the Supreme in the heart of every being; the second, known as *Udgithavidyâ*, emphasizes the cosmic presence of God as centred in the sun, and the third, called *Madhu vidyâ*, takes reality in its totality, the cause and the effects, the sun and its rays. The *mahâvâkyâni* start with the fact that Brahman is consciousness (*prajnânam Brahma*), identify the self of each being, Atman, with Brahman (*Ayam Atma Brahma*), show that Brahman is to be seen as one's own deepest self (*Aham Brahmâsmi*), and complete the picture by stating that that Self is the real in everything (*Tat tvam asi*). We do not intend here to make any textual study of this Upanishadic doctrine, but only briefly to explain how these metaphysical meditations and the *mahâvâkyâni* provide us with an integral vision of reality. We therefore restrict ourselves to their metaphysical relevance.

THE 'DAHARA VIDYA': BRAHMAN IN THE HEART OF EVERY BEING

Dahara vidyâ strives to realize the nature of the macrocosm of reality in the microcosm, especially of the human being. Owing to its physiological function, the heart is considered a symbol of the

[2] *Br S Sank Bh,* IV, i, 15.
[3] *Brih Up Sank Bh,* IV, iv, 8.

human self itself. The heart enshrines all knowledge.[4] It is considered the seat of all virtues, including faith and truth,[5] as well as the symbol of stability.[6]

Like all symbols, the heart, too, has a certain polyvalence in this context. It stands for the subjective attitude in the approach to reality, the basic reality itself, and what flows from a true knowledge of reality—namely, satisfaction and joy in the object. As Sankara points out, though one who has a direct realization of Brahman may simply ignore the world of beings, one bound in worldly existence has to rise to the transcendental Brahman by an integral vision, starting with his own individual being, his own heart as the seat of Brahman. Though Brahman is qualityless in Himself, He has to be conceived as comprehending all qualities. To one steeped in sense experience, the way to realization is an integration of experience itself; for him, even the Ultimate Reality has to be localized.[7]

What has fascinated the Hindu thinkers in the heart-symbolism is the fact that inside the heart is a space, âkâsa separated from all outside space, beyond the touch or taint of other gross matter. It is empty, and the external voice cannot reach it. It is the ideal of the void, a symbol of the Absolute. This cave of the heart is conceived as the abode of the Supreme Being who, from there, sees and guides all things.[8] Brahman who is greater than all that is great like the earth, is at the same time subtler than the subtlest things entering even the impenetrable heart.[9]

The whole body is conceived as a city of God, and in it the heart, His palace; the senses, the mind, and intellect are all considered his servants ready to obey the master.[10] The Supreme is hidden in the cave of the heart,[11] the city of eleven gates, namely the faculties of knowledge.[12] The space, or âkâsa, of the heart also symbolizes the subtle Brahman, because He is bodiless and all pervasive, while hridaya, or heart, stands for the buddhi, or intellect.

[4] Brih Up, II, iv, 11.
[5] Brih Up, III, ix, 21.
[6] Brih Up, IV, i, 7.
[7] Chând Up Sank Bh, VIII, 1, Introduction.
[8] Pras Up, III, 6.
[9] Chând Up, III, xiv, 3; VIII, i, 1; Kath Up, II, vi, 17; BG, XVIII, 61.
[10] Chând Up Sank Bh, VIII, i, 1.
[11] Kath Up, I, ii, 20; Tait Up, II, i, 1.
[12] Kath Up, II, v, 1.

Critique

The metaphysical importance of this vision of Brahman as seated in the heart is that is presents an integral view of reality, with Brahman as the core and centre of human life. What realizes and communicates to other faculties this presence of Brahman is the *buddhi*. *Chândogya Upanishad* extends the presence of Brahman in the heart of the microcosm to the macrocosm itself : 'The *âkâsa* inside the heart is as much as this *âkâsa*. . . . Whatever is of it here and whatever not, all are truly stored in it.'[13] It is by understanding the divine in oneself that one can proceed to understand the Divine in the universe.

THE 'UDGITHA VIDYA' : GOD IN THE UNIVERSE

The *Chândogya Upanishad* starts on its metaphysical inquiry by proposing the *Udgîtha vidyâ*, which is the central point of the *Sâma Upâsana*, or hymn worship, in which, through the mystic syllable *ôm* one tries to rise to the unity of all beings in the macrocosm with the sun in the centre of the universe. Sun is conceived as the abode of Brahman, on account of its illuminating all things through its rays.[14] Man rises to the cosmic level through *Udgîtha*, which is composed of man's *vâk*, speech, and *prâna*, life or vital air,[15] a combination of *jnâna* and *karma*, reason and action. What is life in man is the sun in the universe. Life is liberated by *vâk*, or speech; sun removes darkness by light. *Udgîtha* means a lifting up. What is required is to project the integral unity of one's own vital self into the cosmic realm with the sun, the symbol of Brahman.

The three syllables of the word *Udgîtha* stand for three movements in this transcendence from the psychic to the cosmic level. *Ut*, an uplifting of one's own spirit, *gî*, a conscious utterance of the implied realization, and *tha*, stability of thought in the ultimate ground and support of all things.[16]

This threefold movement of thought is required of all who wish to attain a complete view of reality. Through it, the mind attains a conscious convergence of all things in the comprehensive totality of Brahman. But, as *Dahara vidyâ* concluded with a reference to

[13] *Chând Up*, VIII, i, 3.
[14] *Chând Up*, II, ii, 8; I, i, 1–10; *Pras Up*, I, v, 7.
[15] *Chând Up*, I, i, 5.
[16] *Chând Up*, I, iii, 6–7.

the cosmic order from the psychic, *Udgîtha,* starting from the cosmic order, concludes with a reference to the internal self. One should direct thought from the universe back to one's own self, resting the Self in the centre of one's own self.[17]

'Madhu Vidya': God, the Essence of Things

The third metaphysical meditation proposed by the Upanishads is called *Madhu vidyâ.* It has two interpretations, one proposed by the *Chândogya Upanishad,* and the other by the *Brihadâranyaka Upanishad.* The former, according to Sankara, is a meditation for rising from the sacrificial honey, which is the essence of the sacrificial offerings, by way of knowledge through the sun to final realization. In the Brihadâranyaka version, *madhu,* or honey, means the cause-effect interrelation between the various categories of objects falling within our experience. In this, one proceeds by seeking the honey or spiritual ground or essence of things.

Thus, the elements earth, water, fire and wind, the sun, the quarters of heaven, the moon, lightning, thunder and space, truth and moral law, and even the human race itself, are conceived as unifying the essence or honey of things below them. They all finally lead to Brahman, in whom everything finds its final unity. 'This Atman is honey for all things, and all things are honey for this Atman.'[18] This means that Atman is the overlord and ruler of all things. All things are centred and unified in Him. 'In this Atman all things, all gods, all worlds, all breathing things, all these selves are held together.'[19]

The Metaphysical Meaning of these Meditations

The metaphysical meaning of these meditations may be summarized as follows:

(1) Brahman, the Supreme Reality, is not a mere abstract ideal for unifying the things of experience, nor a mere external cause. He has to be looked at as the deepest reality present in all things. In the human individual, He is as intimate as the subtle space in the inner cave of the heart, attained only by *buddhi;* in the universe, He is the self of the sun that illumines and vivifies all

[17] *Chând Up,* I, iii, 12.
[18] *Brih Up,* II, v, 1–14.
[19] *Brih Up,* II, v, 15.

things. In the totality of beings, He is the supreme ruler and central axle of the wheel that unifies all the spokes.

(2) The correct vision of reality is not a mere abstract idea of the absolute, nor a partial view of things that excludes the basic unity. The true vision is to see Brahman in all things, and all things in Brahman.

(3) There is a parallel between the microcosm of the human self and the macrocosm of the universe. Both find their integration in the Absolute from whom all things proceed and in whom all things are rooted and stabilized.

(4) The ultimate metaphysical category is the One. Other categories, being, truth, goodness, and the like, are not absolute. They do not embrace all things of the world of reality in the same way, or in the same sense. Finite things are not being, true, or good, in the sense in which the Supreme Being is being, truth and goodness. The two cannot be embraced under any one of these categories. The only category that embraces the Supreme Being and the finite beings is 'One'.

Moreover, it is not the negative 'one' of Plotinus, which simply isolates the Absolute from everything else, as transcendent and ineffable, excluding being and even intelligence. Neither is it the amorphous one of the *pleroma* of the Gnostics, which is simply a non-distinguished crowd of entities. Nor is it the 'one' of Plato, which is merely an ideal and model for all to imitate, but outside all. The One, perceived as the ground of all things in Indian thought, is a positive category. All things are in the One without adding anything to its superabundant fullness, yet it is in the heart of each being as its innermost reality. This 'One' does not leave any metaphysical residue. All are in Him in His supreme unity, and He is in all without being multiplied.

The 'Mahavakyani': The Four Great Statements

The four great statements, or *mahâvâkyâni,* recognized by the whole Hindu tradition, present the same metaphysical synthesis explained above as four insights into the basic aspects of reality. They show how the human mind proceeds from one insight to another in four principal steps, to gain an integral vision of reality. I shall briefly explain here the four *mahâvâkyâni* and indicate the insight implied in each.

Prajnanam Brahma[20] : *Brahman is consciousness*

The most basic intuition of the Indian tradition is that the Ultimate Reality is consciousness. This is a direct conclusion arrived at from the desire to know—namely, the tendency to unify all experience in an ultimate ground. The Aitareya Upanishad sets forth the principal arguments for the conclusion in this matter : (1) Sight, hearing, smell, and all internal experience through mind and intellect are all modes of becoming conscious; (2) Perception, discrimination, wisdom, insight, thought, thoughtfulness, and even desire and will, are only different aspects of this *prajnâna*, or intelligence; (3) All beings in the universe, from the celestial ones down to the least earthly ones, are all ordered and guided by intelligence. The Ultimate Reality, which is the ground of all these forms, modes and expressions of reality, should be pure intelligence : 'All this is guided by intelligence, is based on intelligence. The world is guided by intelligence. The basis is intelligence. Brahman is intelligence.'[21]

Metaphysical meaning

The statement defining Brahman as *prajnâna*, or pure intelligence, marks an upward or transcendental movement of thought. In all the things coming within our experience, the noblest and most comprehensive one is consciousness. Things have meaning for us only to the extent to which they are known. Even among the grades of knowledge, pure consciousness, which is light without subject-object dichotomy, is the most comprehensive. The object is presented to thought only in the intelligibility it shares with the subject. When this intelligible aspect is separated as the area of the knowing subject as distinct from the object, the object itself is mutilated. Knowledge of reality has to be focused at a point where the subject and object meet together. This point is *prajnâna*, or consciousness.

This shows that Brahman is not a mere object. A God that is represented in our thought as an 'it' circumscribed by a definite essence cannot be God. Something corresponding to our thought is finite and correlative to our finite subject. Such a thing cannot be God, and if it is taken for God, it will be an idol.

[20] *Ait Up*, III, v, 3.
[21] *Ibid*.

Nor is God a 'He'. 'He' circumscribes consciousness in a definite essence. Any determination contradicts the very meaning of the Ultimate Reality.

God can be conceived only as pure consciousness. *Taittirîya Upanishad* describes God as *satyam-jnânam-anantam*, infinite immutable consciousness. As Sankara rightly notes, these three terms do not define Brahman, though they do refer to Him in their primary meaning. According to Ramanuja, they do not represent His ultimate substance, but only aspects and modes of the divine reality manifested to us. Thus, Brahman is the pure consciousness, the ground and source of all that can be affirmed and conceived, but defined or exhausted by none of them.

Ayam Atma Brahma :[22] *this Atman is Brahman*

The transcendence of Brahman, as affirmed in *prajnânam Brahma*, should be counterbalanced by a downward or outward movement which affirms the immanence of Brahman in all things : Brahman is the Atman in all things. 'He became corresponding in form to every form. This is to be looked upon as a form of Him,'[23] says the *Brihadâranyaka Upanishad*.

There is nothing real in which Brahman is not the Atman, the self and the ground. 'Everything here is Brahma; this Atman is Brahma,'[24] says the *Mândûkya Upanishad*. All things are enveloped by the Lord. He is above everything, outside everything, beyond everything, yet also within everything.[25] He is the hearing of the ears, thought of the mind, voice of speech and breathing of breath.[26]

Metaphysical meaning

(1) The important point emphasized by this affirmation of the immanence of Brahman is that the Supreme Reality cannot be placed outside finite things, even if it be above them. A transcendence without immanence will make the finite beings something outside of, and additional to, the Supreme. The transcendent reality is, therefore, also immanent in all beings.

[22] *Brih Up*, II, v, 19; *Mândy Up*, 2.
[23] *Brih Up*, II, v, 19.
[24] *Mândy Up*, 2.
[25] *Isa Up*, I, iii, 5.
[26] *Ken Up*, I, 2.

(2) The *ayam âtma Brahma* formula has another important point to emphasize : Atman is Brahman, but not *vice versa*. Atman stands for the Supreme Reality as far as He is the ground and ultimate self of the finite individual being. When this Self is identified with Brahman, the implication is that finite things are in the Supreme, rather than the Supreme being received and contained by the finite.

(3) By seeing the Atman as identical with Brahman, one also obtains a realization of the all-comprehensive unity of absolute reality. This is a passage from change and instability to calm and tranquility which is termed *sânti*. *Sânti* is not a negative concept like *stirata* and *niscalata,* which indicate absence of disturbance and involvement in external multiplicity. It is a tranquility of peace which implies rest in the supreme plenitude of Brahman. Hence, the identification of Atman and Brahman shows that the individual discovers in its own depths the cosmic plenitude of God, and thus attains *sânti*.[27]

Aham Brahmasmi : *I am Brahman*[28]

But the most important movement in the whole process is an inward one, by which Brahman is perceived as the *Aham*, the ultimate ground of I-hood, the ultimate self of our own personal being. Our phenomenal self is only an *ahamkârâ*, egohood, individuality. Most of it is constituted by material conditions and time-place factors, and only the immutable central point is conscious personality. The Supreme Consciousness, of which our own intelligence is only a mere reflection and participation, is more intimate and central to our being than all that we have as our individual being.

Metaphysical meaning

The basic fact here is that the ultimate reality cannot in any way be stated with an 'is'. The third-personal 'is' exteriorizes God. The second-personal 'art' is also inadequate; it divides reality into two camps, the I and the Thou. God is not a Thou, as opposed to our 'I'. Hence, the only possibility of attaining the Divine without

---

[27] *Brih Up*, IV, iv, 23.
[28] *Brih Up*, I, iv, 10.

exteriorization and conceptual mutilation is to discover God in the depth of the 'I am'.

As Sankara rightly remarks, the authentic way of attaining the Ultimate Reality is *anubhava,* realization. Sense experience gives only a view of the outside of reality. Inference from experience cannot take us far from the finite world. Even Scripture can give only a reported account of the Real. To know the Real, one should become one with the Real, be united with it in the intimacy of realization. In this connection, a general statement of medieval Hindu scholars is relevant : One who says 'God is' does not know God; only one who says 'I am God' knows God. He who says 'God is' makes God an alien, an object, a thing among other things, something corresponding to and on a level with his own finite intellect. Such an object cannot be the finite and all-embracing God.

On the other hand, the statement 'I am God' does not mean that my individual finite being is identical with God. 'I' is deeper than all that is finite, far beyond our *ahamkârâ,* individuality. The meaning is that my real 'I', the ultimate ground of my reality and selfhood, is God. This is the only statement that cannot objectify or circumscribe absolute reality.

It appears clear from this that God is not an object, an 'it' nor a 'he', nor even a 'thou', but the transcendent 'I' that unites and centralizes in itself all reality, even my own self. The Absolute Reality is not far away from our intimate self. One does not have to reconstruct it by one's own efforts. It is already present in the depth of one's very being, as the truth of truth, the authentic ground and source of the intellectual light in us.

This view of God being the intimate Real in one's own being is affirmed by all the great mystics over the ages. St Augustine spoke of God as *'interior intimo meo et superior summo meo'.*[29] 'Do not go out,' he exhorts in his treatise on True Religion. 'Return to yourself; in the interior of man resides Truth.'[30] 'God is nearer to me than I am to myself,' wrote Eckhart.[31] St Thomas Aquinas also often refers to this intimate presence of God in us.[32]

This intimate presence, when realized, becomes *anubhava,* a

---

[29] St Augustine, *Confessions,* III, 6, 11.
[30] St Augustine, *De Vera Religione,* I, 39, n.72, PL. 34, 154.
[31] *Deutscher Predigten,* Nr. 36.
[32] *Summa Theologica,* I, q8, a1; q105, a5.

'becoming one with'. 'He who knows Brahman, becomes even Brahman,' says the Upanishad.[33] This does not mean that one is transformed into Brahman. The very meaning of consciousness indicates an active becoming. Knowledge is not a physical transformation, but rather a spiritual 'in-formation'. The knowing intellect becomes one with the object known, both in spirituality and in suchness. To say that I know this table is to mean that my intellect assumes the suchness of the table, not descending to its materiality, but raising it to the level of the spirituality of consciousness. But as for the suchness of the thing, it is a sort of descending and going out to the status of the table. In knowing God, the process is in the reverse order. The knower who belongs to a lower level has to be raised to the spiritual level of supreme consciousness, both in spirituality and suchness. Only in God and by God can we know God. Hence, to know God is to be centred in God as the source and principle of our knowledge, as well as the immediate term and object of it.

Brahman is knowledge and bliss : This statement emphasizes another aspect of the interiority implied in *Aham Brahmâsmi*. We have discussed in a previous chapter how Brahman is known through *Brahmajijnâsa,* the very desire to know Brahman. The realization, *aham Brahmâsmi,* brings this desire to its fulfilment, and so culminates in bliss. Bliss is the self-possession of reality in itself. The realization that the Supreme is not something outside and remote, but resides within the depth of one's own self, is the most satisfying self-possession. Brahman is designated as *saccidânanda,* pure existence, consciousness and bliss : subsistent existence attains itself fully in infinite consciousness, and in that complete self-possession is also the plenitude of bliss. The finite self which realizes its own finiteness and participation from God finds Him as the true self, the ultimate ground of its unity and intelligibility, and the fulfilment of its aspirations. The *aham Brahmâsmi* is the pregnant expression of this liberating discovery. It sets the individual self free from its isolation, ignorance and misery.

Tat Tvam Asi : *That Art Thou*[34]

The fourth great statement is a reassertion of the centrality and all-comprehensive perfection of the Self, but from a privileged

[33] *Brih Up,* IV, iv, 25.
[34] *Chând Up,* VI, viii, 7; ix, 4; x, 3.

point of view. It is the *guru*, the master who has already attained
realization of the Absolute, who solemnly utters it for the benefit of
the disciple, so that the latter also may obtain the same realization.

Thus, Uddalaka Aruni makes the solemn statement to Svetaketu
his son : 'That which is the finest essence, this whole world has
that as its *âtman*. That is reality. That is Atman. That art thou,
Svetaketu.' This statement is supposed to be a solemn declaration
made at the exact moment when the disciple is all prepared for
the final realization, as if it were the spontaneous breaking forth of
the divine reality itself in the heart of the disciple, through the
medium of the mouth of the master who is Brahman in visible form.
In the same *Chândogya Upanishad*, Prajâpati makes the solemn
declaration about Brahman being the unique and ultimate reality
to Indra the god, but only after the latter had waited upon him
a long time and had repeatedly returned to him with insistence to
know the ultimate explanation. In the *Katha Upanishad,* the god
Death makes the solemn announcement about the nature of ultimate
reality to Naciketas, by which the latter attains realization.

This statement, 'That art thou,' is like the reassuring declaration
of the wise person who tells someone frightened by what appears
to him to be a snake, 'Do not be afraid; it is a rope; this snake
is a rope'. The different metaphysical opinions of Indian thinkers
have been focused on this statement. According to the Buddhists,
what is crucial in the rope-snake-hallucination or confusion is 'this',
which combines the two mental forms of the rope and the snake,
taking one for the other. When the 'this' is dissolved, all the cause
of ignorance is got rid of. Ultimate reality is the void, or *sûnya*,
which will be left by the denial of the 'this'.

According to Sankara, in the erroneous perception one form is
falsely superimposed. The snakehood superimposed on the rope is
false. Hence, it has to be denied, and the realization attained that
it is rope alone. All conception of duality implies such a superimposition. The path of action which is based on the idea of duality
imagines the self as an agent and enjoyer, as ultimate aspects of
it. Since Brahman is the ultimate and Supreme Self, all these
superimpositions of agent, enjoyer, etc., devolve on Him and
bring Him down to the level of finite individual selves. The statement 'That art thou' is to deny this false attribution and to affirm
Brahman as the unique Reality and Ultimate Self.

According to Ramanuja, the meaning is slightly different. One does not perceive the rope as a snake by mere imagination or superimposition. There is an objective reason for the mistake. Certain aspects of the snake, its shape, colour and coils are found in the rope too. What is wrong is the combination and reference. Error is referring certain attributes to one subject instead of another, referring the perceived qualities to the subject of snake rather than to the subject of rope. *Tat tvam asi* demands the correction of such a wrong attribution. The error of individual consciousness is that it attributes all actions, qualities and relations to individual selves, as if they were ultimate and independent grounds. In truth, all these, including the individual selves, have to be referred to Brahman as their ultimate ground and authentic centre.

Hence, according to both Sankara and Ramanuja, *Tat tvam asi* is not a mere indicative statement. It is a dynamic declaration of the identity of *tat* and *tvam*. 'That' is your real thou-hood. *Tvam* has a double meaning here. At the beginning of the statement it stands for the individual self considered as the agent of actions and enjoyer of results. But when it is identified with *Tat*, 'That', the Supreme Being, it denotes the authentic Self, the Ultimate Reality.

Metaphysical meaning

There are several metaphysical points involved in this fourth step towards the total reality.

(1) The finite beings cannot be isolated from the Supreme Being, either as independent absolutes, or as metaphysical residues. To the extent they are, they are grounded in the Absolute, and totally dependent upon it.

(2) The dual meaning of the *tvam* explained above shows the intimate relation, and at the same time a certain tension and polarity, between the individual self and the Ultimate Self. In passing from the one to the other, there is a certain denial of the former; a negation of the objective and finite 'thou' in order to affirm in its place the absolute 'Thou', the real *Aham*. On the other hand, there is a certain continuity between the two moments of the *tvam*. This phenomenal *tvam* has ground and meaning only in the *tat*, which is the absolute and real *tvam*. Not only that, in all our being, the *tvam*, our selfhood, is the focal point where the Supreme Self is most clearly reflected. Hence, the finite self is a symbol and a pointer to the Absolute Self.

(3) More important in the personal conception of reality is the relation between the *guru* who pronounces the *Tat tvam asi* and the *sishya*, or disciple, who is made to realize it in reality. The master has already reached the realization and is the symbol of the Supreme for the disciple, yet the master also belongs to the phenomenal level and is only a transitional means towards realization. However, he still presents the authentic condition of the finite self in this earthly existence. He is not beside the Absolute Self or in opposition to it, but only a symbol, a reflection of the Ultimate Self. Hence, the transformation required of the finite is not a destruction of its individuality, but rather the right orientation. From an isolated and independent being, it has to become totally orientated to and dependent upon the Supreme Self.

(4) There is therefore no I-Thou relation to God from the side of the finite self. Even the selfhood of the finite is derived and reflected from the Absolute Self.

(5) On the other hand, what the individual self *is* is constituted by the Ultimate Self, who is the source and ground of all its perfection. *Tat tvam asi* declared by the *guru*, the authentic representative of the absolute Self, in a way constitutes the finite self in its authentic selfhood as a reflection of the Supreme. In spirit and meaning, it is equivalent to saying 'You are my son', for you are of my own self. We shall develop this point in more detail in the next chapter.

Conclusion

Thus, following the Upanishadic procedure, one can obtain an integral vision of reality.

(1) If the Ultimate Reality is viewed as residing in the heart of every being, the finite beings appear as organically united with the Absolute as members and faculties in a body. The Supreme is intimately immanent, not only in the whole body, but also in each member, yet it totally transcends them all.

(2) The cosmic vision which conceives the Absolute as residing in the Sun presents a cosmic unity of beings parallel to the human microcosm.

(3) *Madhuvidyâ* emphasizes that the psychic and cosmic realms should be unified in the subtlest aspect of reality which is the Ultimate Self.

(4) But the four *mahâvâkyâni* indicate the four steps of a complete metaphysical evaluation of reality. Metaphysics starts with the realization of the intelligibility of reality. Ultimate Reality is pure intelligibility, absolute consciousness. In its light, other things should be evaluated—in other words, evaluated according to the grade of consciousness they imply and involve.

(5) When one proceeds to evaluate finite beings in their intelligibility, it becomes evident that their *âtman*, their sufficient reason and ultimate ground, is Brahman Himself. Hence, the ultimate ground of beings and the Supreme Reality are the same.

(6) This leads to the realization that Supreme Reality is not a mere 'it', nor a 'he', nor even a 'thou', but an 'I'. *Aham Brahmâsmi* declares that our authentic self, the ultimate ground of our existence and intelligibility, the real *aham*, is God.

(7) *Tat tvam asi* completes the circle by casting a look on the finite world, the apparently individual and isolated selfhoods, and declares that *Tat*, the Supreme Reality, is their Self. Their apparently independent individuality is only a symbol of a deeper and all-comprehensive Self. This Ultimate Self makes them what they are.

This polarity between the transcendent Self and the finite selves will be examined more closely in the next chapter.

CHAPTER XIII

PERSONALITY FROM THE POINT OF VIEW OF CONSCIOUSNESS

TAT TU SAMANVAYAT = 'THAT BEING THE HIGHEST OBJECT OF HUMAN PURSUIT'

The culminating point of Vedanta philosophy is that Brahman is the highest object of human pursuit. The fourth Sûtra of Bâdarâyana reads: *Tat tu samanvayât* = 'that being the highest object of human pursuit'. The meaning of the statement, according to Ramanuja, is that the final goal of all search for reality is not action or attainment of finite results, but the knowledge of Brahman as the Ultimate Self. Worship and loving surrender are the means by which Brahman, who is the Supreme Person, is attained by man. The human being is a conscious self, capable of knowing and loving. Brahman, too, is a person, a conscious Self. The whole process of liberation is governed by man's attitude to the Divine Person, and the help the Divine Person renders the human person to attain the right knowledge.

This brings us to the explicit consideration of personality, the personality of God, the supreme Self, and the personality of the loving and devoted finite self. Personality is the most important category in Ramanuja's conception of reality. First, I shall briefly indicate how the notion of personality is obtained through rational analysis and then, in the light of this, explain the concept of personality from the point of view of consciousness. It will become clear that personality is the converging point for the two approaches to reality.

THE RATIONAL EVALUATION OF PERSONALITY

Here again, the two approaches are different and complementary. In the rational approach, we start analyzing the concept of the person and defining him. The Greeks were not very conscious of the value of personality. In Plato's Republic, people were organized, not with any adequate appreciation of man's freedom and natural rights, but rather according to the needs of the political society. According to Aristotle, man is by nature a political animal; but 'the state is by nature clearly prior to the family and to the individual, since the whole is of necessity prior to the part'.[1] In metaphysics, person was almost equivalent to substance.

The term 'persona' itself is said to come from an Etruscan word meaning a mask. 'Personare' was to act out the role of somebody wearing his mask. But since only important personalities were presented on the stage, *persona* gradually came to mean the important individual, and finally the human person. It was Christian Theology which gave a new impetus to the examination of the notion of personality: there is only one God, but three Divine Persons; in Christ there are two substances, the divine and the human, but only one person. This forced a detailing of the elements essential to the notion of personality, as distinct from that of substance or nature.

Person could not be defined merely as an intellectual substance, since in God one intellectual substance was identical with three Divine Persons. Hence, St Thomas gave the definition of person as 'a distinct subsistent in an intellectual nature'. The person is first of all an intellectual individual, but what characterizes him is his distinct subsistence, conscious of himself and opposed to others.

The drawn-out discussions of scholars about what precisely constituted personality in its formal aspect have only a historical value today. Some conceived it as a kind of special mode, qualifying either the essence or the existence; others confused it with individuality, while yet others identified it with existence, either as opposed to or as inclusive of the proper essence.

However, all agreed that person is the highest ontological value, *perfectissimum quid in natura,* the most perfect aspect of the self-manifestation of being.

Intentionality and inter-subjectivity

The shift of emphasis from objective nature to the subject of thought itself gave a new angle to the rational investigation of per-

[1] Aristotle, *Politics,* Book I, ch. 2, 1253*a*.

sonality. This appears especially in the Phenomenology of Edmund Husserl, who seems to have made a synthesis of the scientific approach of Descartes and the subjectivism of Kant.

Reason, by its very nature, is intentional and constitutive. It is only by constituting the subject that the objective essence is formally constituted. But the evident fact of the existence of other subjects has to be integrated into this universally valid scientific phenomenology. Other subjects are not mere objects, otherwise mutual communication of ideas and a common understanding would be impossible. This dilemma can be solved only by a re-examination of the self-constituted subject. If the self is not to be confused with a vague transcendental ego as the unifying point of all intentionality, it must be concretized by reflexion and, in a sense, objectified. By the very universal validity of intentionality, this objectified subject is concrete and multiple : each of these subjects, my own self and other subjects, is self-constituted, otherwise it would not be intentionality. They have to be subjects, not merely in their conceptions, but in other subjects too, otherwise, again, mutual communication and common understanding would be impossible. If my idea should be communicated to another, and I must have common understanding with him, I must be constituted in him, not as an object, but as a subject as I am to myself. If not, we will end up with a monadological system of isolated and closed-up subjects. This means that our self-constitution in intentionality is at the same time the constitution of other selves, and also of an inter-subjective world in which the subjects commune with each other in a common ground of understanding.[2]

The 'there-being'

Thus, in a sense, the whole world of reality is caught up in a dialogue among subjects. The real beings are selves or persons. It is a dialogue rather than a colloquy. In a colloquy, all kinds of diverse opinions and criss-cross communications take place. In a dialogue, there is a common ground or Logos in which two or more share, but at the same time preserving their inalienable identity. It is this openness to the intelligibility of the common field

---

[2] Cf. J. Quentin Lauer, S.J., *The Triumph of Subjectivity* (New York: Fordham University Press, 1958), pp. 148–51.

of intentionality that makes the human being the There-Being (to make use of the terminology of Heidegger). The very capacity to ask the question of being shows that the questioner stands there, open to reality, open to its self-manifestation. Being is the intelligibility of beings as they are presented to the questioning There-Being. There-Being is not a mere subject, an individual and closed ego. It is not a mere entity, but a privileged being, open to the Being of other beings. Though it is, as it were, thrown among beings, found in their midst, it still stands out, distinguishing itself by its freedom and responsibility.

Though it is with others, it transcends them. In a world of being and becoming and self-dissipating activity, the There-Being alone understands the unifying Logos. It is free, not only because its activity is spontaneous, but also because it is autotelic; it has in itself the Logos. Hence, There-Being is, in a sense, the focal point of being. 'The ontological structure of the self is the ecstatic nature of existence; it is essentially not a substance enclosed within itself, but a process which comes to pass as transcendence.'[3]

The pure 'for-oneself' and being

Standing in the midst of beings, yet transcending them all, the Person presents a peculiar aspect of reality. It is not a thing among other things. It is a subject of reference. He is the 'by whom' and 'for whom' of things. In this sense, the Person is opposed to mere being : he is not a thing, but he by whom and for whom a thing is, and he is for himself. The positive element, which may be recognized and acknowledged in Sartre's theory of the conscious self as mere 'for-oneself' and absolutely opposed to the 'in itself' of things, is this transcendence of the person : the Person is the point of reference who desires to be all things and to have all things, yet cannot be identified with any of them, under pain of distorting him into a mere thing.

But this is not a purely negative openness to reality, the 'useless tendency' of Sartre. It is a positive openness and orientation, either to give oneself totally, or to receive one's total reality. This total openness of personality can be understood if we analyze the

[3] William J. Richardson, S.J., *Heidegger—Through Phenomenology to Thought* (The Hague : Martinus Nijhoff, 1963), p. 181.

commonplace examples of personality : a father is a person in relation to his son, and *vice versa*. Anyone who produces anything is not a father. Only one who communicates the whole reality that he is, is a father. Thus, a father is a person because he is open to communicate his whole being. The son is a person because he is open to receive his whole being from another. A son, as son, has received all that he is and all that he has from the father. Hence, in reference to his father, his personality is a point of reference, a radical openness or receptivity.

Similarly, an act is personal when it implies the freedom and responsibility of man. It is an expression of the total disponibility of the person. In some manner, it is an expression of his total orientation. Hence, it deserves absolute praise or absolute blame, and makes him good or bad.

The inter-subjectivity

This openness of personality shows that reality is not a crowd of isolated beings, but an inter-subjectivity. Man finds in his own being all kinds of perfections, faculties and qualities. But he never identifies his own self with any of them : I am not my body, I am not my intellect, nor my will, nor even my soul. All these are in me. But looking into the world outside and seeing the things there, I realize that what I have is what they are. I have received a share in them. My humanity itself is the same humanity found in other men. A child is born from two parents, they from four other men, they from eight others, and so on. A human being is the child of thousands of men gone before it, a child of the whole human race. It receives what other men received, or what they together are. They all received it, and passed on to others what they received as a sacred trust. This is true about all other perfections. They are all received. Hence, they have meaning to a conscious self reflecting on them only as a trust received from an eternal and all-embracing Person. Hence, all perfections in me put me in dialogue with other human beings, and through them and in them with God Himself.

Thus, to know reality is to know oneself, not in isolation, but in communion with other beings and with the Supreme Being. To know things properly, one has to know oneself and be oneself. But this knowledge of ourselves is possible only if we know our openness to others, receiving what they are, thus entering into a communion with the Supreme Person. An isolated being has no meaning. Material beings are symbols in our dialogue with other conscious beings and with God.

Even in our daily experience, only a personal communion with other persons brings a meaningful understanding of reality. Human beings are opaque to the processes of registration, classification, codification and statistical analysis. We never get through these objective processes to what something or someone means to a person. A human person is known only through love.

Love is a radical expression of the openness of a person to other persons. It is the response of the receptive person to the Fullness of what he actually is, the supreme, subsistent, conscious good, the Supreme Person. Hence all love is symbolic. Since we have no direct intuition of the Supreme, we constantly keep going out to him under the symbols of finite things. I love myself most because I am the symbol of the Absolute closest to me. I love myself, but not in order to close myself in my petty self: a finite closed in itself can only stagnate and perish. Nor is the goal of love to increase my own self by little additions, because however much I may add to myself, I shall remain finite and incomplete. The only reasonable goal of love is to surrender oneself totally to the One who is the Good of all good. Hence, love by its very nature is outgoing and transcendental.

Our love goes out to other persons because it finds in them the best reflexion of the communion with the Supreme Good. They have with me a similarity of condition, since they too are bound by the sense of trust, creative fidelity and hope. They, too, have received all that they are and all that they have and feel bound by the converging movement of all reality to the ultimate goal, that, too, in a conscious manner. They, too, show the spontaneous resistance to the corroding effect of time and the effort to transcend the limitations of matter.

Material things are also caught up in this movement of personal love. I know them only to the extent that they mean something. And what they mean is that they are precisely symbols of communication between the Supreme Person and human persons. They are for men, and, in that respect, words of the conscious Supreme Person addressed to conscious beings. In loving them, man is unconsciously loving the Supreme Good.

I-Thou relation of social living

This I-Thou relation embracing the whole of reality is not something arrived at by abstract thought. It underlies the very process of human learning and development. The very need for speech and self-expression shows that there is somebody to speak to, somebody with whom I am already in communion; I cannot speak unless I realize that the other will understand me, that we are bound in a common understanding. A child learns even commonplace truths, such as that two and two make four, not by personal research, but by faith from its mother or teacher. All the important fields of human self-expression and development—music, poetry, art, language and ritual—have meaning only in the context of the person-to-person encounter.

Thus, the world of reality is not a mere 'it'. Nor is it the isolated 'I' of Descartes, or the absolute Transcendental Ego of Kantian subjectivism. It is the field of encounter for the 'We'. The child, in its immature stage, is unconscious of itself and concentrates on the objective world. It speaks of itself as if it were someone else. At the time of puberty, a boy becomes self-conscious and asserts himself and his rights against others in a militant sort of self-defence. But at adulthood, he realizes his responsibility for others and identifies himself with others. Perhaps this was also the course of Philosophy. In its early immature stage, it was totally concerned with 'nature'. Even man was treated as a nature, and the human person as an individual. At its awakening period, Western Philosophy became a little over-conscious of the knowing subject and proposed a kind of closed subjectivism. But the more mature human thought becomes, the more it feels that reality is not an isolated 'I', but a 'We' to whom the world of beings serves as a place of encounter.

PERSONALITY FROM THE ANGLE OF CONSCIOUSNESS

Approach from the side of consciousness confronts reality in the sense of the 'I'. For it, the difficult task is to reach a stage of encounter, the sense of the 'we'. Sociological values do not get their proper emphasis when attention is riveted on the 'I' and its ultimate depths.

The *Advaitin* starts with the I-Thou and subject-object confrontation and confusion of empirical knowledge, and fixes on the 'I' as the pure and unmixed reality. Actually, the whole Advaita philosophy is a search for the Self, and it conceives several empirical selves in concentric circles around the one ultimate Self. But these empirical individual selfhoods are mere constructs of the evolutes of *mâyâ*. The approach to the Ultimate Self has to be one of self-denial and transcendence : *Aham Brahmâsmi*, I am Brahman; *Tat tvam asi*, That art thou; my real *Aham*, Self, is not this individual ego, which is a mere *mâyâ*, a shadow, an illusion, but is Brahman, who is the Self of all selves.

Hence, it does not develop into a dialogue except on the empirical level. The reason for *Bhakti*, or devotion, according to the Advaitic approach, is merely to concentrate attention and to realize that these empirical constructs are transitory and unreal, that the Self alone is the Real.

Obligation and personality

However, with self-consciousness as the point of departure, personality and personal encounter appear at the heart of reality itself. The basic fact that appears in self-consciousness is the sense of obligation and the call to action. The Advaitins explain away all action as modifications of the *gunas* falsely superimposed on the Self. But Ramanuja rightly points out that this will make the very idea of liberation contradictory; there is someone to be liberated, and he has to strive for that. It is not a mere passive role, but an active challenge.

As Ramanuja clearly explains, this sense of obligation places the human person in a sort of dual dialogue, a dialogue with the world of beings, and a dialogue with the Supreme Person. Obligation is not a blind necessity, but an appeal to free action. This means that there is someone who commands, someone who is commanded, and something commanded about.

Here, Ramanuja employs an *argumentum ad hominem* when he draws upon the etymology of the word *Sâstra* (Scripture, which is the chief authority, even for the Advaitins), which is derived from the root *sâs* = to command. Only an intelligent person, free and responsible, can be the addressee of the do's and dont's of *Sâstra*.

This shows the basic characteristics of the finite person; moral freedom and responsibility. These are the two poles of the human person. Concerning material objects, the person is not necessitated; he is not their slave, but master and disposer. If he had no choice, discretion and dominion over things, the sense of 'ought' and command would have no place or meaning. On the other hand, responsibility shows man's subordination to a higher Self from whom he takes orders. If he were all alone, this would have no meaning; material things which are inferior to him cannot create an obligation in him. Nor can he bind himself. The sense of 'ought' is, therefore, the beginning of a dialogue with the Supreme Person.

The structure of the finite person

The consciousness of obligation reveals, first of all, the structure of the finite person himself. He is a knower who can understand a command, and also to a certain extent is immutable, and certainly immortal.[4] All perishable things are provided for the spiritual person, who is the enjoyer.[5] All appeal for acting rightly in opposition to bad actions is a command to return to one's authentic self, shedding the false and inauthentic self. This means that one has an authentic self to return to, a self that is immortal and eternal.

The Supreme Person as Lord and Guide: the Antaryamin

Once the personal aspect of the command is realized, the one who issues the command appears as a Person. As obligation is not a blind necessity, the command is not an impersonal oracle. It is not for his own benefit that He gives the command. Only the Lord and Guide of everything can be the universal source of the command, since he alone has transcendence over the finite self. He is the innermost self of every self, residing in the heart of every being and directing them to their authentic self, calling the finite person from transitory things to the ultimate, immutable reality.

Thus, a second level of dialogue implied in the sense of obligation reveals itself, between the Director and the directed, the Inner Ruler and the ruled, the Teacher and the pupil. This changes the very face of Absolute Reality: Ultimate Substance is not a mere

---

[4] *Sri Bh,* II, iii, 18.
[5] *Sri Bh,* II, iii, 33.

âdhâra,[6] ground, not merely the *satyasya satyam*, impersonal Truth, but *Purushottama*, the Supreme Person.[7]

Even with the Karma doctrine, this role of *Antaryâmin* or Inner Ruler has a special meaning for Ramanuja. Karma is the inner law on the unconscious level of reality, expressing itself in action and results, which by their own force bring about retribution in further actions. But *Purushottama* or *Nârâyana* (lit. Leader of men), who is also the heart of all reality, shows the counter-balancing law of conscious Person. Even the force of Karma is derived from Him, and hence can be controlled by Him. He appears as the discerning Ruler who makes use of the punishment of Karma as a means to turn the attention of the finite person back to Himself, to seek the resolution of the blind Karma in the conscious centre. The Lord is, therefore, the mediating link between the blind fruition of desire and the fulfilment of reasoned and free choice. In this personal outlook, even Karma and liberation assume aspects of punishment and reward.[8]

The Sesha *and* Seshi

This personal dialogue reaches a cosmic level when the consciousness of obligation is understood, not as an individual phenomenon, but as the law of finite self, and as such embracing all individual persons; every individual soul is bound by the law of the Lord and guided by Him. He is *Nârâyana*, the provident guide of men. Here the *Antaryâmin* appears as Brahman, the Lord of the universe. The individual souls communicating with Him, together with the material world, constitute His cosmic body. The Sâmkhya philosophers had already explained that the composite of individual souls and the material world evolving out of *Prakriti* is not a meaningless mass, but a purposeful project, working for the liberation of individual *Purushas*, in the realization of their own spiritual selves. When this purposeful world-system is seen against the background of the one Inner Ruler guiding and directing all things, it becomes a sort of cosmic programme of which Brahman is the principal mover.

In this cosmic plan, Brahman appears as the *Seshin*, the Chief and Ruler, under whom the multitude of persons constitutes *sesha*,

[6] *Sri Bh,* II, i, 28; II, iii, 30.
[7] *Sri Bh,* I, ii, 3.
[8] *Sri Bh,* II, iii, 41.

or subordinate agents. He appears 'engaged in the control and ordering of all beings without exception, the *Seshi* for whom all beings exist,' says Ramanuja.[9]

This is a reversal—from the soul's condition of bondage and subordination to material things to obedient and willing submission to the Lord : 'In individuality, the self is a means to the ends of matter and sensibility. Autonomy is the return of the self to its independence, like the Sâmkhyan *Purusha* when he is freed from the stain of *Prakriti*.'[10] But, when the idea of personality develops and the individual's limitations are realized, the finite persons realize that they are subordinate agents in a cosmic plan.

Loving surrender

This dialogue reaches the level of total openness of love when the soul realizes that the Lord's commands and guidance are not for His benefit, but for its own. The initiative comes from the Lord. Consciousness of duty appears as a loving personal invitation from the Lord. 'In mercy only to them, dwelling in their hearts, do I destroy the darkness born of ignorance, with the brilliant light of knowledge,' says the Lord in the *Gîta*.[11]

Hence, the soul's refusal to listen becomes rebellion, and its turning away to material things, sin, bringing down the displeasure of the Lord. Turning back to Him in repentant response to His grace opens the way to liberation. In submitting itself to the injunction of the Lord, the soul finds Him 'the refuge of the whole world without any exception and regardless of all consideration', 'the ocean solely of love' to those who depend on Him.[12]

In this loving encounter with the Lord, the soul realizes Him as the fullness of all reality, and all works are turned into acts of homage to the Lord. The soul does not lose its identity, though it finds its joy in submitting itself totally to the Lord. Hence, in this approach, devotion is not a transitory expedient, but the authentic condition of the finite person in communion with the Supreme Person. This total self-surrender is the goal of the whole of human life. According to Ramanuja, the goal of all search for reality is

[9] Ramanuja, *Saranâgatigadya*, no. 5, trs. M. R. Rajagopala Ayyangar (Madras), p. 10.

[10] P. N. Srinivasachari, *op. cit.*, p. 41.

[11] *BG*, X, 8–11. Cf. *Sri Bh*, II, iii, 41.

[12] *Saranâgatigadya*, trs. cit., p. 9.

to find all one's joy in rendering worship to the Lord, inspired by the 'unlimited and unsurpassed love arising from the boundless and unsurpassed delight in the full, continuous, eternal and extremely pure enjoyment of Bhagavân'.[13]

PERSONALITY AND THE DIVINE TRINITY

In a sense, the highest point of metaphysics is understanding the Trinity of persons in the one God. Indeed, the fact of the Trinity is a mystery which the human mind could attain only through divine revelation. Still, the need to understand the mystery in some manner has encouraged metaphysics to refine its own conceptions. Besides, the advance of human thought has played no minor part in the progressive revelation of the divine mystery itself.

In Judaism itself, there was a subtle and gradual historical evolution that attained fulfilment in Christ's revelation of the Trinity of God. In the Old Testament, two lines of thought appear : one personalistic and anthropomorphic, the other abstract and impersonal. The uniqueness of Christ's revelation is that in his teaching these two lines suddenly attained a synthesis and fulfilment and a certain transcendence over the limited modes of previous thought. On the one hand, God is the Creator of all things, the victorious Lord, the lawgiver, the tribal Deity who enters an exclusive covenant with Israel, *viz.*, He to be their God and they His people—the King, Father and Husband of the small nation. On the other hand, He is the ineffable Divinity, Yahweh, whose name even cannot be pronounced, the transcendent God of the universe who inhabits unapproachable light, that no one can see Him and live.

Similarly, there is the slowly evolving concept of the Messiah, the promised Leader, Judge, Prophet and King, the suffering Servant of Yahweh, the Redeemer, Prince of Peace, the Son of God, a title first applied to the whole Israelite people, then symbolically to their king, and finally focused on the future Son of Man who was to deliver the people. By the side of this line of thought appears the concept of the *sod*, the secret counsel of God about the governance of the world, the mystery He hides in His mind, the *dabar*, word of Yahweh which goes out of His mouth and effects all things, the Wisdom which was from the beginning with God

[13] *Ibid.*, p. 7.

and in whom and by whom all things were made. The two lines of thought meet in Christ, who is declared to be the well-beloved Son of God, sent by the Father, and yet lives with the Father and is one with the Father. All that is of the Father is given to the Son; the Father and the Son are one; he who sees the Son, sees the Father.

Finally, there is the invisible, yet powerful force of God which broods over the primordial waters and creates all things, the Spirit of God who moves the Judges of Israel, inspires the Prophets and gives wisdom to the kings, and a special outpouring of which is promised to mark the messianic times. This spirit descends like a dove on the Messiah and as tongues of fire on the Apostles. At the same time, He is announced as a person, a special consoler who will remain with the Church till the end of days, specially sent by the Father, a Teacher who would remind the Apostles of all things taught by Christ. He dwells in the hearts of men, pours out divine love in them, prays and works in and with them. He receives from the Father and the Son, and lives and works in a divine manner with and like them.

Thus, in the revelation of the Trinity, the two lines of thought—anthropomorphic and absolutist—reach a synthesis. The three Divine Persons are not three Gods, nor are they merely three aspects of the one Absolute. The three are identical with the one divinity and yet are clearly distinct from each other. No absolute perfection separates or distinguishes them. Father is pure paternity, the Son pure sonship, and the Holy Spirit pure spiration. The personality of the Father is in His total givability by which He expresses Himself totally in the Word, the Son; the personality of the Son is in His total receptivity and reflectivity, the capacity of being a complete and perfect reflection of the Father, the capacity of being a Word and nothing else. The Father giving Himself fully does not empty Himself, nor does the receptivity of the Word presuppose a previous void. It is the gift of the fullness that does not imply any emptying, and the receptivity that does not mean a filling-up.

Similarly, the Holy Spirit completes the circle of the internal dynamism of the Godhead : this movement starts as the self-reflexion of the Father in the Word and culminates as the divine self-gift in the subsistent love of the Holy Spirit.

In the plurality of the Trinity, number has no place; it is not a numerical multiplicity of absolute perfection, but the opposition of personal relation in the substantial identity of the one Divinity. It is also incorrect to apply the apophatic method to designate the ineffable Father. By expressing the Word, the Son, the Father does not empty Himself, or exist as absolute void and silence analogous to the *sûnya* of the Buddhists. Even the *sûnya* is too mathematical (being zero) to be applied to the Divine Person. The One who eternally speaks the Word is never silent. Nor are the Son and the Holy Spirit absolute entities opposed to a Father : the eternal Word of the Father cannot be a totally different entity; nor can the total self-gift in love constitute a divisive entity between the lovers.

The Trinity of God in internal experience

However, one thing has to be admitted : the Trinity of persons in the one God can never be properly understood by objective analysis, because the method of analysis is applicable only to entities. But the Trinity in God excludes all entitative division. Nor is mere conceptual distinction sufficient to account for the real distinction that exists among the Persons of the Divinity. But where the method of rational analysis seems to be inadequate, the approach from internal experience and consciousness seems to be very helpful. Even St Paul sets forth the mystery of the Trinity in the context of the internal experience of sanctifying grace, which is an extension of the loving self-gift of God represented by the Holy Spirit : '. . . you have received the spirit of sonship. When we cry Abba ! (Father !) it is the Spirit himself bearing witness with our spirit that we are children of God' (Rom. 8, 15–16). Experience of God begins in the experience of the testimony of the Spirit who pours forth his divine charity in us and makes us go beyond our limitations and look on the Divine Good as our own good. This gives us the spirit of freedom, the characteristic of the children of God; those who are led by the Spirit of God are the children of God. This freedom is not something conferred from the outside, but welling up spontaneously in the depth of our own being, where the Spirit becomes the principle of our thinking and willing. He makes us believe and will, and himself prays in us.

But this intimate experience of the spirit of the children of God, with its necessary limitations, bears with it the stamp of the unique Son of God. Those who are made the children of God by the Spirit of the Son are only sharers in the sonship of the one Son, the Word.

They experience their sonship in the one Son. Hence, the internal experience of the spirit spontaneously leads to a direct experience of the Son. But to be in the Son is to open one's heart to the Father and cry 'Abba!' There can be no experience of the Son without, at the same time, there being a sharing in his filial sentiment towards the Father.

Internal experience of God in Indian tradition

However, such an explicitation of the internal experience of God could not be found without the aid of Divine Revelation, and is not, as such, found in Indian tradition. Still, the Indian tradition, with its interioristic approach, is closer to it than any rational analysis of the concept of the Divinity. In Indian tradition, too, two parallel currents of thought about God exist, one anthropomorphic and devotional, the other abstract and absolutist. On the one hand, Brahman is conceived as the One without a second, the pure Being that was in the beginning, the truth of truth, the Ultimate Self, *the satyam-jnânam-anantam*. On the other hand, God is considered as the Prajâpati, Varuna, or Iswara, who creates all things, the Vishnu who is born in visible form from age to age to protect the just, destroy the wicked and preserve the balance of *Dharma* or righteousness, and the Maheswara or Siva who destroys all things to bring them back to fulfilment and tranquillity in their own source. He is also conceived as the *arca*, or *Ishtadevata*, the Deity beloved of the particular devotee, the *Nârâyana*, the loving guide of men, who directs each individual internally to attain the final *sânti* in the possession of the Divinity.

These two lines have never been brought to a perfect synthesis. Still, the interioristic way in which both lines are conceived spontaneously generates a certain synthesis. The personal and devotionalistic conception, with all its symbolism and affective overtone, is not the final view of the Divinity, but only a means adapted to the particular individual in order to direct his attention inwards into his own ultimate depth. Even for Ramanuja, *bhakti* is not sentimental devotion, but loving knowledge in which the element of knowledge, the realization that the Lord is my real Self, predominates. In the depth of one's own self, one discovers the Divine Self as the ground of all and acknowledges Him as one's own Self.

In this interioristic experience of the Ultimate Self, the designation *saccidânanda* (*sat-cit-ânanda*), which is a modified form of the *satyam-jnânam-anantam* of the *Taittirîya Upanishad,* is very significant. According to both Sankara and Ramanuja, the three terms do not constitute a definition of Brahman, nor are they synonyms. For Sankara, they only point to an absolute beyond, in which all the three are reduced to absolute unity. According to Ramanuja, these three terms only indicate three positive modes of the One who is existent, conscious and blissful. However, both seem to admit that these three terms contain an irreducible contrast among themselves, even though they stand for absolute and simple perfections which do not imply any limitation or division.

Hence, the experience of God as *saccidânanda* implicity contains an experience of the Trinity of God. *Sat* means that which is in itself and by itself, the immutable 'I am'. *Cit,* on the other hand, stands for the perfect intelligence and perfect intelligibility of the Divine, the one who illumines all things and also illumines and expresses himself fully, the perfect and absolute 'I know'. *Anantam,* infinite, which is the fullness without any lack or defect is also *ânanda,* perfect bliss of complete self-attainment; it stands for the final *anubhava,* realization, expressed as 'I attain my Self'. These are three irreducible moments in the internal dynamism of the Absolute Self : Self being in itself and by itself, fully expressing and illumining itself in the plenitude of consciousness, and completing the circle in the complete and blissful self-possession. These are not three actions, because neither action nor change is admissible in the immutable and infinite Self. Nor are they three aspects or modes of the Divinity, because aspects and modes are partial and accidental, while each of these moments embraces the whole Self and is totally identical with it. Yet these three moments are irreducible to each other : absolute subsistent does not contain or imply by itself self-expression or self-illumination, nor *vice versa*; similarly, self-realization is in contrast to self-existence and self-expression.

These three irreducible moments of the Self are best apparent in the intimacy of the *brahmajijnâsâ,* my intense desire to know Brahman. If I examine my *mumukshutva* closely, the intense desire to attain liberation and go beyond my finiteness and attain perfect bliss in complete self-possession, I can find that the desire does not have its source in my *ahamkâra,* the finite individual self. It is a far cry from the immense drawing force of the absolute Self, the *paramâtman* which pulls together all things in a total 'I-possess-

myself'. The infinite Self is in me, totally given to me, and at the
same time drawing me to my own deepest centre, towards the final
self-realization. My desire is only the shadow of an infinite love
within which I am caught up.

However, this movement towards the Self is not a blind force.
It is a *jijñâsâ*, a desire to know. This desire proceeds from an
initial knowledge, and draws me to a deeper and fuller knowledge.
My present knowledge is *avidyâ*, non-knowledge, yet it tends to
break all limits and to become *vidyâ*, true knowledge, and *parâ-
vidyâ*, transcendental and all-comprehensive knowledge. This
dynamism discovered in my limited light, the finite knowledge, is
a sign that it is not an isolated light but the reflexion from a subsistent consciousness, and also a guarantee that it has its fullness
and perfection in the absolute 'I know' deep within my own self,
the *anubhava* by which the knower of Brahman becomes Brahman
itself.

This desire for the fullness of knowledge carries me to the deepest
centre of my own self : through the expansion of my consciousness,
I wish to be more authentically myself. My own existence is finite;
it is inauthentic and anomalous. I am, yet I am not fully; I am *mâyâ*,
a shadow, an illusion in comparison with absolute existence. But the
shadow tends to be the real as far as possible, to be all that it can
be in itself and by itself. This, again, shows that my existence is not an
absolute. My finite 'I am' is only a reflexion of the absolute 'I am',
in which and by which I subsist.

This third moment in my experience is different from the first,
because the first is an outward movement in search of an object,
the absolute self that will integrate me to itself. This third moment,
on the other hand, is, by its very nature, an inward movement in
search of my authentic self, the absolute 'I am'. The first is the
movement of love towards self-fulfilment, the second the dynamism
of knowledge that seeks perfect self-expression and self-illumination,
and the third is the self-consistency of existence which seeks to be
authentically and totally itself.

The 'I love' of the *bhakta* corresponds and calls to the all-
possessing and all-drawing moment of the Divinity, the Lord who
gives Himself totally to His devotees. The 'I know' calls to the pure
cit, the subsistent consciousness of the Divinity in whose light everything else shines, itself being illumined by none. The 'I am' of the
human self is the content of the 'I know' and finds its full meaning

in the *Aham Brahmâsmi*; it recognizes the absolute Self as its ultimate source and ground.

In this dialectic of the human self with the trans-absolute and tri-personal Self of God, we find the full meaning of the *Tat tvam asi*, That art thou. The individual *tvam*, the finite self, is inspired and drawn by the *Tat*, the absolute Self to attain its self-realization in the divine *Tvam*, where the *Tvam* becomes the *Aham*, my own Self. Here, the three moments of the Divine Self are clearly seen. The *Tat*, the absolute subsistence which is in itself and by itself, the *Atman-Brahman*, is not apprehended as a thing, but as a *Tvam*, a realized self, the Self that is consciousness, *prajnânam brahma*. The *Tat* manifests himself in consciousness. Nobody can know God, unless God manifests Himself to him, and in a way becomes the light by which his finite consciousness is replenished and expanded. But the deep gulf between the *Tat* and *tvam* is bridged only when one cries Abba, Father, in the intimate realization in which *Tat* is recognized as one's own *Aham* : *Aham Brahmâsmi*. There he finds that the divine Self is not an 'other', but the Self of his own self.

THE POINT OF CONVERGENCE

In this conception of personality and the experience of the Trinity of God, Eastern and Western philosophies do converge. Both require a synthesis between the anthropomorphic and absolutist trends of thought, correcting the drawbacks of both lines of conception. Both place the concept of personality, not in any absolute entity, but in a unique point of reference, which stands both for total self-possession and for total self-disponibility or responsibility.

The two conceptual dangers

In the transition from the level of absolute entities to the level of personalities, especially on the divine level, there are two conceptual dangers to be avoided, namely anthropomorphism and absolutism, corresponding to tritheism and pantheism.

Accustomed to conceive things as substantial entities, we easily tend to translate the same entities to the personal level and to identify persons with individual substances. The same misconception is implied in conceiving the three persons of the Trinity in the fashion of human selves. This will make them three Gods, three knowing and willing subjects. In fact, there will here be four absolutes, since the Divinity which is subsistent consciousness also has to be taken into account.

The fact is that the selfhood, or personality consciously experienced in us, bears a certain similarity, if at all any, only to the Son, the second person of the Trinity. The Holy Spirit who conforms us to the Son, and the Father to whom we cry 'Abba', are outside the range of the type of personality found in our conscious self. Though we are directly related to the Father and to the Holy Spirit, to apply any human idea of paternity or love on those Divine Persons will be anthropomorphism. Only through the Son can the Father, as the Father of the unique Son, be approached; so also the Holy Spirit is the Spirit of the Father and of the Son, the subsistent self-gift and love. The three persons present totally different personality types which cannot be comprehended under any one concept.

Absolutism also is a conceptual error. It takes one idea, selfhood or being, and makes it the whole reality. All plurality is either denied, or the many conceived as forms and modifications of the One. This is the error of pantheism, which conceives everything as a form or mode of God. Thus extending the human idea into the Absolute, one fails to recognize the limitation and inadequacy of human conception in grasping the Supreme Reality. Failure to take note of the immense and infinite distance between the Infinite and finite is at the root of all Pantheism and Panentheism.

Thus, *Sat, Cit,* and *Ananda* are not three layers of the Divinity, nor three modes or aspects or functions or powers, but three unique and mutually irreducible moments of the dynamism of the Divinity, each one of them totally identical with it.

The metaphysical notion of personality that emerges from this experience of the Trinity is that of a point of reference, identifiable with complete self-possession, and at the same time coupled with total disponibility or response. Father, *Sat,* is person because He is totally in himself identical with and possessing the whole divinity, and yet is capable of giving himself totally to the Son. Son is person because he possesses the whole divinity, and yet totally responds to the Father as His comprehensive Word. The Holy Spirit, the plenitude of *ânanda* or bliss, is person because He is the unique point of reference which receives the total self-gift of the Father in the Son and completes the circle by His total response of love.

CONCLUSION

Thus, the highest perfection and ultimate meaning and goal of the human reality are found in the personal encounter with the personality of God. The method of rational analysis and conscious experience approach this personal encounter from different directions, yet arrive at the same realization.

(1) Rational analysis examines the knowing subject and discovers inter-subjectivity in its openness to other subjects and to the eternal subsistent subject. Conscious experience finds its own selfhood as open to and grounded in the Ultimate Self. For both, inter-subjectivity is the ultimate dimension of reality.

(2) Rational analysis finds the Trinity of God in the transcendent fecundity of the Father who, possessing the Divinity in its plenitude, expresses Himself fully in the Son, the Divine Word, and in the total response of the Son which breathes forth the Spirit as the loving self-gift of the Divine Persons, thus completing the circle. In consciousness, the *sat-cit-ânanda* of the Divinity appear as the three irreducible moments of the dynamic selfhood of the Ultimate Reality, the Self of all selves. But in both approaches, the three are not numerical entities, nor absolute substances, nor even mere aspects or modes of the same amorphous self, but three irreducible points in the total self-possession and total response of the dynamic Divinity.

(3) In both approaches, the divine personality is best understood in the depth of our own finite personality, which, as a reflexion of the divine selfhood, in loving desire seeks to realize itself more and more fully, crying Abba to the ultimate *Aham*.

(4) In both approaches, the ultimate dimensions of the human personality are freedom and responsibility, which open out our vision to other persons and to God. Only one who knows oneself and in a way possesses oneself fully can respond to others as one ought. Hence, the person as the radical note of reality constitutes the basic and converging point of metaphysics.

CHAPTER XIV

THE GENERAL WORLD VIEW

SUMMARY OF THE TWO METAPHYSICAL POSITIONS

We have examined so far the approach to Reality from consciousness, as distinct from the rational metaphysics which has been traditional to the West. The difference is radical and affects the solutions to all the main problems of metaphysics.

In the first part, we traced the evolution of this approach to reality in the long philosophical history of India, and indicated how it came to be systematically expressed in the six schools of Hindu thought. This study of reality from the angle of consciousness attained maturity in the metaphysics of Sankara and Ramanuja, who are opposed to each other in the conception of consciousness itself : Sankara takes the abstract and distinctionless notion of consciousness as the standard for reality, while Ramanuja takes self-consciousness as the model with which to measure beings. In spite of their apparent divergence, these two leaders of Indian thought complete each other and have much of a common ground to present : both start from consciousness, seek an integral vision of reality, and strive to interpret the world of finite beings in relation to the Absolute Consciousness, Brahman.

In the second part, we have taken the fundamental problems of metaphysics and tried to explain how each problem is solved from the angle of consciousness, but always after briefly stating how the question is faced from the rational angle, drawing inspiration from the various systems that have developed in the West. To sum up the main points :

(1) Western Philosophy proceeds towards reality by a rational analysis of thought, whether it be of its object, or of its structure as a process, a phenomenon, an action or as a self-manifesting existence; the laws of thought reveal the laws of reality. But the Indian approach takes our conscious self-awareness as the authentic reality and tries to discover its immutable ground and authentic condition in the multiplicity of daily experience.

202

(2) The approach from rational analysis takes the multiplicity as a fact, and tries to solve the problem of unity in terms of the analogy of being, participiation of all finite beings from the one First Cause, and their communion with Him. In contrast to this, the study from the angle of consciousness takes the absolute unity of all things in Supreme Consciousness as a fact, and proceeds to resolve the problem of multiplicity, not in exact definitions and categories, but through analogies which may familiarize us with the ineffable mystery of reality : the coexistence of the finite beings with the Supreme, Infinite Consciousness is like the effluence of the word from the knowing subject, like the relation of the body to the spiritual soul, etc.

(3) In rational metaphysics, the key to resolving the anomaly of finite being is causality. Among the four causes, the formal cause predominates, since even the efficient cause acts in virtue of the form immanent in it. But according to the approach from consciousness, causality which explains the relevance of finite beings is of secondary importance in the study of reality as such. Among the causes, it gives pride of place to the material cause in the special sense explained above—namely, as the ultimate ground and maternal principle of all things, operative and formal causes have only instrumental functions and merely limit and define reality from the outside.

(4) The real point of convergence between the two trends of thought is the concept of personal encounter. In both, a basic fact is the freedom and responsibility of the conscious finite self, the rational being. According to rational analysis, this shows the openness of the intelligent subsistent to other human beings and to God. Freedom shows his superiority over finite things. But his responsibility binds him in loyalty and trust to other men from whom he has received his humanity, and to the Eternal Person from whom he has received all that he is and all that he has. Every finite being coming into his experience finds meaning only in the context of his communion with other persons and the Supreme Person.

The approach from consciousness, too, starts with the facts of freedom and responsibility discovered in the consciousness of obligation and duty. Looking into the nature of obligation, it discovers in it the Supreme Person as the lawgiver, guide and benevolent and loving Lord, as the other member of a person-to-person dialogue. However, it is not an equal partnership : even the personality of the individual self is totally received from the Supreme Self. Hence, the finite person is the subordinate and disciple and the humble devotee.

THE TWO WORLD VIEWS

But what is perhaps more important than all these differences on particular problems is the general attitude to life and reality, which appears radically different. Only an appreciation of each other's world vision and outlook can prepare the ground for a fruitful dialogue. This difference of outlook may be summarized under a few principal headings; though these may appear to be oversimplifications and overgeneralizations.

General mode of thought

Rational thought is exteriorized and static.[1] Since its main function is to report things, it insists on details. Hence, it cannot tolerate even an inaccuracy or falsehood. This insistence on accuracy often may appear as intolerance of other possible views.

Tolerance is, on the other hand, the keynote of the approach from the side of consciousness. Being introspective and dynamic, it fixes on the total vision of reality as the goal. In the light of the unattainable goal of direct vision, every system of thought and formulation appears inadequate, but nevertheless to be tolerated for the partial vision it contains. As Dr. S. Radhakrishnan says, 'Toleration is the homage which the finite mind pays to the Infinite'. Proceeding from details to unity, every detail is important, and any false element can mar the final picture. Starting from full vision and proceeding to details, every detail is partial, and in a sense distorted and refracted, and in every detail a certain amount of inadequacy has to be recognized and tolerated. For one introducing Robert to an assembly, to say, 'Robert is an animal' will be quite wrong and inappropriate. But a biology teacher may speak of Robert, who is well known to the class, as an animal. Tolerance of error as a partial truth supposes a mode of thought which goes, first, directly to the totality of truth, and from there comes to

---

[1] Even a proponent of dialectics based on consciousness, like Hegel, ends up with an iron-clad objective system owing to his strictly rational method!

various expressions, formulations and definitions, which are mere approximations to reality.

Manner of looking at the universe

The rational outlook is interested in the object, the being which is independent of our thought and presented to it. Hence, the Greek was a willing contemplator of the universe which was conceived as a *theatron*, a well-arranged play, a *cosmos*, a perfect and harmonious totality, which orders the infinite forms to which Physis, eternal motion of procreation, gives reality. This *cosmos*, which means splendour, order, adornment, etc., imposes itself equally on all. Even the gods who presided over it were in some manner bound by it.

On the contrary, the attitude and approach of the Hindu to the objective world is quite different. For him, the world is simply 'existence'—something which is outside itself, an extrapolation of reality. It is simply a projection from the absolute, and it therefore obscures our vision and hides the Self. Hence, it has only a symbolic and pedagogical value : to lead us back to the core of reality. This is why *Bhagavad Gîta* calls all action, all knowledge, all devotion and all faith 'yoga', because they all lead us back to the Self.

Conception of history

For the Greek who places the emphasis on the immutable cosmic order, the idea of time is cyclic. It is the measurement of a movement within the well-ordered system. The regular and immutable course of stars gives its image to things and events. History has no special meaning as a definite plan or progress. It is merely the chronological succession of events. True values exist out of time. It was the Judeo-Christian conception of salvation that gave the West a sense of history as a well-ordered plan gradually being carried out. But this Christian conception is being rejected by profane historians who, seeking the meaning of events, try to reduce everything into economic, sociological and cultural laws, inexorable in their course, calculable and foreseeable, and therefore cyclic in character.

The Indian concept of history, on the other hand, tries to combine the cyclic and personal aspects into one. Since all time and history is a mere projection of eternity, by its very nature it tends to fall back into the eternity of the source. Hence, time has a corroding effect, reducing everything back to the original calm of the Divinity. On the other hand, since eternity itself is the personal existence of God, it has—implied in its evolution—a certain benevolent plan : it is a self-manifestation of God himself. 'I am time', says the Lord in the *Gîta*. The purpose is the education and liberation of souls bound in bodily existence. Hence, the whole history is a drama, with a symbolic and religious value for man. This is the basic idea of Hindu ritual : stone and water, the Lotus and the Banian tree, ashes and oil, all have a certain divine virtue present in them, and they help to lead man to the realization of the Divine.

Idea of truth

From the rational point of view, truth is *a-letheia,* a removal of the veil, the manifestation of the objective, clear and immutable. *Logos* is the unifying basis of multiplicity.

But from the angle of consciousness, *satyam* is not an absolute value, but a combination of the Real and unreal, a mere designative term of the Ultimate. *Sabda,* or word, is not the unifying factor, but the diffusing and diversifying *mâyâ* individualizing things through name and form.

Nature and psychology of man

Rational approach follows a strict dichotomy in the conception of man, distinguishing in him matter and spiritual form, body and soul. The soul is the principle of actuality, unity and finality in man, and matter pure potentiality, *Soma,* the Greek word for body, originally meant a dead body, and was assumed in philosophy to designate the purely potential and material principle in man.

The Indian approach from the side of consciousness has concentrated on the spiritual aspect of man, but has not made his material part a pure potency. Of course, spirit transcends time and space and is not subject to change. Still, in its presence the active principle of evolution, *Prakriti,* brings out all variety and diversity through the varying combination of the functions of *sattva, rajas* and *tamas.*

The goal of human life

For the rational approach, what is important is right order. For the Greek, what was considered ideal was neither to become nor to owe, neither to be able nor to will, but solely to be, be in the perfect order. This order was the ideal for the moral life of man in the Western tradition. The cardinal virtues were prudence, justice, temperance, and fortitude, which were calculated to keep man in perfect balance within himself and in relation with others. The final goal is contemplation, as opposed to action.

The ideal from the angle of consciousness is to reach the stage of immutability free from change, illusion and error. Hence, the striving is to go down deeper and deeper into the immutable core of one's own self and discover there the Absolute Self. Self-realization is therefore the goal.

Concept of God

Even in the approach to God, each tradition shows its particular attitude. For the Greeks, God, the Supreme Being, is the climax of the cosmic order. Hence, He is conceived as the One, the unifying point of everything, the absolute Good and Beauty from which everything else gets its share. Even the Five Ways of St Thomas do not deviate significantly from this pattern. The personal aspect of God in Christianity is a patrimony from Judaic monotheism and the Revelation given us by Christ.

Approach to God from consciousness interiorizes God. God, who is called Brahman, the one who is really big, the all, is also the Atman, the real self of every being. An exteriorized God is no God, but a mere phenomenon—at best, a symbol of the divine, with only a psychological and pedagogical value.

PRACTICAL CONSEQUENCES OF THE DIVERGENCE

This divergence of outlook does not remain on the merely theoretical level, but affects even the last details of life and thought. This is true even in the field of religion.

(1) For the Judeo-Christian and Islamic religions, which leaned heavily on the Greek philosophical tradition, there is only one God and He is the God of all; every other God is a false God. Since the

world belongs to God by right, the law of the one God should be binding on everybody, whether Hindu, Muslim or Christian.

On the other hand, for the Hindu, the world is not a reality outside and distinct from God, and He does not impose a law on it from the outside. The law is the *rita*, the harmony of things with their Ultimate Ground. Hence, the gods, avatars, *gurus* or teachers are not competitors for the position of the Supreme, but are only partial manifestations of the Supreme. The more there are of them, the better can they manifest the nature of the Supreme, and man can make a better choice according to his own station and psychological condition to understand the Divine. There is no uniform and absolute law binding on everybody in the same way, but only *dharma*, which is proper to each individual, state, class and condition.

(2) From the rational point of view, idolatry is a denial of the true God, and so is the greatest sin. But for the Hindu, idol worship is a great virtue, since recognizing the divine in the material realm is the highest honour he can pay to the Supreme.

(3) From the rational angle, belief in the existence of a personal God is the basic requisite of religion, and hence the Atheist is the worst criminal possible; by the denial of God, he denies all the human values. But for the Hindu who looks from the angle of consciousness, the monotheism of Islam and Christianity is a naive absolutization of the particular, which may be tolerated only on the level of popular devotion. Theism is only a step towards the final realization of God who is supreme consciousness. Hence, Atheism may not be a mere negation, but an emphatic affirmation of the ineffable God beyond human conceptions.

COMPLEMENTARITY AND DIALOGUE

In this divergence of approaches, the final question is not one of truth and error, right and wrong. Besides, it may take a more detailed study of individual points to pass the judgement of right and wrong about each point in its proper context. What is important is to recognize that the two approaches are from different angles, and so are not contradictory, but rather complementary. Only misunderstanding of the approaches can give rise to the total incomprehension and misunderstanding that have kept East and West poles apart, down the centuries.

It may also be futile to ask which approach is better. Both have their strong points and weaknesses: rational approach provides clarity of conception and accurate understanding of distinctions. But it does not mean an understanding of reality as it is in itself. It is easy to project one's own conceptions into systems and take them for the reality. Besides, one often fails to grasp one's own deep involvement in the reality which one tries to understand. On the other hand, consciousness presents reality in one's own self, within reach of immediate understanding. But it tends to forget distinctions, and smooth out and obliterate the limits which define the finite in contrast to the Infinite. Hence, for an adequate understanding of reality, both approaches are necessary.

It may also not be possible to fuse the two approaches into one. They proceed in opposite directions. Fusing them will destroy their special value. Therefore, the best procedure may be to maintain their proper character, and keep up the dialogue that makes them complement each other and correct each other's defects.

SELECT BIBLIOGRAPHY

Ahirbudhnya Samhita, ed. M. D. Ramanujacharya and F. Otto Schrader, Madras: Adyar Library, 1916.

Aurobindo, Sri, *The Life Divine,* 3rd ed., Calcutta: Arya Publishing House, 1947 (2 vols.).

Aurobindo, Sri, *Essays on the Gîta,* Calcutta: Arya Publishing House, Sri Aurobindo Library, 1926–44.

Barlingay, S. S., 'Theories of Language in Indian Logic', *International Philosophical Quarterly,* 4 (1964), 94–109.

Barlingay, S. S., *A Modern Introduction to Indian Logic,* Delhi: National Publishing House, 1965.

Barnett, Lionel David, *The Heart of India,* London: John Murray, 1913.

Barnett, Lionel David, *Brahma-Knowledge, An Outline of the Philosophy of the Vedânta as set forth by the Upanishads and by Sankara,* London: John Murray, 1907.

Barua, Beni Madhab, *Pre-Buddhistic Philosophy,* Calcutta: University of Calcutta, 1921.

Bhaduri, Sadananda, *Studies in Nyâya-Vaiseshika Metaphysics,* Poona: Bhandarkar Oriental Series, 1947.

Bharadwaj, Krishna Datta, *The Philosophy of Ramanuja,* New Delhi, 1958.

Bhattacharya, Benoytosh, *An Introduction to Buddhist Esoterism,* Mysore: Wesleyan Mission Press, 1932.

Bhattacharya, Gopikamohan, *Studies in Nyâya-Vaiseshika Theism,* Calcutta: Sanskrit College, 1961.

Bhattacharya, Krishna Chandra, *Studies in Philosophy,* Vol. I, ed. Gopinath Bhattacharya, Calcutta: Progressive Publishers, 1956.

Burch, George Bosworth, 'Principles and Problems of Monistic Vedânta', *Philosophy East and West,* II (1961–2), 231–8.

Carpenter, Joseph Estlin, *Theism in Mediaeval India,* London: Williams and Norgate, 1921.

Chakravarti, Prabhat Chandra, *The Philosophy of Sanskrit Grammar,* Calcutta: University of Calcutta, 1930.

Chakravarti, Sures Chandra, *The Philosophy of the Upanishads,* Calcutta: University of Calcutta, 1935.

Chatterji, Jagadisha Chandra, *The Hindu Realism, being an Introduction to the Metaphysics of the Nyâya-Vaiseshika System of Philosophy,* Allahabad, 1912.

Chaudhuri, Anil Kumar Roy, *The Doctrine of Mâyâ,* Calcutta: Das Gupta & Co., 1950.

Chaudhuri, Anil Kumar Roy, *A Realistic Interpretation of Sankara Vedânta,* Calcutta: University of Calcutta.

Chaudhuri, Anil Kumar Roy, *Self and Falsity in Advaita Vedânta,* Calcutta: Progressive Publishers, 1955.

Conze, Edward, *Buddhist Thought in India,* London: Allen & Unwin, 1962.

Cowell, E. B. and Gough, A. E. trs., *The Sarva Darsana Samgraha, or*

Review of the Different Systems of Hindu Philosophy, London: Kegan Paul, Trench, Trübner & Co., 1904.

Dandoy, G. S. J., *Essay on the Doctrine of the Unreality of the World in the Advaita*, Calcutta, 1919.

Daniélou, Alain, *Les Quatre Sens de la Vie. L'Inde Traditionnelle*, Paris: Librairie Académique Perrin, 1963.

Dasgupta, Surendranath, *A History of Indian Philosophy*, Cambridge: University Press, 1922–55 (5 vols.).

Dasgupta, Surendranath, *Hindu Mysticism*, New York: F. Ungar, 1959.

Deussen, Paul, *The Philosophy of the Upanishads*, trs. A. S. Geden, Edinburgh: T. & T. Clark, 1906.

Deussen, Paul, *The System of the Vedânta*, trs. Charles Johnston, Chicago: The Open Court Publishing Co., 1912.

Deussen, Paul, *The Elements of Metaphysics*, London: Macmillan, 1894.

Devaraja, N. K., *An Introduction to Sankara's Theory of Knowledge*, Delhi: Motilal Banarsidass, 1962.

Dharmaraja, *Vedântaparibhâshya*, ed. M. Anantakrishna Sastri, Calcutta: University of Calcutta, 1930.

Dutt, N. K., *The Vedânta and Its Place as a System of Metaphysics*, Calcutta: 1931.

Ghate, V. S., *The Vedânta. A Study of the Brahma Sûtras with the Bhâshyas of Sankara, Ramanuja, Nimbarka, Madhava and Vallabha*, Poona: Bhandarkar Oriental Research Institute, 1926.

Glasenapp, H. V., *Madhvas Philosophie des Vishnu Glaubens*, Bonn: K. Schroeder, 1923.

Govindacharya, Alkondaville, *Ramanuja's Commentary on the Bhagavadgita*, Madras, 1898.

Govindacharya, Alkondaville, *The Life of Ramanujacharya*, Madras, 1906.

Grimm, George, *The Doctrine of the Buddha*, Berlin: Akademie Verlag, 1958.

Griswold, Hervey Dewitt, *Brahman. A Study in the History of Indian Philosophy*, New York: Macmillan, 1900.

Guénon, R., *L'homme et son devenir selon le védanta*, Paris: Les éditions traditionnelles, 1952.

Gupta, Anima Sen., 'Ramanuja on Causality', *Philosophy East and West*, 8 (1958–9), 137–48.

Hacker, Paul, 'Eigentümlichkeiten der Lehre und Terminlogie Sankaras', *Zeitschrift der deutschen Morgenländischen Gesellschaft*, 100 (1950), 246–86.

Hacker, Paul, *Untersuchungen über Texte des frühen Advaitavada*, Mainz: Akademie der Wissenschaften und der Literatur, 1950.

Harrison, Max Hunter, *Hindu Monism and Pluralism as found in the Upanishads and in the Philosophies dependent upon them*, London: Oxford University Press, 1932.

Heimann, Betty, *Facets of Indian Thought*, London: Allen & Unwin, 1964.

Hirayanna, M., *Outlines of Indian Philosophy*, London: Allen & Unwin, 1951.

Hohenberger, A., *Ramanuja—ein Philosoph indischer Gottesmystik*, Bonn: Selbstverlag des Orientalischen Seminars der Universität Bonn, Bonner Orientalische Studien, Band 10, 1960.

Hooper, J. S. M., *Hymns of the Alvars*, Calcutta: Association Press, 1929.

Hume, Robert Ernest, *The Thirteen Principal Upanishads, translated with an outline of the Philosophy of the Upanishads and an annotated bibliography*, 2nd ed. revised, Madras: Oxford University Press, 1949.

Ingalls, Daniel Henry Holmes, *Materials for the Study of Navya-Nyâya Logic,* Cambridge, Mass: Harvard University Press, Harvard Oriental Series, Vol. 40, 1951.

Karmarkar, R. D., *A Comparison of the Bhâshyas of Sankara, Ramanuja, Kesavakasmirin and Vallabha on some crucial Sûtras,* Poona: The Oriental Book Supplying Agency, 1920.

Keith, Arthur Berriedale, *Sâmkhya System,* Calcutta: Association Press, 1918.

Keith, Arthur Berriedale, *Buddhist Philosophy in India and Ceylon,* Oxford: Clarendon Press, 1921.

Keith, Arthur Berriedale, *Indian Logic and Atomism,* Oxford: Clarendon Press, 1921.

Keith, Arthur Berriedale, *The Karma Mîmâmsa,* Calcutta: Association Press, 1921.

Keith, Arthur Berriedale, *The Religion and Philosophy of the Vedas and Upanishads,* Cambridge: Harvard University Press, Harvard Oriental Series, Vols. 31 and 32, 1925 (2 vols.).

Krishna Warrier, A. G., 'Brahman as Value', *The Adyar Library Bulletin,* 25 (1961), 477–510.

Krishna Warrier, A. G., 'A New Angle on the Problem of Unreality in Advaita', *Prabuddha Bharata,* 69 (1964), 108–115.

Krishna Warrier, A. G., *The Concept of Mukti in Advaita Vedânta,* Madras: Madras University Philosophical Series, No. 9, 1961.

Kumarappa, Bharatan, *The Hindu Conception of the Deity as culminating in Ramanuja,* London: Luzac & Co., 1934.

Kunjan Raja, C., *Some Fundamental Problems in Indian Philosophy,* Delhi: Motilal Barnarsidass, 1960.

Lacombe, Olivier, *Les Grandes thèses de Ramanuja, traduction annotée du siddhanta,* Paris: Adrian-Maisonneuve, 1938.

Lacombe, Olivier, *L'Absolu selon le Védanta,* Paris: P. Guthner, 1937.

Lazarus, F. K., *Ramanuja and Bowne, a study in Comparative Philosophy,* Bombay: Cetana, 1962.

Macnicol, Nicol, *Indian Theism from the Vedic to the Mohommedan Period,* London: Oxford University Press, 1915.

Madhavacharya, Sri, *Brahmasûtra Bhâshya with Jagannathayatistika,* Madras, 1900.

Mahadevan, T. M. P., *The Philosophy of Advaita,* with a foreword by S. Radhakrishnan, Madras: Ganesh & Co., 1957.

Mahadevan, T. M. P., *Outlines of Hinduism,* Bombay: Cetana, 1960.

Mahadevan, T. M. P., *The Idea of God in Saiva Siddhânta,* Annamalai-nagar: Annamalai University, 1955.

Maitra, Susil Kumar, *Studies in Philosophy and Religion,* Calcutta: University of Calcutta, 1941.

Mallik, G. N., *The Philosophy of Vaishnava Religion,* Lahore: Motilal Banarsidass, 1927.

Mehta, S. S., *A Manual of Vedânta Philosophy as revealed in the Upanishads and the Bhagavadgîta,* Bombay, 1919.

Mukerji, J. N., *Sâmkhya or the Theory of Reality,* Calcutta: S. N. Mukerji, 1930.

Mukhopadhyaya Govindagopal, *Studies in the Upanishads,* Calcutta: Sanskrit College, 1960.

Murti, T. R. V., *The Central Philosophy of Buddhism,* London: Allen & Unwin, 1955.

Nagarjuna, *Mûlamâdhyamakârika with the Madhyamikavritti of Candrakirti,* ed. M. Poussin, St. Petersburg, 1903.

Northrop, F. S. C., *The Meeting of East and West,* New York: Macmillan, 1947.

Nyâya Sûtras of Gotama, ed. B. D. Basu, Allahabad: The Sacred Books of the Hindus, No. 8, 1930.

Osborne, Arthur, *Ramana Maharshi and the Path of Self-Knowledge,* London: Rider & Co., 1954.

Otto, Rudolph, *Vishnu-Narayana,* Jena: Eugen Diedericks, 1917.

Otto, Rudolph, *Siddhanta des Ramanuja, Texte zur indischen Gottesmystik,* Jena: Eugen Diedericks, 1917.

Prabhavananda, Swami, *The Spiritual Heritage of India,* London: Allen & Unwin, 1962.

Radhakrishnan, Sarvapalli, *The Vedânta according to Sankara and Ramanuja,* London: Allen & Unwin, 1928.

Radhakrishnan, Sarvapalli, *The Brahma Sûtra, the Philosophy of Spiritual Life,* Princeton, 1960.

Radhakrishnan, Sarvapalli, *Indian Philosophy,* London: Allen & Unwin, Vol. I, 1923: Vol. II, 1927.

Radhakrishnan, Sarvapalli, *The Philosophy of the Upanishads,* Allen & Unwin, 1953.

Radhakrishnan, Sarvapalli, *A Sourcebook in Indian Philosophy,* ed. with Charles A. Moore, Princeton, 1967.

Raghavachar, S. S., *Introduction to the Vedârthasamgraha of Sri Ramanujacharya,* Mangalore, 1957.

Raja, C. Kunjan. *See* Kunjan.

Raju, P. T., *Idealistic Thought of India,* London: Allen & Unwin, 1953.

Raju, P. T., 'Morality and Self-Realization', *Volume of Studies in Indology presented to Prof. P. V. Kane,* Poona: Oriental Book Agency, 1941, 362–9.

Ramanujacharya, Sri, *Sri Bhashya of Ramanuja,* ed. with trs. R. D. Karmarkar, Poona: University of Poona, Sanskrit and Prakrit Series, Vol. I, 1962; trs. M. Rangacarya and Varadaraja Aiyangar, Madras: The Brahmavadin Press, 1919; trs. George Thibaut, Sacred Books of the East, Vol. 48, Oxford University Press, 1904; Delhi: Motilal Banarsidass, 1962.

Ramanujacharya, Sri, *Vedârthasamgraha,* ed. with trs. J. A. B. Van Buitnen, Poona: Deccan College, 1956.

Ramanujacharya, Sri, *Sri Bhagavad Ramanuja Granthamala,* nine works of Ramanuja, ed. Sri Kanchi P. B. Annangaracharya Swamy, Kancheepuram, 1956.

Ramanujacharya, Sri, *Vedântasara,* ed. V. Krishnamacharya, trs. N. B. N. Ayyangar, Madras: The Adyar Library, 1953.

Ramanujacharya, Sri, *The Three Tatvas,* Kumbakonam, 1932.

Rawson, Joseph Nadin, *Katha Upanishad,* London: Oxford University Press, 1934.

Riepe, Dale, *The Naturalistic Tradition in Indian Thought,* Seattle: University of Washington Press, 1961.

Sankaracharya, Sri, *Brahmasûtrabhâshya,* ed. M. S. Bakre with *Ratnaprabha,* the *Bhâmati,* and *Nyâyanirnaya,* Bombay: Nirnayasagar Press, 1934; trs. George Thibaut, Oxford: Clarendon Press, Sacred Books of the East, Vol. 34, 1890, and Vol. 38, 1896.

Sankaracharya, Sri, *The Gîta Bhâshya,* ed. Dinkar Vishnu Gokhale, Poona: Oriental Book Agency, 1950.

Sankaracharya, Sri, *The Bhâshyas on the Ten Upanishads,* with Anandagiri's Gloss., ed. Anandasrama Sanskrit Series, Poona.

Sankaracharya, Sri, *The Chândogya Upanishad with the Commentary of Sankara,* trs. Ganganatha Jha, Poona: Oriental Book Agency, 1942.

Sankaracharya, Sri, *Brihadâranyaka Upanishad Sankara Bhâshya,* trs. Swami Madhavananda, Mayavati, Almora: Advaita Asrama, 1934.

Schrader, F. Otto, *Introduction to the Pancarâtra and the Ahirbudhnya Samhita,* Madras: Adyar Library, 1916.

Senart, Émile, *Chândogya Upanishad,* Paris: Société d'édition 'les belles lettres', 1930.

Sharma, B. N. K., *Philosophy of Sri Madhvacharya,* Bombay: Bharatiya Vidya Bhavan, 1962.

Sharma, Chandradhar, *A Critical Survey of Indian Philosophy,* London: Rider & Co., 1960.

Shastri, Dharmendra Nath, *An Outline of Critique of Indian Realism—A Study of the Conflict between the Nyâya-Vaiseshika and the Buddhist Dignaga School,* Delhi: Institute of Indology, 1964.

Shastri, Gaurinath, *The Philosophy of Word and Meaning—Some Indian Approaches with Special Reference to the Philosophy of Bhartrihari,* Calcutta: Sanskrit College, 1959.

Shastri, Prabhu Dutt, *The Doctrine of Mâyâ,* London: Luzac & Co., 1911.

Silburn, Lilian, *Instant et cause, le discontinu dans la pensée philosophique de l'Inde,* Paris: J. Vrin, 1955.

Sinha, Debabrata, *The Idealist Standpoint—A Study in the Vedantic Metaphysics of Experience,* Visva-Bharati: Santiniketan, 1965.

Sircar, Mahendranath, *Hindu Mysticism according to the Upanishads,* London: Kegan Paul, Trench, Trübner & Co., 1934.

Sircar, Mahendranath, *The System of Vedantic Thought and Culture,* Calcutta: University of Calcutta, 1925.

Srinivasa Aiyengar, C. R., *The Life and Teachings of Sri Ramanujacharya,* Madras: R. Venkateswar & Co., 1908.

Srinivasa Chari, S. M., *Advaita and Visishthadvaita—A Study based on Vedanta Desika's Satadushani,* with a foreword by S. Radhakrishnan, New York: Asia Publishing House, 1961.

Srinivas Iyengar, P. T., *History of the Tamils from the Earliest Times to 600 A.D.,* Madras: C. Coomaraswamy Naidu & Sons, 1929.

Srinivasachari, P. N., *Ramanuja's Idea of the Finite Self,* Madras: Longmans, Green & Co., 1928.

Srinivasachari, P. N., *The Philosophy of Bhedâbheda,* Madras: The Adyar Library Series, No. 74, 1950.

Srinivasachari, P. N., *The Idea of Personality,* Madras, 1951.

Srinivasadasa, *Yatîndramatadîpika,* trs. and notes Swami Adidevananda, Madras: Sri Ramakrishna Math, 1949; ed. Abhyankar Vasudevasastri, Poona: Anandasrama Sanskrit Series, No. 50, 1908.

Stcherbatsky, Th., *Buddhist Logic,* New York: Dover Paperback, 1962 (2 vols.).

Stcherbatsky, Th., *The Conception of Buddhist Nirvâna,* Leningrad, 1927.

Suzuki, Daisetz Täitaro, 'Reason and Intuition in Buddhism', *Essays in East-West Philosophy,* ed. Charles A. Moore, Honolulu, 1951.

Suzuki, Daisetz Täitaro, *Studies in the Lankâvatâra Sûtra,* London: Routledge and Kegan Paul, 1957.

Thani Nayagam, Xavier S., *Nature in Ancient Tamil Poetry,* Tuticorin: Tamil Literature Society, 1952.

Thomas, Edward J., *The History of Buddhist Thought,* New York: Kegan Paul, 1933.

Tiruvacagam, trs. G. U. Pope, Oxford: Clarendon Press, 1900.

Tiruvalluar, *Tirukkural,* trs. V. R. Ramachandra Dikshitar, Madras: Adyar Library, 1949.

Van Buitnen, J. A. B., *Ramanuja's Vedârthasamgraha,* ed. with Introduction, Poona: Deccan College, 1956.

Van Buitnen, J. A. B., *Ramanuja on the Bhagavadgîta,* 's Gravenhage: H. L. Smits, 1954.

Varadachari, K. C., 'Isavâsyopanishad, A Study according to Sri Vedânta Desika', *Festschrift für Prof. P. V. Kane,* Poona: Oriental Book Agency, 1941, 538–44.

Venkatarama Iyer, M. K., *Advaita Vedânta,* Bombay: Asia Publishing House, 1964.

Venkata, Ramanan K., *Nagarjuna's Philosophy, as presented in the Mahâprajnâpâramîta Sâstra,* Rutland: Charles E. Tuttle Co., 1966.

Warren, Henry Clarke, *Buddhism in Translation,* Cambridge, Mass: Harvard University Press, 1953.

Warrier, A. G. Krishna. *See* Krishna Warrier.

Zaehner, R. C., *The Comparison of Religions,* Boston: Beacon Press, 1962.

Zaehner, R. C., *Hinduism,* London: Oxford University Press, 1962.

INDEX

Index prepared by Brenda Hall, M.A.,
Registered Indexer of the Society of
Indexers.